Welcome aboard! ... knowledge of Navy ... phrases? This workbook is your new best mate, filled with puzzles that will challenge even the saltiest sailor. And because we know you sometimes need a break from all that intellectual heavy lifting, we've thrown in some coloring pages too. So, grab your gear, and prepare to dive deep into the sea of Navy jargon. It's educational, it's fun, and who knows—you might even learn something that could save your six out there.

—Non sibi sed patriae

VETCOLOR

VETCOLOR.COM

PUZZLE 1

ACROSS:

5. Refers to a room or compartment onboard ship.
8. Receiving orders to move from one island to another.
9. A simple cupholder on a submarine, often riveted to any available vertical sheet metal.
12. The most senior nuke onboard a nuclear-powered vessel.
13. Inbound missile to the ship.
14. Officer, who flies alongside the pilot as a weapons officer.
15. The wives of sailors who are on deployment, usually found in bars near their husbands' naval base.
16. Night before graduation from Boot Camp spent with family.
17. A term used to remind sailors how to tie a dress uniform neckerchief.
19. Sailor with 99 or less days until his/her "End of Active Obligated Service", or EAOS.

DOWN:

1. Command-wide urinalysis test.
2. Front flap on trousers part of the dress uniform for E-6 and below.
3. An Officers Candidate School graduate.
4. Imaginary group of sailors activated by the commanding officer to ensure low morale.
6. Imaginary appliance in a ship's galley used to dry (like toast) otherwise good pieces of cake.
7. A sailor known for being good at their job but having poor military bearing.
10. Casual for "Get busy!" From formal daily announcement Turn to ship's work, often given as direct order Turn to!
11. Temporary Assigned Duty
18. Hamburgers or cheeseburgers.

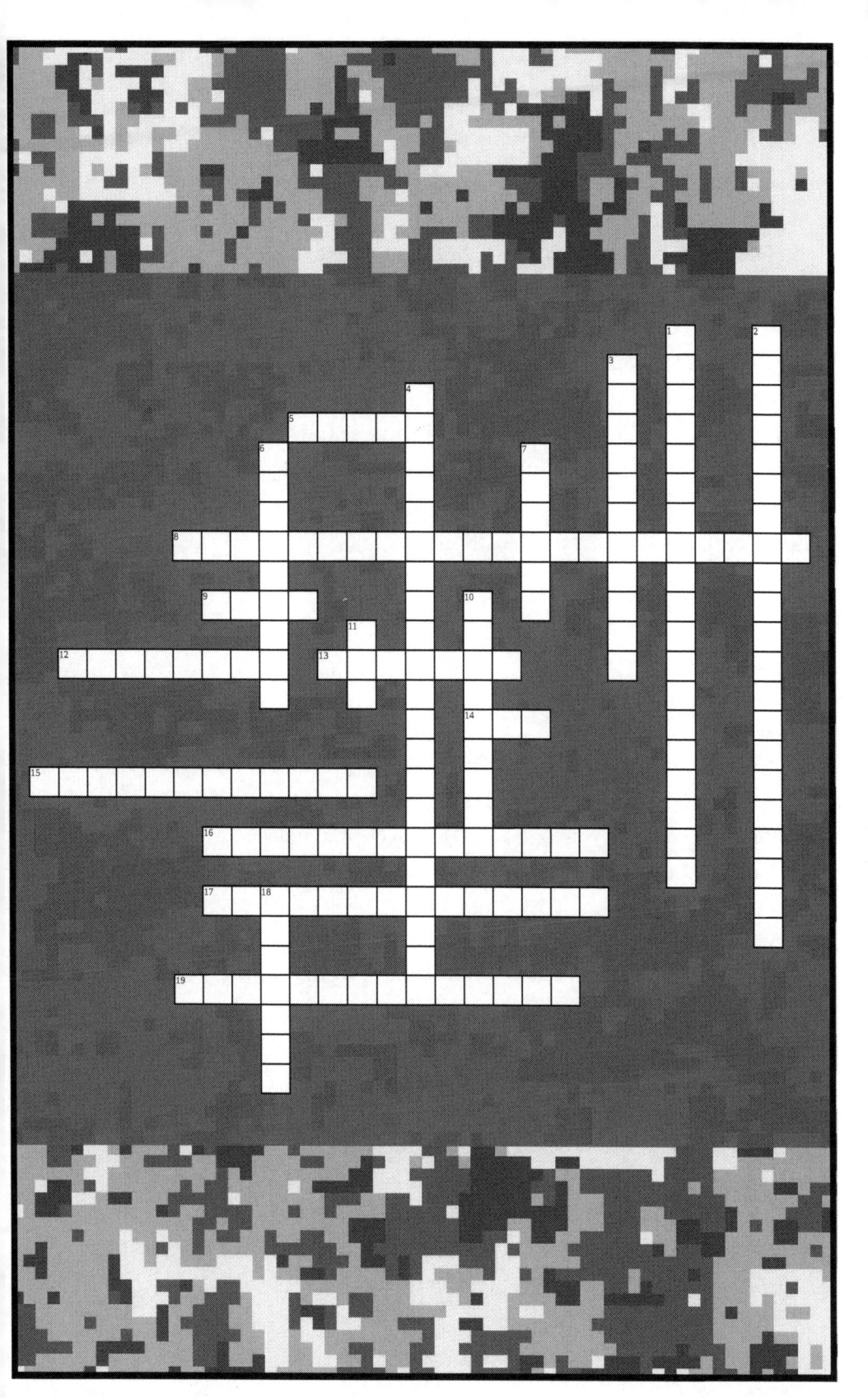

PUZZLE 2

ACROSS:

4. When a sailor is volunteered into a collateral duty by his superior.
6. Ceiling.
9. Derisive term for the city of Chula Vista, CA.
10. Term for unidentifiable meat eaten nonetheless.
13. Civilian clothes typically worn by those described as WUBA.
16. The watch responsible for monitoring the forward spaces of a submarine while in port.
18. Term for a sailor advanced to E-4 because they graduated top of their "A" school class. The Navy 'rents' them for an extra year in return for being promoted.
19. Confusing day in any Wardroom.

DOWN:

1. Form DD-214 transfers you from COMSUBLANT to CIVLANT.
2. A naval term for someone who has not crossed the equator, part of a traditional ceremony involving both officers and enlisted personnel.
3. Collected unclaimed personal items or confiscated items auctioned to the crew.
5. Captain's Mast or Non-Judicial Punishment.
7. To fall between ship and pier onto a floating log, which is often fatal.
8. Sea-sickness pills.
11. Typical Officer Dude. A weak attempt by TEDs to come up with a nickname for officers.
12. Seagull. Pronounced "See-Gee-Yuu-Eleven." Similar to "bulkhead remover," an inexpensive way to derive enjoyment from inexperienced personnel on watch.
14. Junior Officer Requiring Guidance.
15. Acronym for "No One Gives a Shit," used to dismiss junior personnel.
17. Other than ethical means of procurement.

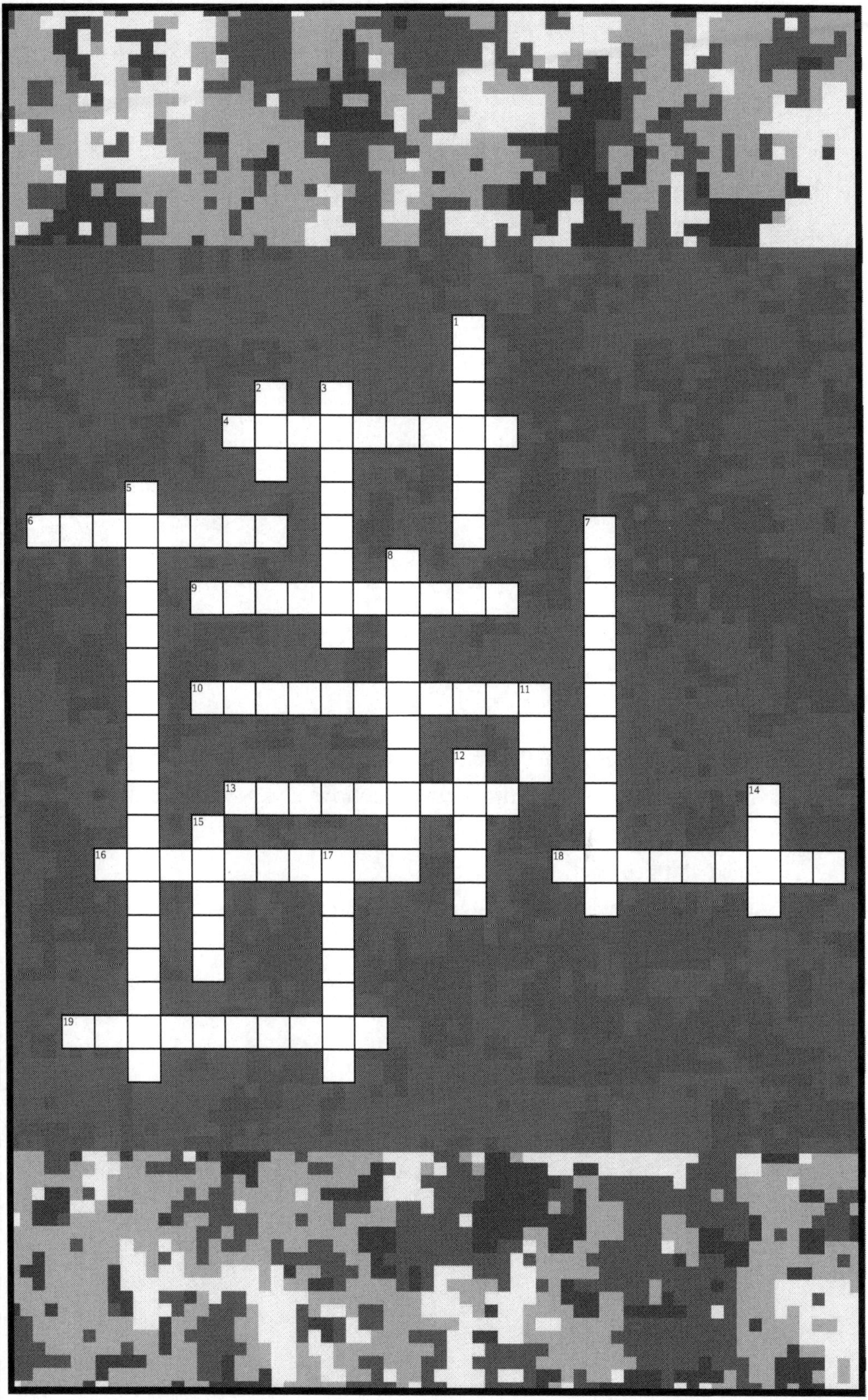

PUZZLE 3

ACROSS:

3. Slang for Armed Forces Radio & Television Service.
4. A submarine tender, or other non-combat ship that is comprised nearly completely by female sailors.
5. Stairs aboard a ship.
10. (Submarine Service) Affectionate term for Missile Technicians on Ballistic Missile Submarines.
11. Abbreviation for Junior Officer.
13. To eject from an aircraft.
16. Hour long field day held daily onboard USS Cape St. George (CG-71).
18. Birth Control Glasses. Standard Navy-issue corrective eyewear.
19. Information that is dubious, exaggerated, or outright false.
20. Sailor who avoids work while not being detected.

DOWN:

1. An expression voiced when a subordinate strongly disagrees with a superior's order and the subordinate takes actions he knows to be the correct procedure, counter to the order.
2. Creamed chipped beef.
6. Extended periods wearing Emergency Air Breathing devices.
7. Navy preferred term for exercise.
8. Similar to the 1MC, except that it is only heard on the flight deck of an air-capable ship.
9. Ravioli
12. Procedure allowing a sailor to wear higher rank insignia temporarily.
14. A submarine crewman who is not part of the engineering department.
15. Intercom or amplified circuit used to communicate between spaces of a ship.
17. A 6-month (or longer) deployment on a ship. Work-ups precede cruise.

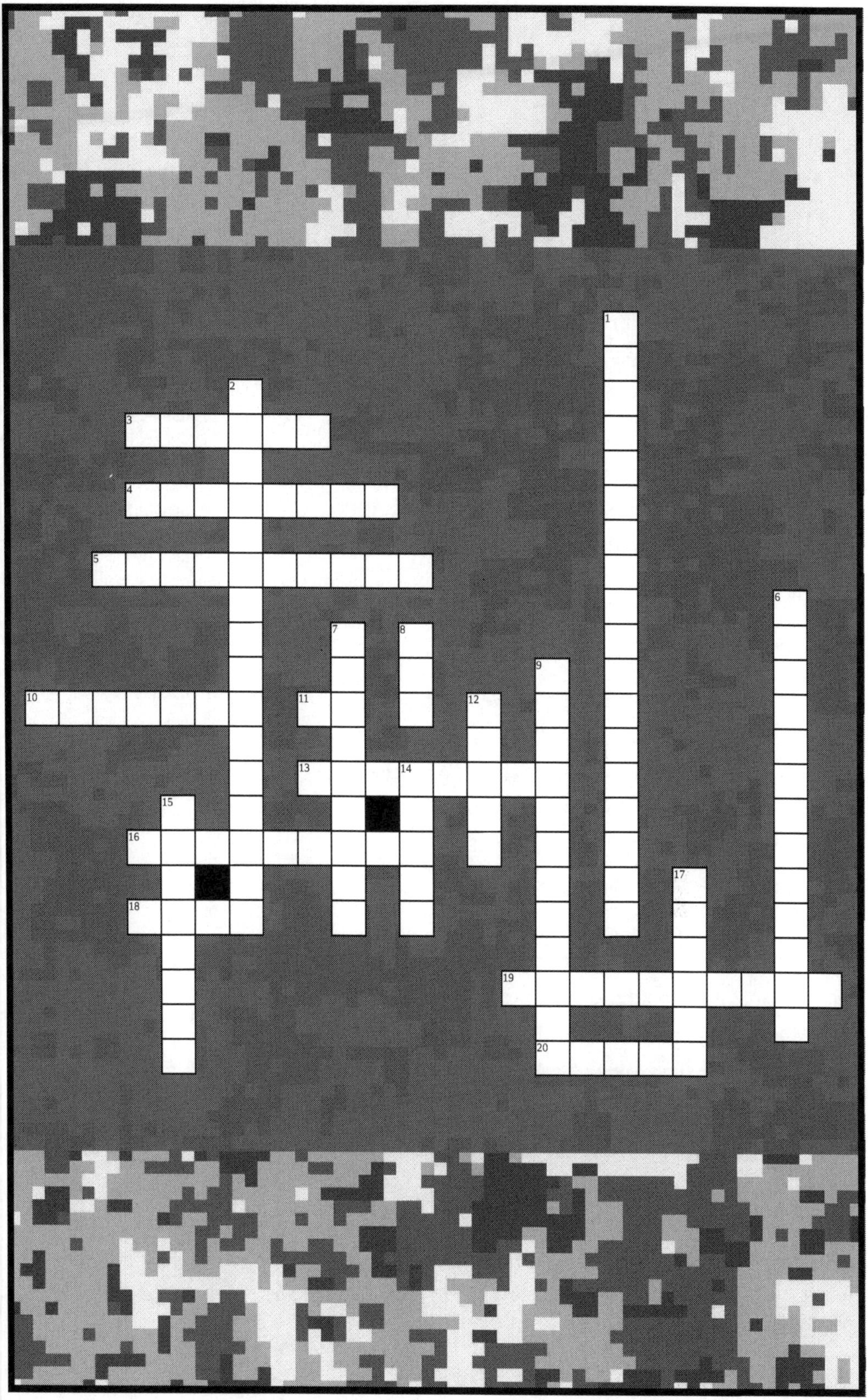
1
2
3
4
5
6
7
8
9
10
11
12
13
14
15
16
17
18
19
20

PUZZLE 4

ACROSS:

1. An expression voiced when a subordinate strongly disagrees with a superior's order and the subordinate takes actions he knows to be the correct procedure, counter to the order.
2. Creamed chipped beef.
6. Extended periods wearing Emergency Air Breathing devices.
7. Navy preferred term for exercise.
8. Similar to the 1MC, except that it is only heard on the flight deck of an air-capable ship.
9. Ravioli
12. Procedure allowing a sailor to wear higher rank insignia temporarily.
14. A submarine crewman who is not part of the engineering department.
15. Intercom or amplified circuit used to communicate between spaces of a ship.
17. A 6-month (or longer) deployment on a ship. Work-ups precede cruise.

DOWN:

1. A feeling that something has been done correctly and will produce the desired results. Most often used in the negative.
4. Two round pieces of metal (Iron) on either side of a ship's magnetic compass to correct for the magnetic field caused by the ship's metal surfaces, also known as Deviation.
5. Either the name for a trash can, or the act of throwing something into the trash.
7. Stateroom where lower-ranking JOs are billeted, known for lack of comfort and privacy.
8. The canvas white hat Sailors wear with their dress uniforms.
9. Container for toiletry articles such as shaving cream, deodorant, after-shave lotion, etc.
10. Someone who works in the engineering spaces.
11. A short cruise for reservists.
12. To center or tighten; derived from tackle.
13. Surface Sailor (used by submariners).
15. Landing Safety Officer or Landing Signals Officer, responsible for aircraft landing safety.
18. Short Little Ugly Fucker, nickname given to the A-7 Corsair.

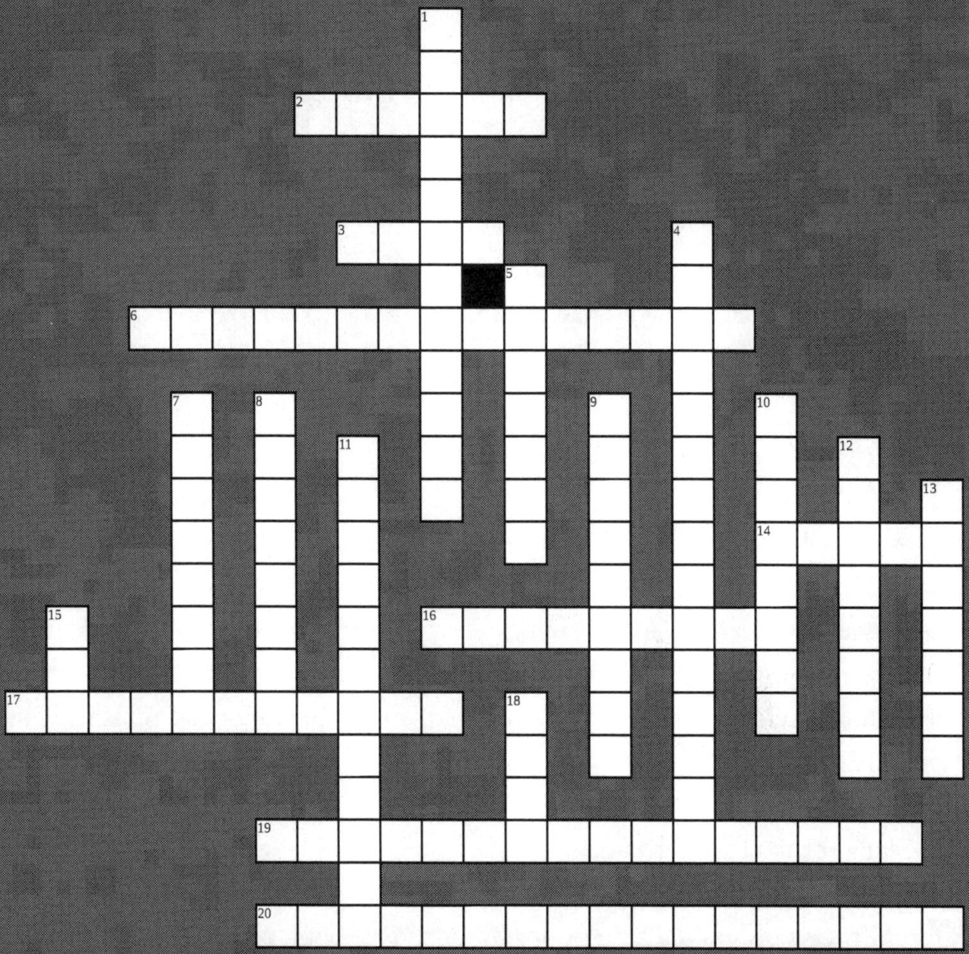

PUZZLE 5

ACROSS:

6. Any task or evolution that is extremely painful or difficult to accomplish, often due to bureaucracy or red tape.
7. Term used to describe an evolution that has gone awry.
12. Formation.
13. Slang for the dress blue uniforms worn by sailors E-6 and below. (see Marine Corps Table Cloth).
15. Right side of the boat or ship (when facing the bow).
16. Before photocopiers were common, such were prepared by typing a mimeo or ditto master, due to the number of copies required.
18. Large space aboard a carrier that is the focal point for each of the squadrons in the airwing.
20. Often exaggerated or embellished tales from previous deployments or commands told by seniors to juniors.

DOWN:

1. Absent Without Official Leave
2. Sailor in the Gunner's Mate rating.
3. Name given to the CAG bird in each squadron in the airwing, with a side number ending with double zeros.
4. Changing clothes without bathing, usually just applying deodorant or cologne.
5. Derisive term for a Hospital Corpsman.
8. Slang for the garrison cap.
9. Failed attempt at an arrested landing on a carrier by a fixed-wing aircraft. Usually caused by a poor approach or a hook bounce on the deck.
10. Aircraft.
11. Term coined by A-Gang for the Officers.
14. Title used when addressing the airwing commander.
17. Aviation water survival training.
19. When the ceiling and visibility at an airfield or over an air-capable ship are below minimums for takeoff and landing.

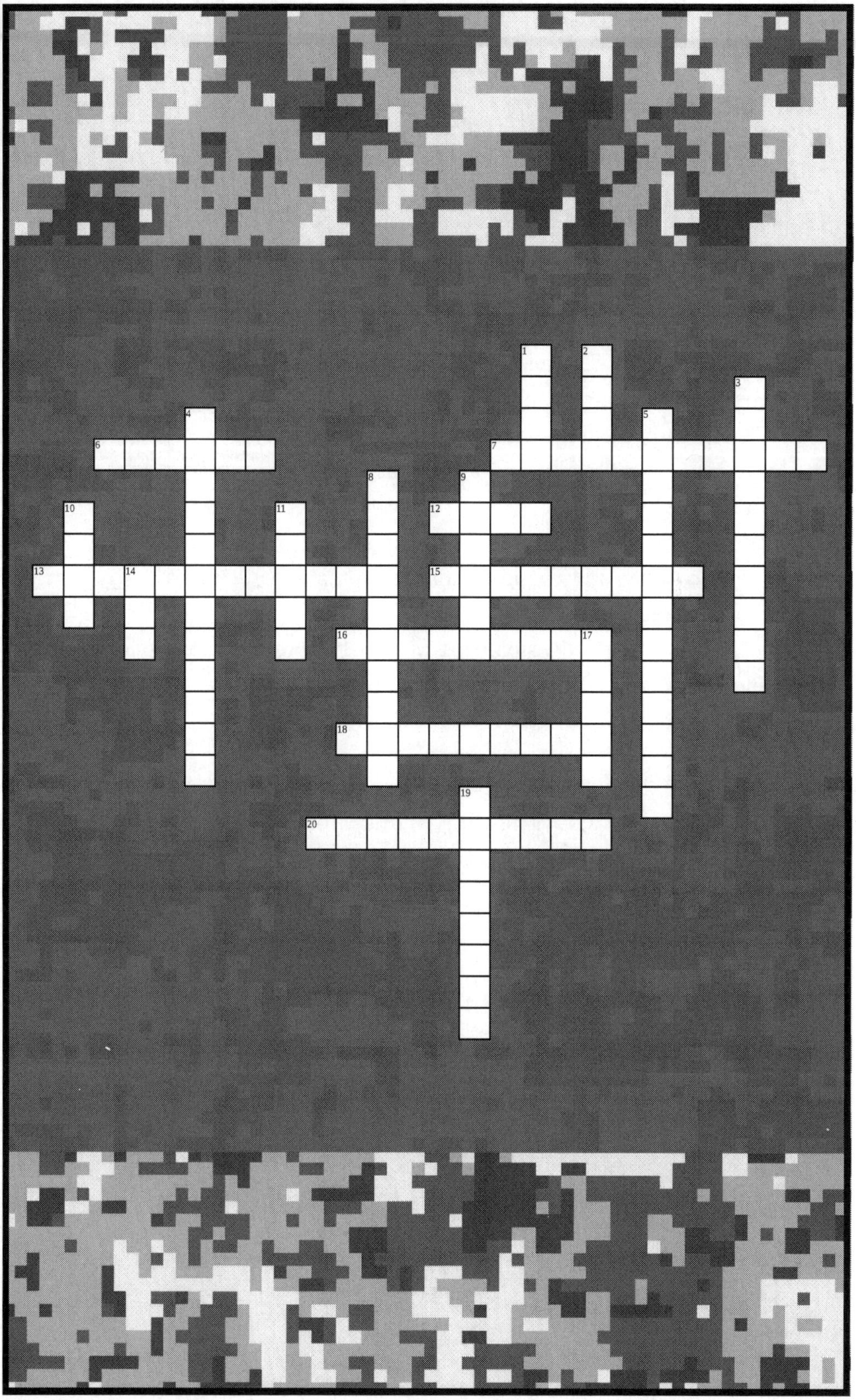
1
2
3
4
5
6
7
8
9
10
11
12
13
14
15
16
17
18
19
20

PUZZLE 6

ACROSS:

1. Absent Without Official Leave
2. Sailor in the Gunner's Mate rating.
3. Name given to the CAG bird in each squadron in the airwing, with a side number ending with double zeros.
4. Changing clothes without bathing, usually just applying deodorant or cologne.
5. Derisive term for a Hospital Corpsman.
8. Slang for the garrison cap.
9. Failed attempt at an arrested landing on a carrier by a fixed-wing aircraft. Usually caused by a poor approach or a hook bounce on the deck.
10. Aircraft.
11. Term coined by A-Gang for the Officers.
14. Title used when addressing the airwing commander.
17. Aviation water survival training.
19. When the ceiling and visibility at an airfield or over an air-capable ship are below minimums for takeoff and landing.

DOWN:

1. Junior Non-Qualified submariner tasked with doing officers' laundry.
3. Pneumatic tool used for removing paint from steel.
6. Is a yellow cloth suit that is worn from head-to-toe by navy "Nukes".
7. Aircraft carrier.
9. Officer's mess, or dining room. Also used to collectively refer to all the officers at a command.
12. Slang for National City, California, near Naval Station San Diego, known for its cheap dive bars frequented by "West-Pac Widows."
18. Slang for the last day of a long deployment when sailors could get laid and still obtain Venereal Disease cures before returning home.

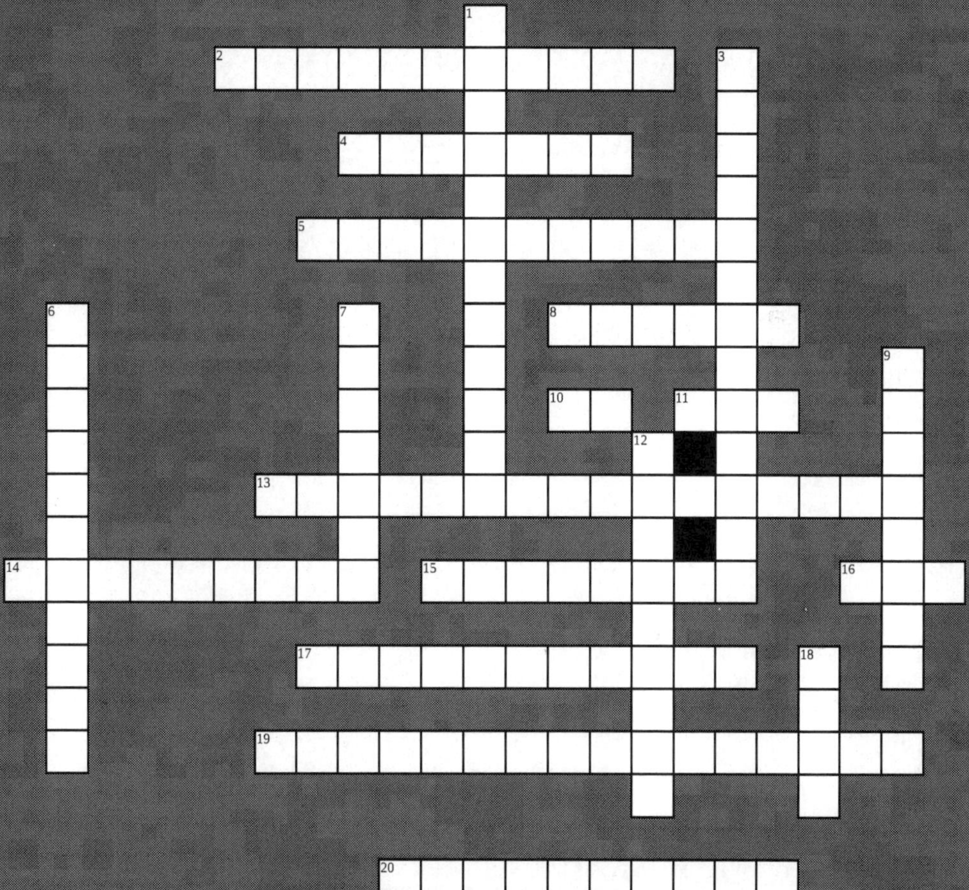
1 2 3 4 5 6 7 8 9 10 11 12 13 14 15 16 17 18 19 20

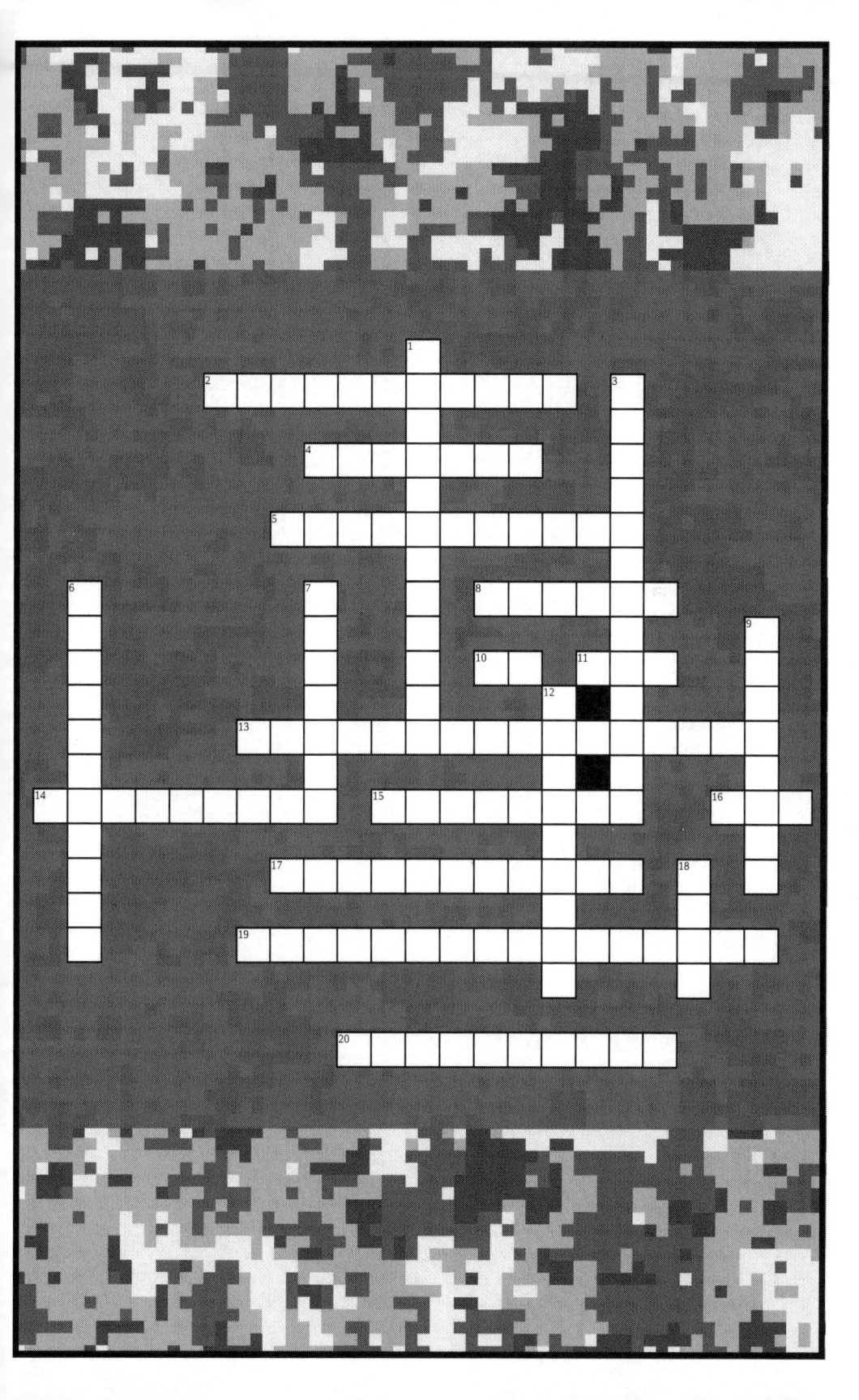

PUZZLE 7

ACROSS:

3. Shower
5. An officers reply to a junior person's call to "attention on deck".
8. Chief Engineer.
10. Individual Augmentation/Augmentee: Program deploying sailors to the Middle East for 6-14 months.
12. Navy female with an unusually broad ass.
14. Baked, candied apples served to midshipmen at the Naval Academy on special occasions.
15. Large mounted binoculars normally found on or near the Signal Shack.
17. Usually a CT, IS or some kind of intelligence type.
18. Reference to the Navy's main base at Norfolk, Virginia, so called because "it's where sailors' careers go to die."
19. Acronym used humorously by disgruntled sailors for "Never Again Volunteer Yourself."

DOWN:

1. Derogatory term for non-natives in Hawaii.
2. Slang for anonymous. Safety system where sailors can drop an anonymous recommendation into a locked box.
4. Term used for a spunk rag.
6. A sailor who spends more time going to medical feigning ailments than doing work.
7. A derogatory term for a sailor who has been awarded punishment at mast, or any less-than-par sailor. Also known as "Shitbird".
9. Enlisted Air Warfare Specialist.
11. Hot dogs (also called "dangling sirloin").
13. A term used to indicate the time of the 0030 security sweep on some bases.
16. Short for an aircraft's propeller.

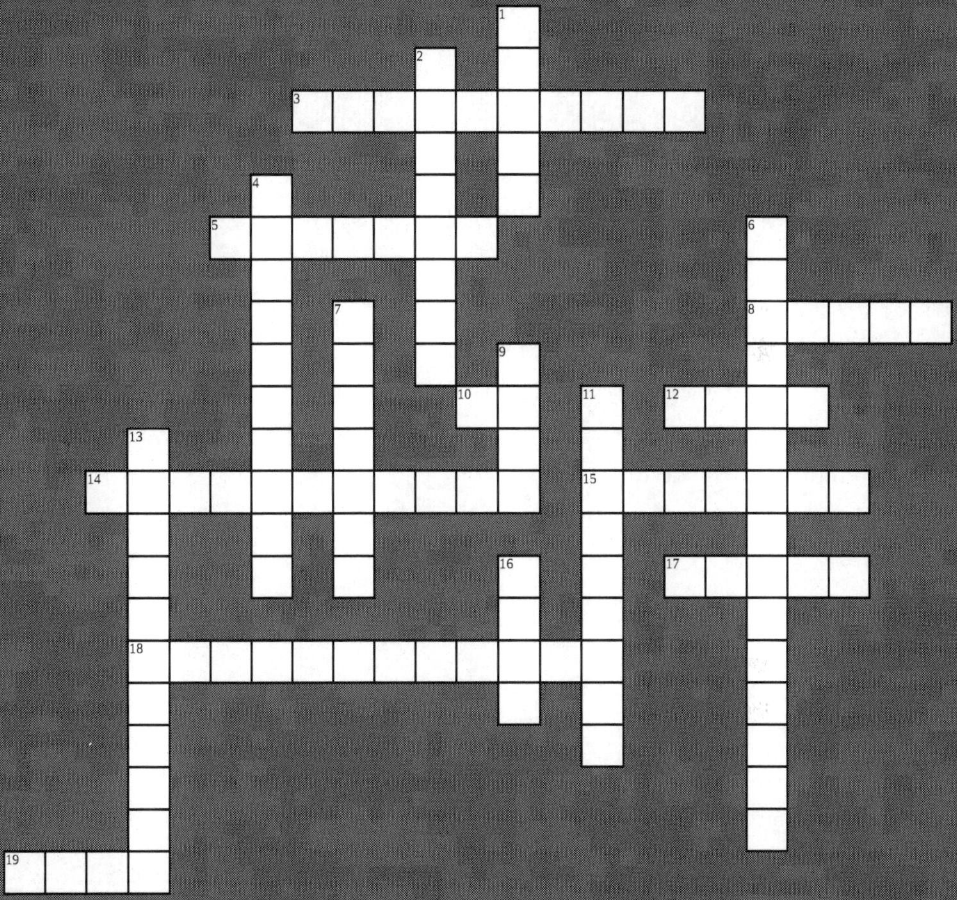
1
2
3
4
5
6
7
8
9
10
11
12
13
14
15
16
17
18
19

PUZZLE 8

ACROSS:

2. Pulling rank.
3. Term for a lifer with no life outside the Navy.
7. A sailor who is on fire and is running around screaming.
10. Personal Qualifications Standards, a card carrying various qualifications for a warfare badge or similar.
11. Officially called the FRS (Fleet Replacement Squadron), although the former is still widely used.
12. A device such as a Leatherman or Gerber multi-tool often carried by those who love the Navy.
14. Helicopter used for transporting chaplains to other ships for services on Sundays.
15. Acronym for belt adornment, worn by nukes to see how much radiation is received in a period of time.
17. Bathroom on a ship.
18. Derogatory term for officers in general, particularly junior officers.
19. Civilian Under Naval Training.
20. Acronym used to describe when things work but the reason is unknown.

DOWN:

1. Your right hand. (AKA-Handeria)
4. Recruits assigned to maintain cleanliness.
5. A sailor's rack. Usually referred to by senior personnel without many daily responsibilities.
6. Pumice stone used for cleaning a wooden deck.
8. A naval aircraft when its wings or rotors/tail pylon are folded and it is parked in close proximity to other aircraft.
9. Anti-Submarine Warfare Officers
13. Nickname for USS Bonhomme Richard (LHD-6)
16. Title sarcastically given to someone stating the obvious.

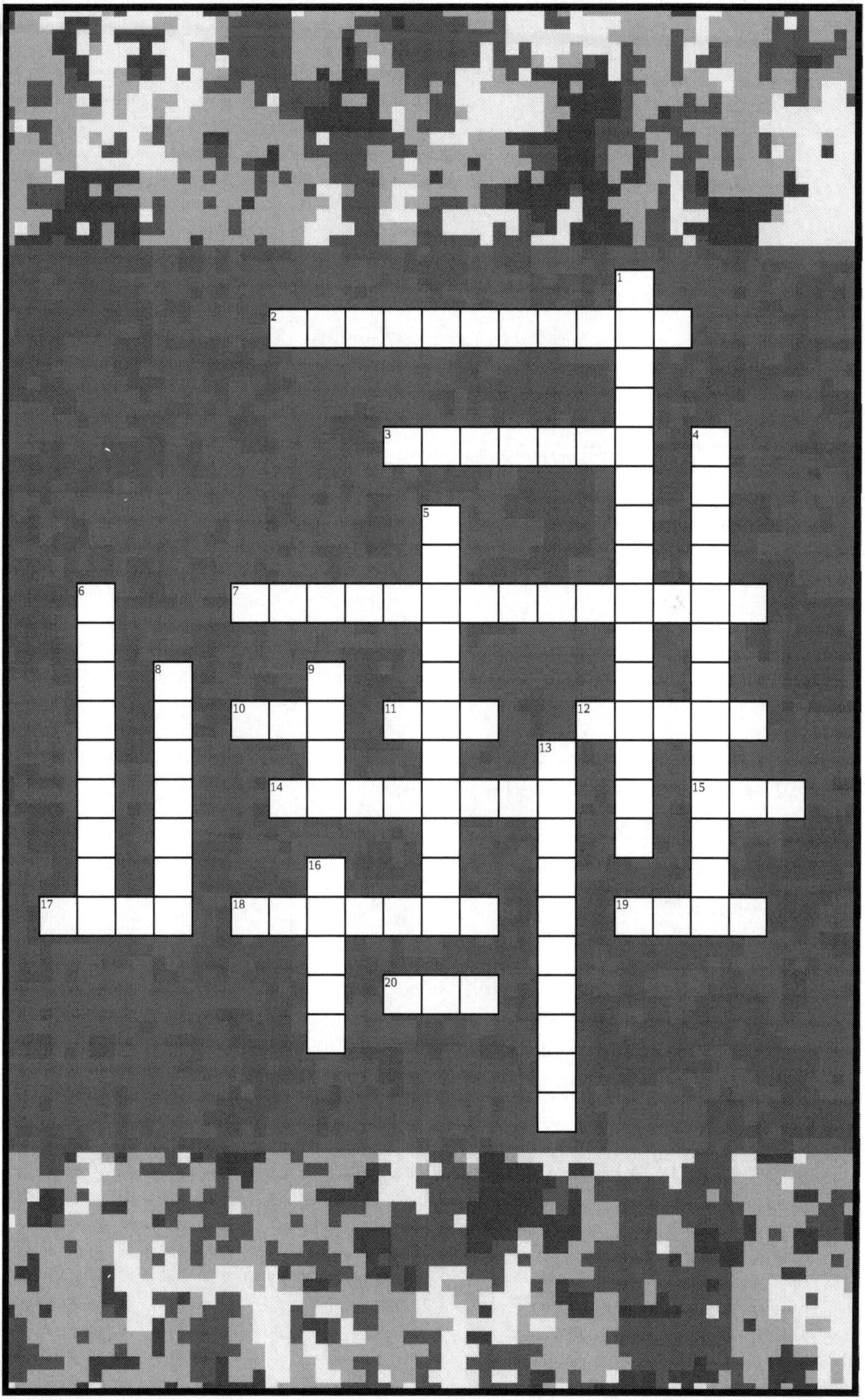
1
2
3
4
5
6
7
8
9
10
11
12
13
14
15
16
17
18
19
20

PUZZLE 9

ACROSS:

2. Acronym for "Eat Shit, Fuck Off, And Die."
9. The interior of a submarine.
10. Expression for confusion or surprise, "What the Fuck, Over."
14. Drunk. The preferred state of consciousness for junior sailors, especially those visiting foreign ports.
15. Joke name for The United States Coast Guard.
16. A rotation of two duty sections, one designated port and the other starboard.
17. Sailor who lands aboard an Aircraft Carrier.
18. A very small screwdriver used by EM's and ET's to make meters indicate correctly.
19. On larger ships like carriers and "gator freighters," this is a small hospital.

DOWN:

1. A fan, painted red, used by damage control parties to de-smoke a space.
3. When a second in command takes over.
4. Answer The Fucking Question. This grading remark often appears on nuke-school exams.
5. Obsolete term for throwing something overboard.
6. Ships Serviceman assigned to do the Ship's laundry.
7. Used to refer to a sailor who convinces a doctor to give them an SIQ chit.
8. To poorly execute a routine task.
11. Situation Normal, All Fucked Up.
12. Large civilian women who prey on the sexual needs of unwary junior enlisted personnel.
13. A derisive term for a SONAR Technician.
20. Short for cannibalize, which is the practice of using one or more of a unit's aircraft strictly for parts to keep the rest of the aircraft flying.

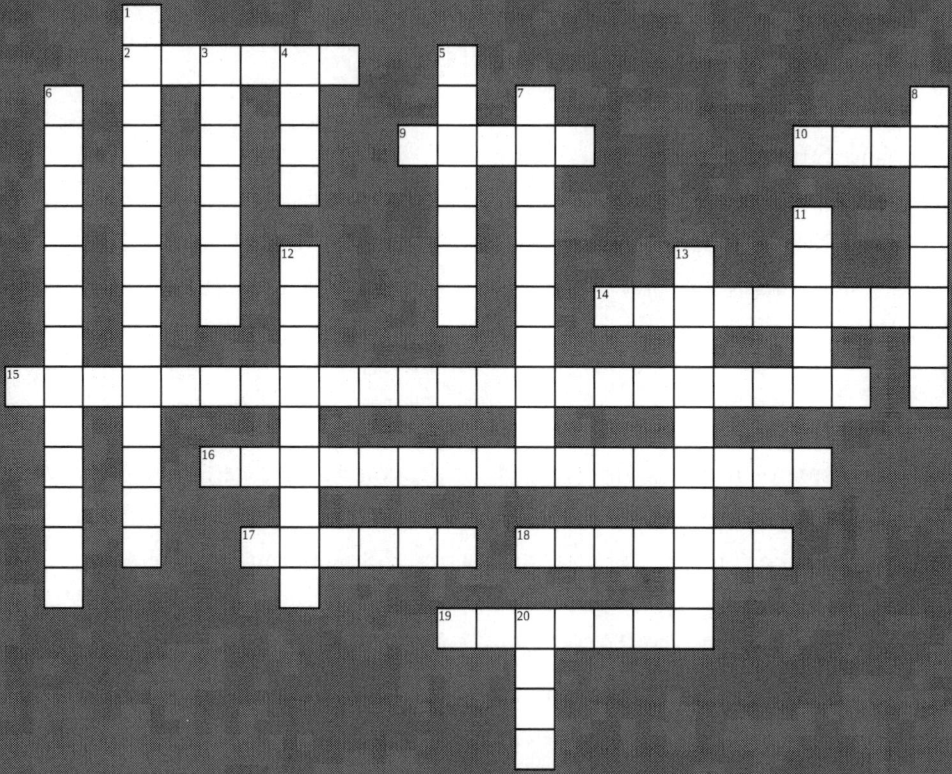
1
2
3
4
5
6
7
8
9
10
11
12
13
14
15
16
17
18
19
20

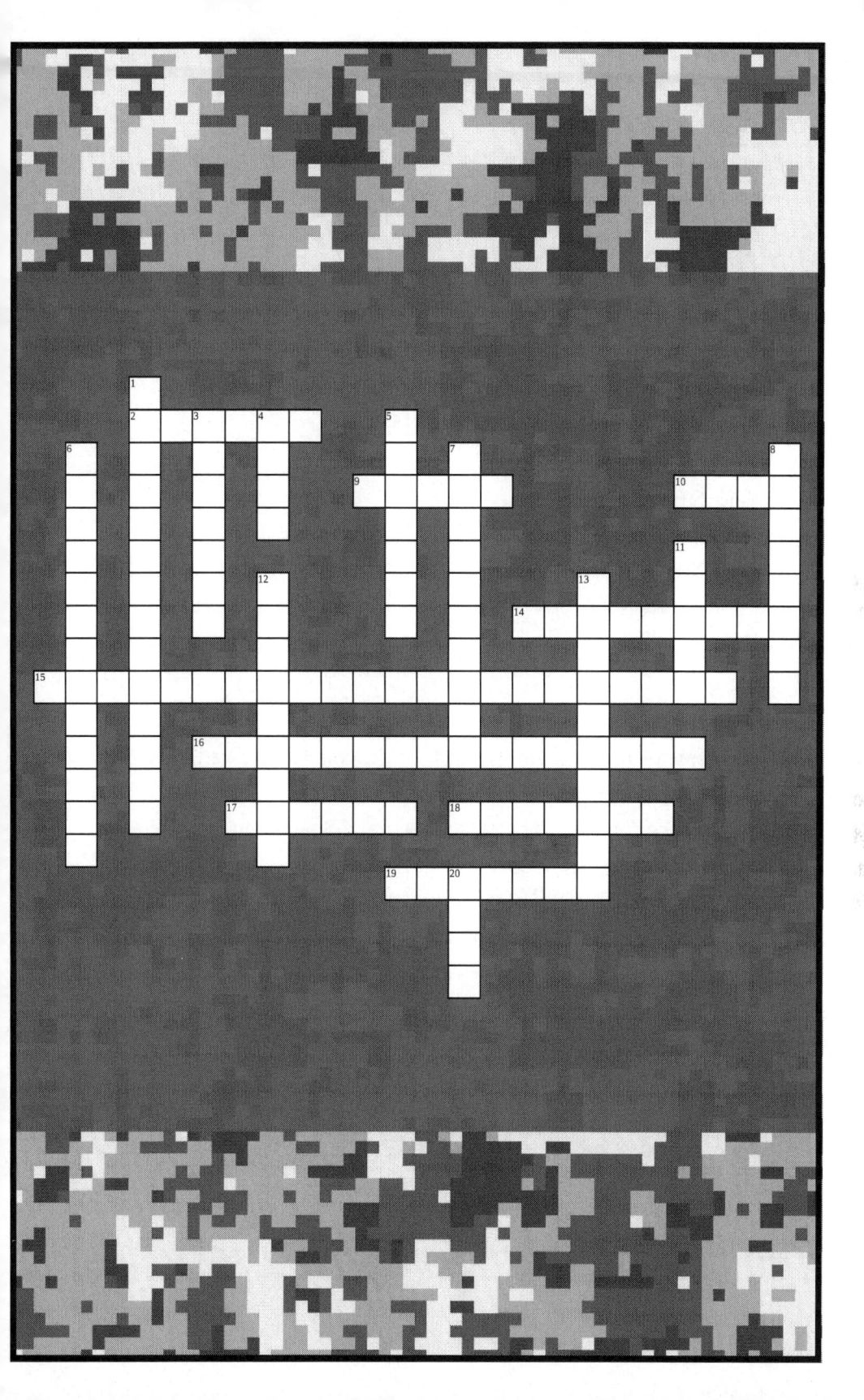

PUZZLE 10

ACROSS:

3. Slang for Dishonorable Discharge.
4. Slang for a slider topped with a fried egg, served at midrats.
8. Imaginary machine used by a ship's laundry to pulverize buttons.
11. Affectionate term for someone who does what you do. In aviation, someone who flies the same type of aircraft as you.
13. Term jokingly referring to the high percentage of female children fathered by naval aviators, attributed to various factors including electromagnetic exposure and lifestyle.
14. Short for autorotation.
15. Short for "tailhook".
18. To leave an area of responsibility.
19. Less than 100 days to EAOS (End of Active Obligated Service).
20. A signature on a qualification card. Also, Naval Air Station Sigonella, Sicily.

DOWN:

1. Fratricide or friendly fire. Named for the color associated with friendly forces during "workups" and exercises.
2. A Sailor that has just reported to his first duty assignment after completing Recruit Training.
5. "Terra firma." Any place that is not covered by water.
6. Leave a place of duty (go on liberty)
7. On a submarine, the confines within the pressure hull, as opposed to other specific tanks.
9. Slang for the F-14 Tomcat.
10. What landlubbers call a "map".
12. Fitness Enhancement Program, mandatory physical training regimen.
16. Particle radiation emitted from naval nuclear power sources or nuclear weapons.
17. The levers in the Maneuvering Room of a diesel submarine that are used to change the settings for the main propulsion motors.

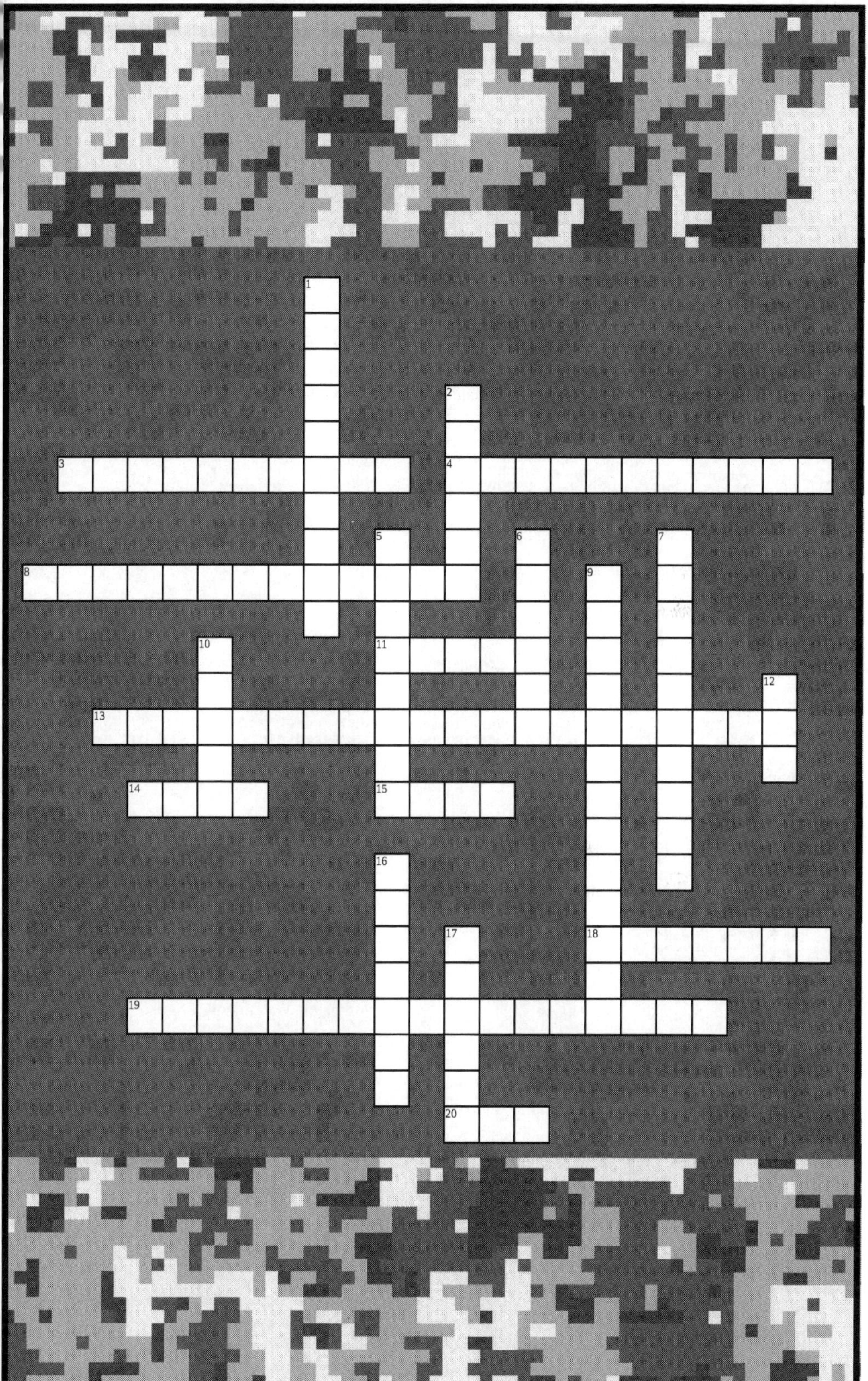
1
2
3
4
5
6
7
8
9
10
11
12
13
14
15
16
17
18
19
20

PUZZLE 11

ACROSS:

4. Similar to Corpsman Candy above, but in this context relating to Motrin.
10. Sore-throat lozenges handed out at sick bay in lieu of any substantive treatment. Sometimes accompanied by two aspirin.
11. "Whiz Quiz" or urinalysis.
13. Trash Disposal Unit. Sophisticated AN-DEEP-6 weapons system.
15. Nickname for Jebel Ali, UAE.
16. Term for the junior most pilots or NFOs in a squadron who are fresh out of the Replacement Air Group (RAG).
17. Refers to the connected silver rank bars of a Lieutenant's khakis.
18. Candy, sweets, or ice cream used as bribes for non-infantry personnel.

DOWN:

1. Daily hour-long mandatory cleaning evolution typically initiated by the executive officer via the 1MC communication system.
2. Military Training Instructor responsible for guiding future submarine sailors.
3. Profane dismissal of the Navy.
5. Short sleeve white dress shirt with black trousers and Combination Cap. Common in the 70's. Basically a less dressed up version of the Bus Driver Uniform.
6. When several aircraft are practicing touch and go landings at the same airfield or ship.
7. When an aircraft gets drastically low while attempting to land on a carrier and strikes the "round down," or stern of the ship, Often with devastating results.
8. Derogatory term for females near a Naval Station who use sailors for money.
9. Slang for a helicopter pilot.
12. Gold embroidered oak leaves decoration on a Commander's/Captain's cover.
14. Small privacy curtain hanging on the outside of a rack.

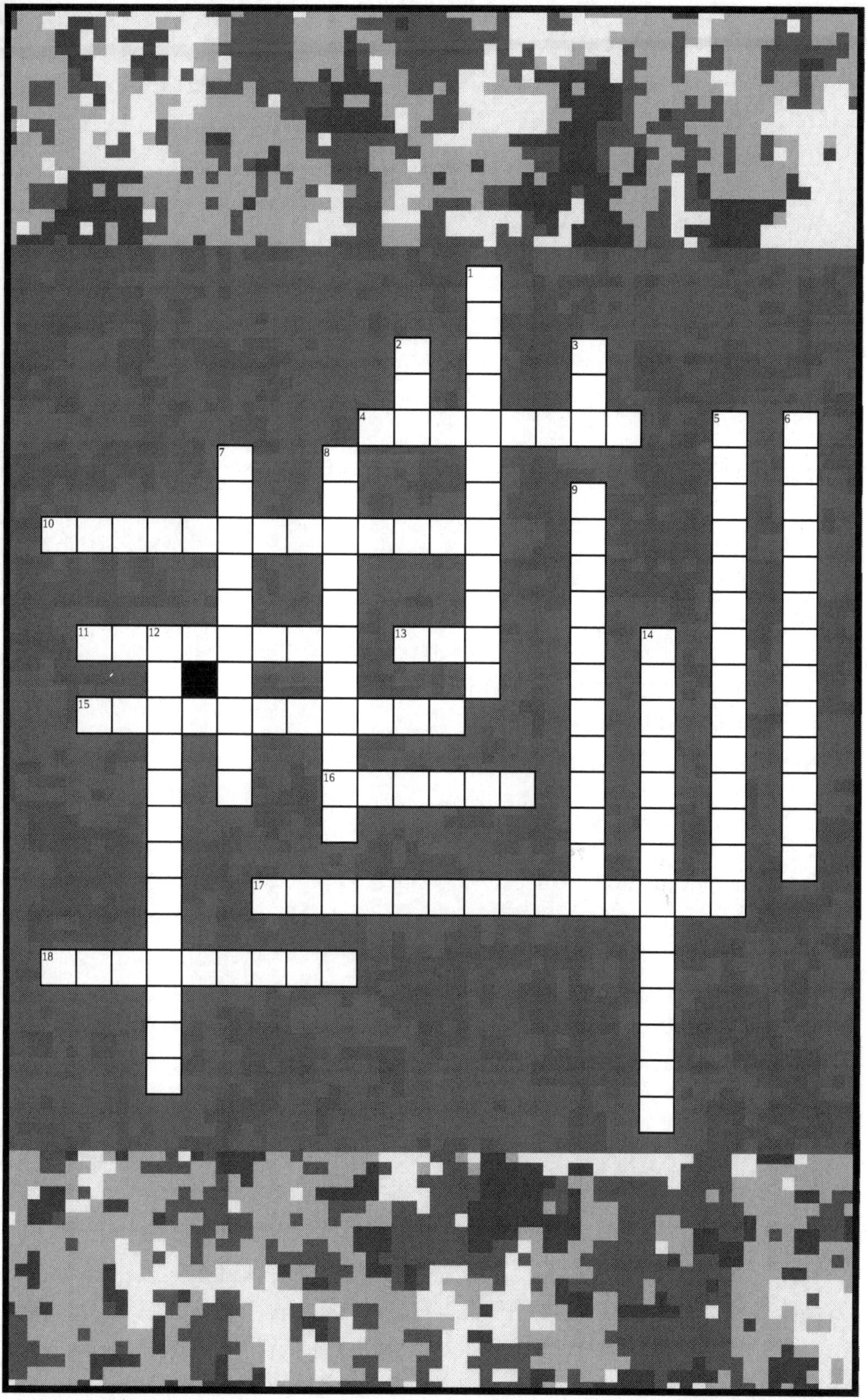
1
2
3
4
5
6
7
8
9
10
11
12
13
14
15
16
17
18

PUZZLE 12

ACROSS:

4. Engineering Officer of the Watch.
6. An adjective emphasizing something as beyond outstanding, used seriously or sarcastically, often by RDCs in boot camp.
12. Dismissive phrase indicating one's independence.
13. Slang for the F-4 Phantom back in the day - presently slang for the F/A-18 E or F Super Hornet.
14. Water craft small enough to be carried on a ship, unless a submarine, which is always called "a boat" or "the boat" when referring to the actual vessel.
15. Buffarilla Bar and Grill (Club outside the Ingalls shipyard in Pascagoula, MS.).
17. Officers Club.
18. Middle organizational level in most naval commands, below department and above branch.
19. Maddening condition aboard ship, especially aircraft carriers, where passageways are "taped off" so that they may be waxed, dried, and buffed in the middle of the night.

DOWN:

1. Area where aircraft are readied for flight.
2. Alternating crews for the same ship - usually applied to submarines, but recently applied to forward deployed "small boys" in the "Sea Swap" program.
3. Drinking fountain or rumor (originated from the rumors that would be spread on board ship while gathered about the water barrel).
5. The senior-most Ensign onboard a surface ship. In charge of various wardroom duties.
7. Emergency radio frequencies.
8. A sock that is sacrificed early in a deployment and used to clean up after masturbating. It is usually kept under the mattress and can stand up on its own by the end of cruise.
9. Maintenance and Material Management.
10. Term used in combat aviation when an enemy aircraft is hit.
11. Green log book hidden in an engineering space where sailors vent frustration through prose, poetry, drawings, or cartoons.
16. Area for corrective exercises in boot camp.

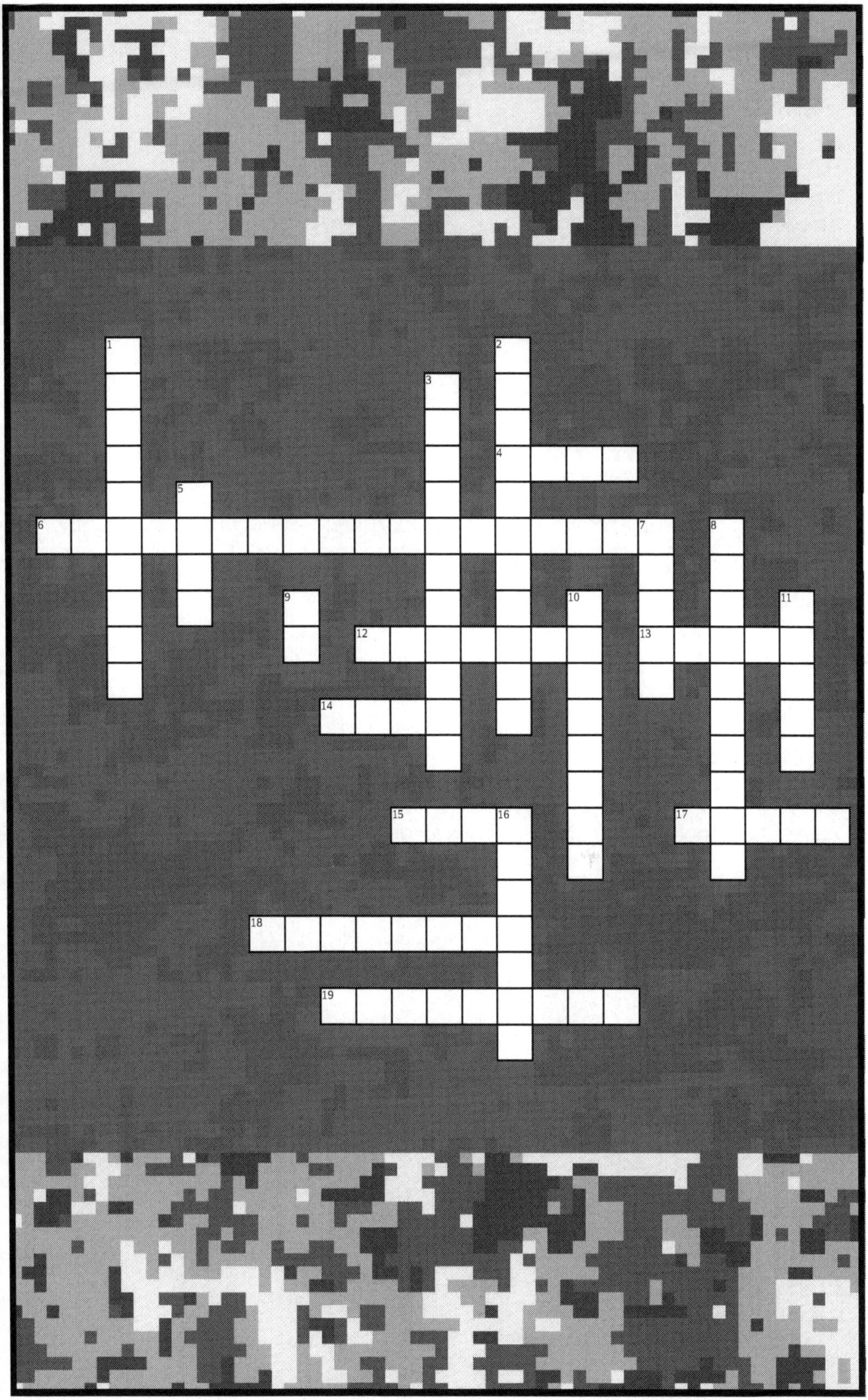
1
2
3
4
5
6
7
8
9
10
11
12
13
14
15
16
17
18
19

PUZZLE 13

ACROSS:

2. Tijuana, Mexico. It is thus labeled because it is dirty, smells like shit, has high crime and drugs, corrupt police officials, and has few redeeming qualities.
4. Term used for various nozzle-shaped implements.
10. Special Liberty, Comp-Time.
13. Side dish during chow that helps identify main dishes.
14. Canvas mattress cover.
16. A term of understanding and acceptance when given an order or other information.
18. Shortest Nuke On Board.
19. Slang term for Motrin (Ibuprofen) distributed by corpsmen in Sickbay.
20. Pronounced "oh dark". Referring to some point really early in the morning, like 0200

DOWN:

1. Officer who rose from the Enlisted ranks.
3. (Aircraft Carrier): Forward wardroom for pilots wearing (sweaty) flight gear. As opposed to formal ship's wardroom.
5. A direction perpendicular to the bow-stern axis of the ship. That is, moving port-to-starboard or starboard-to-port.
6. Slang for a PH (Photographer's Mate) in a fighter squadron.
7. Married sailor who brings his lunch from home in a paper bag (because he is receiving a Commuted Rations or COMRATS cash allowance for his meals).
8. Acronym term indicating supreme indifference; "Gaffer".
9. Sailor in the Electronics or Electrical fields of job specialties.
11. Midnight or 0000Hrs.
12. Sailor who frequents the Honcho bar district.
15. A sailor's rack or bunk, or the engine room on a ship.
17. Commanding Officer and Executive Officer.

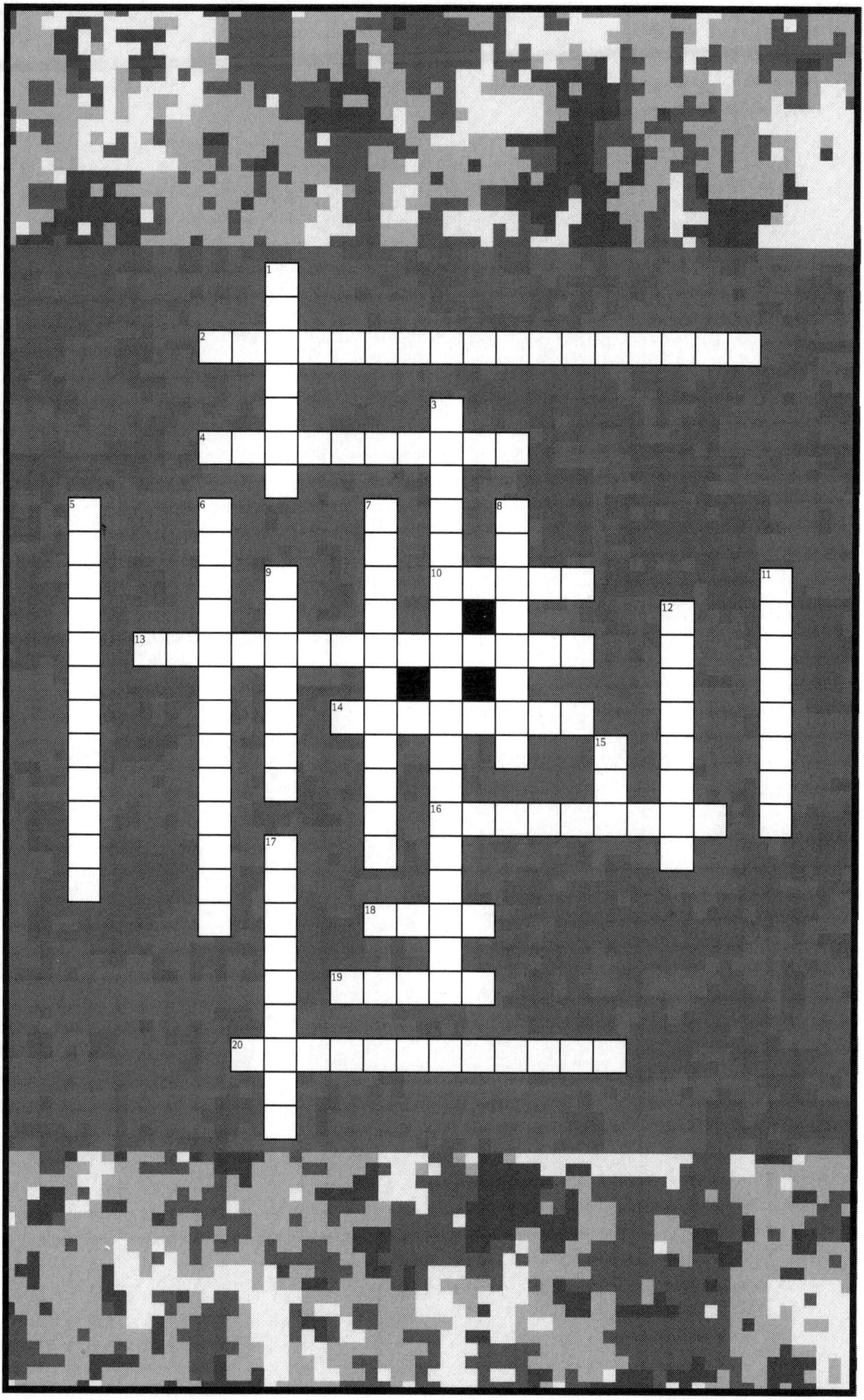
1
2
3
4
5
6
7
8
9
10
11
12
13
14
15
16
17
18
19
20

PUZZLE 1-4

ACROSS:

5. A common form of greeting in the Submarine Service where one man shakes another man's crotch, testing mettle and camaraderie.
8. Designated smoking area aboard ship that is not a weatherdeck space. Quickly fills with a haze of smoke. Also called "Crack shack".
9. Acronym for Profane dismissal.
10. Set of blue sweatpants and sweatshirt issued on arrival at boot camp.
13. The large green bag the army calls a "duffel bag".
14. A group of warships and supply ships centered around a large deck aircraft carrier and its airwing.
16. Refers to the aircraft in the fighter squadron on a carrier with the side number "111".
17. Sailor trying a "little too hard" to make rate by sucking up to superiors.
19. Term for women in the Navy because all the meat is in the tail.
20. Machine in the galley that gives lettuce leaves their brown color.

DOWN:

1. Game in which many promiscuous women give multiple men blowjobs.
2. Things Are Really Fucked Up.
3. Sailor who gets away with doing no work.
4. A derisive name for Marines. Refers to the fact that they pull guard duty aboard ship. A good phrase to use when picking a fight with a Marine.
6. A term used to describe a sailor who is always on point with hair cut and grooming.
7. Marines or soldiers. Derived from the sound they make when tanks roll over them.
11. Acronym for "Over And Fucking Out," similar to "WTFO" (What The Fuck Over).
12. When a sailor is too ill or incapacitated to perform his duties and is required to report to his rack (quarters).
15. Tension caused by high stress during a difficult or dangerous situation.
18. One-night sickness in boot camp after receiving smallpox vaccination.

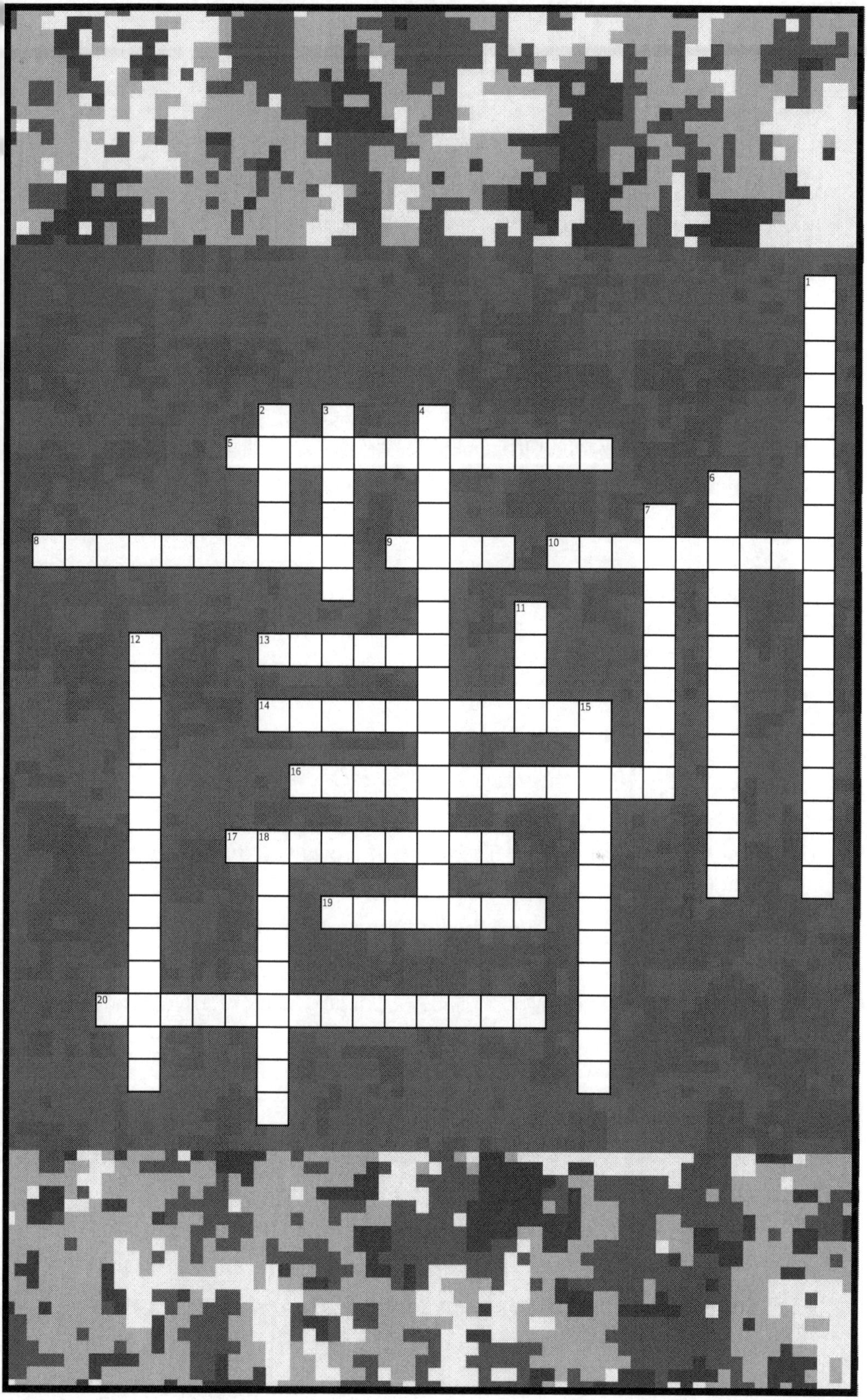
1
2
3
4
5
6
7
8
9
10
11
12
13
14
15
16
17
18
19
20

PUZZLE 15

ACROSS:

6. In general, to prepare something for stormy travel.
12. Any attempt to restart an aircraft's engine(s) after in-flight failure.
13. The computer generated female voice heard in an aviator's earpiece when something is not as it should be.
14. You get to go to real college on a full ride (shorter scholarships are also available) and only wear your uniform once a week.
16. Area aft of maneuvering on submarines often used for telling sea stories.
18. Acronym for Retarded Officer Dude
20. (Submarine Service) missile area, on a boomer.

DOWN:

1. UNless Otherwise DIRected; enables TRUST-based management by exception (MBE).
2. CH-46 Sea Knight helicopter, notorious for its mechanical issues and accidents during takeoff.
3. Area on the mess decks where sailors of Filipino descent congregate.
4. A sailor that would rather stay in his/her rack other than participate in the everyday routine of the ship.
5. Derogatory term for "Boiler Technician," typically from Machinist Mates who attend the identical A school.
7. Unofficial acronym found on the uniforms of Aviation Ordnance personnel.
8. Training and preparation periods before deployment, involving various drills and exercises.
9. Acronym for "Just Another Reason To Get Out."
10. Derogatory term for a reservist.
11. Fictional and clueless cartoon character used in WWII era training material to demonstrate what NOT to do in naval aviation.
15. Anything unwanted or trash that makes a sound when dropped into the water.
17. Sailor receiving on-the-job training for a designated field (or rate)
19. Damage Control Assistant, usually is a junior officer.

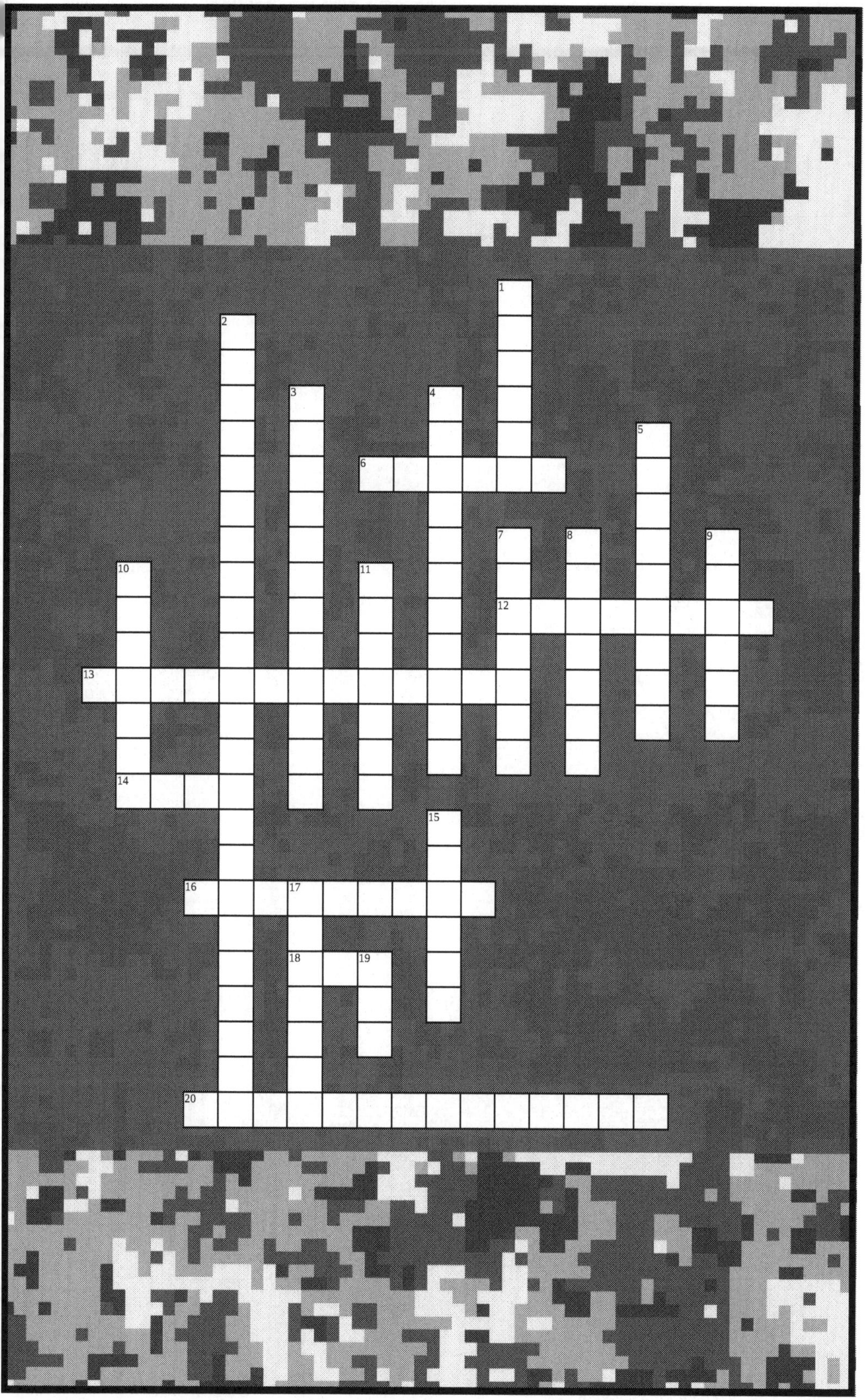
1
2
3
4
5
6
7
8
9
10
11
12
13
14
15
16
17
18
19
20

PUZZLE 16

ACROSS:

2. Pejorative term for sailors who exit the Naval Nuclear Power training program before successful completion.
6. The Commanding Officer or Admiral in command, regardless of gender, usually used when the CO has gained the respect of subordinates.
7. Combat Information Center Acronym
8. Short for Bureau Number - this is a 6-digit serial number assigned to every naval aircraft when it is accepted into service. In no way related to an aircraft's 3-digit "side number."
11. In days of old, a deck hand on his hands and knees holystoning a wooden deck. Now it just means to work hard without rest.
13. A short break during mealtime where sailors report to their rack or an undisclosed location for an hour of sleep.
15. Monitoring the movement of the ship while at anchor.
16. Inside information or advice.
17. To "borrow" a needed item, often condoned to get underway.
18. Evolution of transferring a sick person from a submarine to a helicopter.
19. Refers to a sailor's sea time in terms of the number of cruises or patrols completed.
20. Storekeeper.

DOWN:

1. Navy term for Nonjudicial punishment under Article 15 of the Uniform Code of Military Justice.
3. Toilet (or "Head," see above). Shipboard space where "shit" is both a verb AND a noun. Self-explanatory, really.
4. See "Piss Cutter".
5. Training device simulating a helicopter crash at sea.
9. Acronym for the date before returning home from a deployment to stop masturbating in order to save it up for your wife or girlfriend.
10. United States Naval Academy.
12. Acronym humorously describing the relationship between the Navy and the Marines.
14. The act of taking a peek outside after many days or weeks below decks.

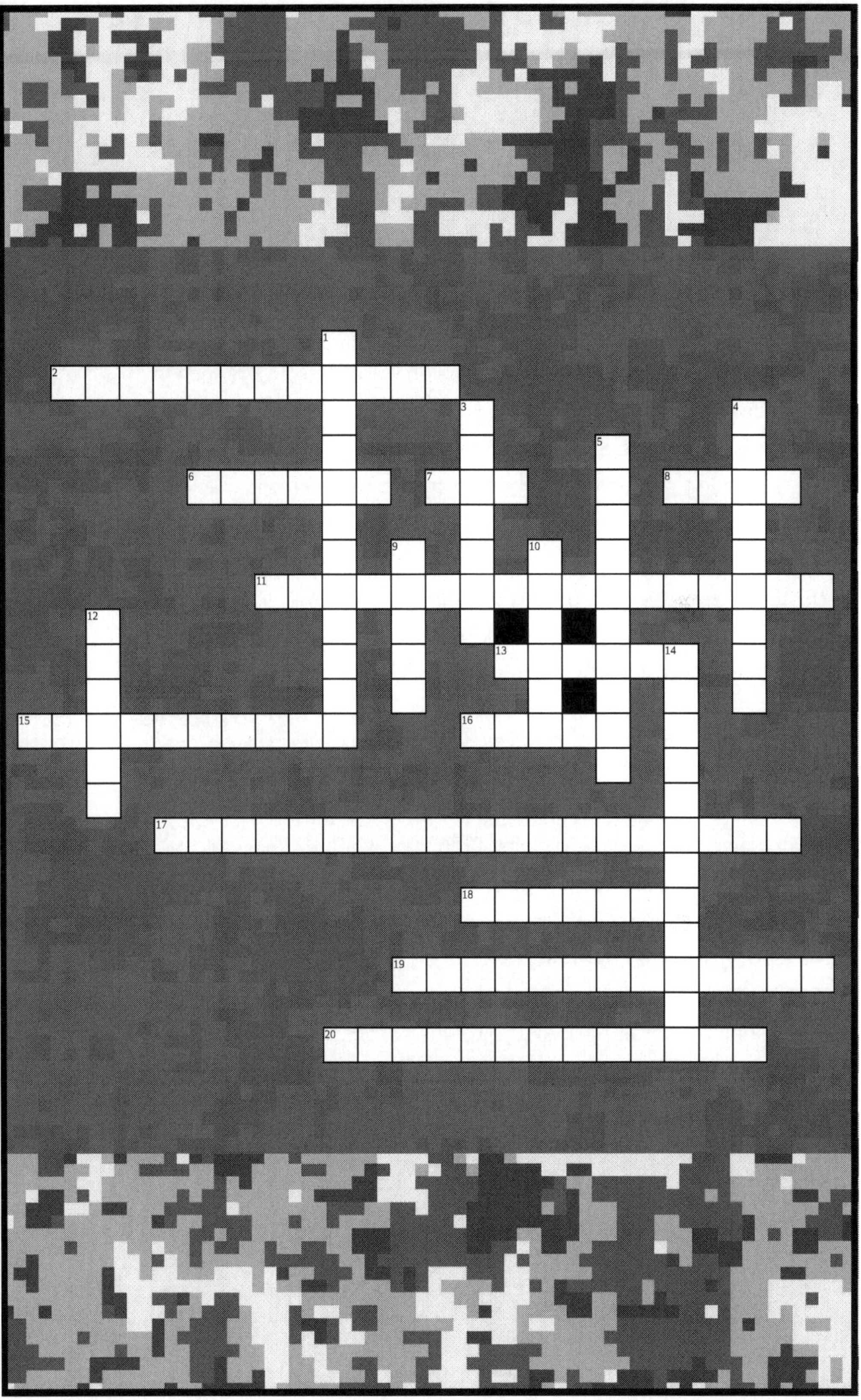

PUZZLE 17

ACROSS:

3. Repeatedly falling asleep in a meeting or a class while trying desperately to stay awake.
5. Lounge for Chiefs.
8. Physical Readiness Test, assessing a sailor's physical fitness.
9. A name used for by RDC's when an anonymous recruit messes up and doesn't take credit for his behavior.
10. A term describing a sailor that has been ordered SIQ(sleep in quarters)by medical.
12. Nickname for USS Enterprise (CVN-65).
14. Large log of baloney or Polish Sausage served for meals.
16. Pulled Directly Out Of My Ass, used by Chiefs when asked where they got a good idea.
17. Engineering sound-powered circuit.
18. End of Active Obligated Service, the normal end of enlistment.
19. Aircraft chronically out of service.
20. Term used by Marines to describe Corpsman that they like within Fleet Marine Force Units.

DOWN:

1. Derisive terms for U.S. Coast Guard personnel.
2. In submarine service, the practice of entering engineering log data that is suspiciously similar to the previous hour's data, derived from "Xerox."
4. A party for a sailor about to leave on a cruise.
6. Flirting with other people aboard the ship.
7. Designated smoking area aboard aircraft carriers.
11. Exercise area on a ship.
13. An enlisted sailor below the rank of E-7 (Chief Petty Officer).
15. Affectionate slang term for the warfare insignia/badge worn by special operations personnel qualified in Explosive Ordnance Disposal (BOMB SQUAD).

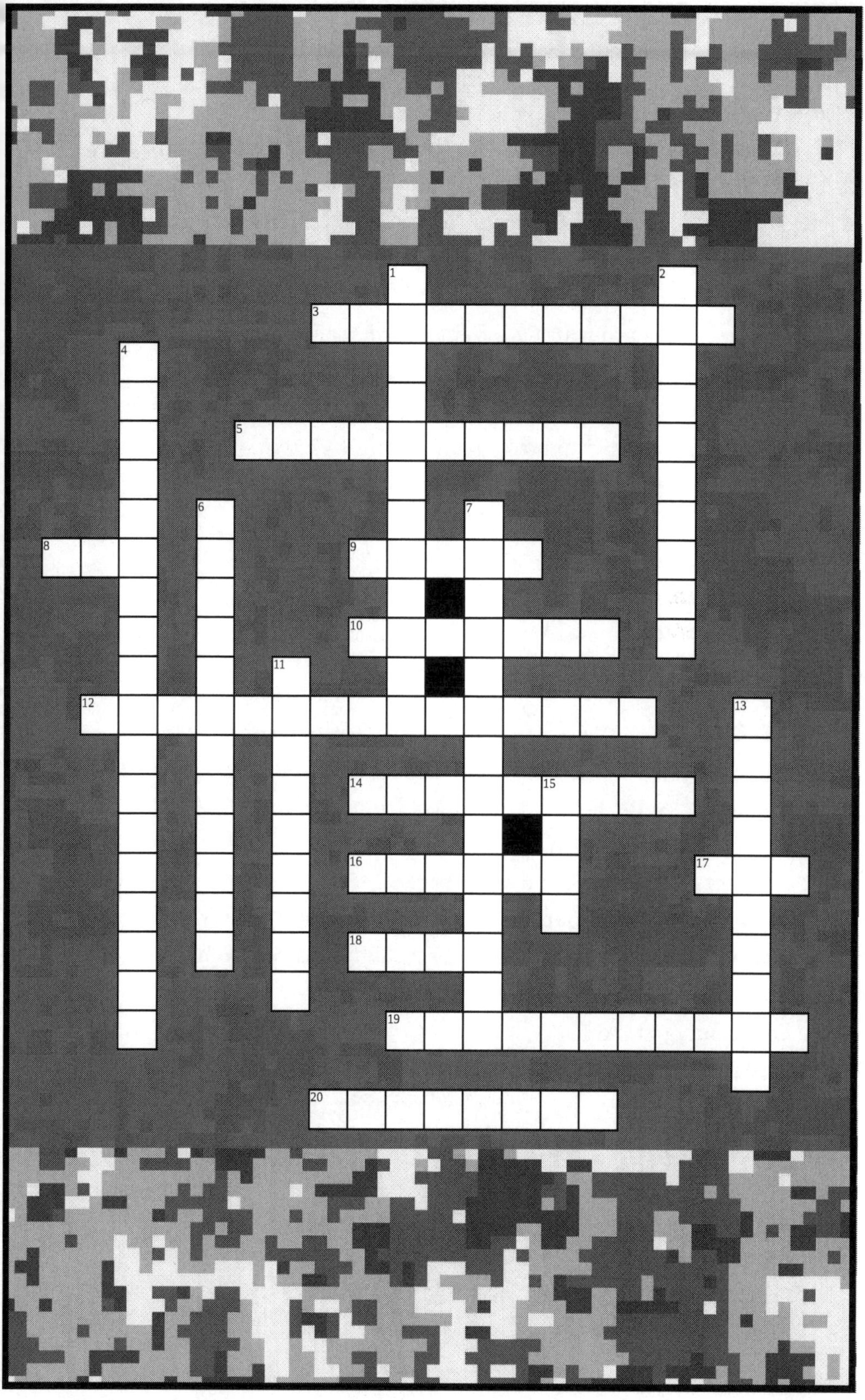
1
2
3
4
5
6
7
8
9
10
11
12
13
14
15
16
17
18
19
20

PUZZLE 18

ACROSS:

2. (Submarines) A prank, similar to the Portable Air Sample snipe hunt, conducted on a NQP that, played correctly, can involve several departments including sonar, engineering, and weapons.
3. Nickname for corned beef, based on color and flavor.
10. Your left hand. (AKA Palmala, Handeria's twin sister)
13. Reporting aboard without a full uniform; deficient in aptitude or intelligence.
15. Inoperative, casualty reported; casually, OOC (out of commission). Often jocularly applied to broken minor items not requiring any report, or to personnel on the binnacle list.
16. Food.
17. Short for "mid-rats"
18. Mildly abrasive scouring pad.
19. When an officer has sex with an enlisted sailor.
20. Aircraft carrier.

DOWN:

1. Nickname for USS Kalamazoo (AOR-6), a Wichita-class Replenishment Oiler that served the U.S. Atlantic Fleet from 1973 to 1996.
4. To correct something that is screwed up.
5. Culinary dish resembling a small rodent.
6. Slang for the USS Mount Whitney (LCC-20), which rarely leaves port.
7. Bright silver helmet worn by officer candidates as part of the "poopie suit" during the first week of OCS.
8. The cleaning of the bilges in Machinery Rooms, generally performed by younger sailors while supervisors poke fun.
9. Card game of trump played by 2 to 4 players (mostly "snipes"). A player unable to make their bid goes set 3 X the bid. Game can be played by partners.
11. Shortest Nuke on Board, refers to the lucky nuke who gets out of the Navy next.
12. Profane term (Acronym) for an electronic device.
14. Term for a chaotic situation.

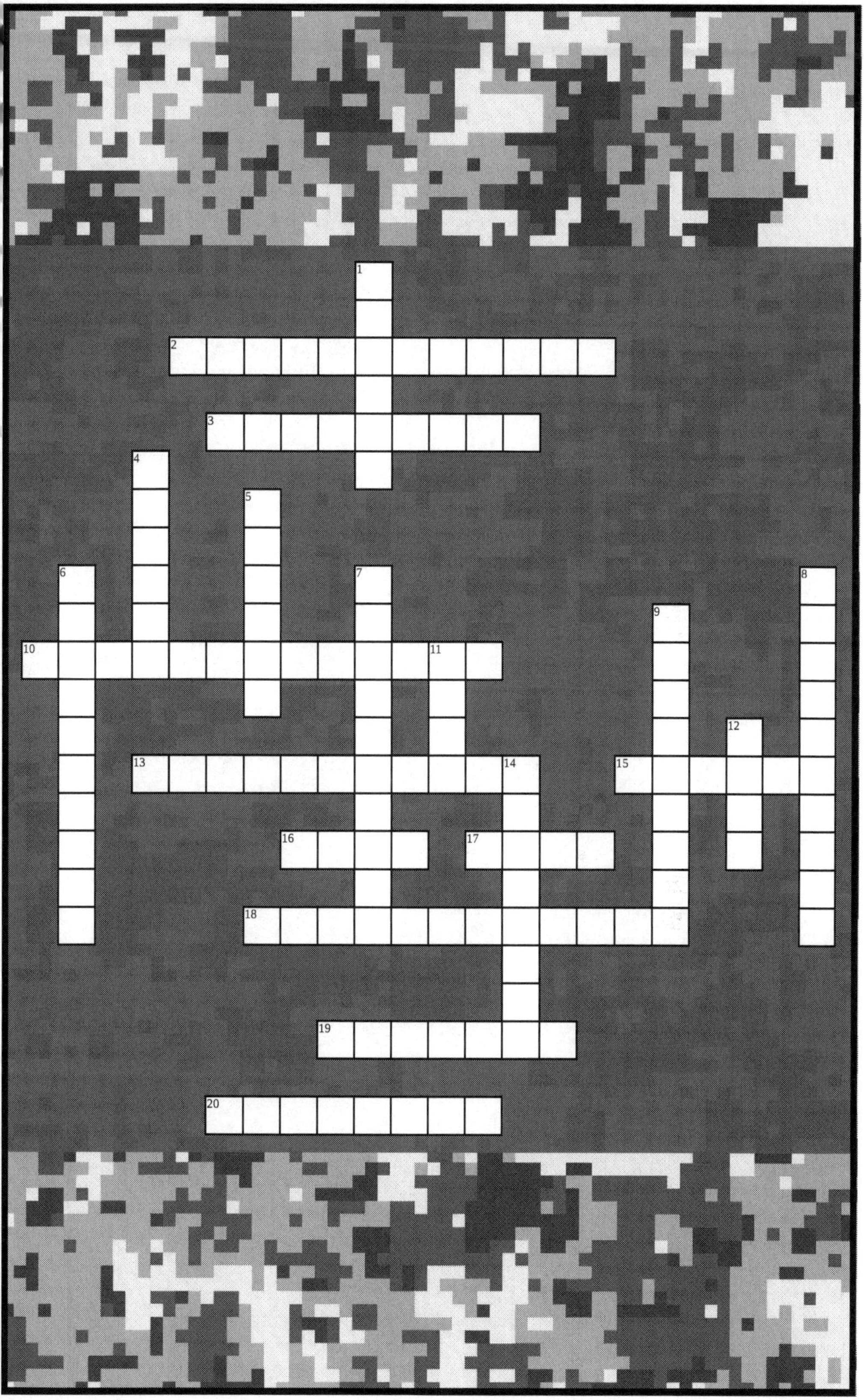
1
2
3
4
5
6
7
8
9
10
11
12
13
14
15
16
17
18
19
20

PUZZLE 19

ACROSS:

5. Mythical concept of a commemorative rivet.
7. Search and Rescue
10. Taking supplies from the supply ship via helo pick up and drop off.
13. Another name for a Battle Group.
14. Line Of Sight Tasking: when a senior officer tasks a junior officer with a time-consuming project.
15. A sailor in the Boatswain's Mate rating. Nickname for a Boatswains Mate.
16. A pair of pants made by cutting off the top half of a coveralls uniform item.
19. A person with eccentric or strange ideas; someone who is perceived as odd or quirky at Mess
20. Pneumatic tube system used for sending documents such as hard copies of radio messages to and from the radio room to other areas of the ship.

DOWN:

1. Term coined by nuclear personnel in response to Ordnance's navy pride.
2. Acronym for "male appendage in the ocular". Usually reserved for undesirable tasks forced on one by superiors.
3. Night Vision Equipment.
4. Individual tasked with ensuring urine samples in a drug test are legitimate.
6. Getting the day off for donating a pint of blood.
8. Also called the barrier, this is a huge nylon net strung across the landing area of a carrier to arrest the landing of an aircraft with damaged gear or a damaged tailhook.
9. To land a fixed-wing aircraft successfully aboard an aircraft carrier via the tailhook and arresting wires.
11. Acronym for group formed to provide guidance and support for young officers.
12. An official document issued by a command listing all activities for the day, including the Uniform of the Day.
17. A useless sailor who does not pull his share of the load.
18. Simulators.

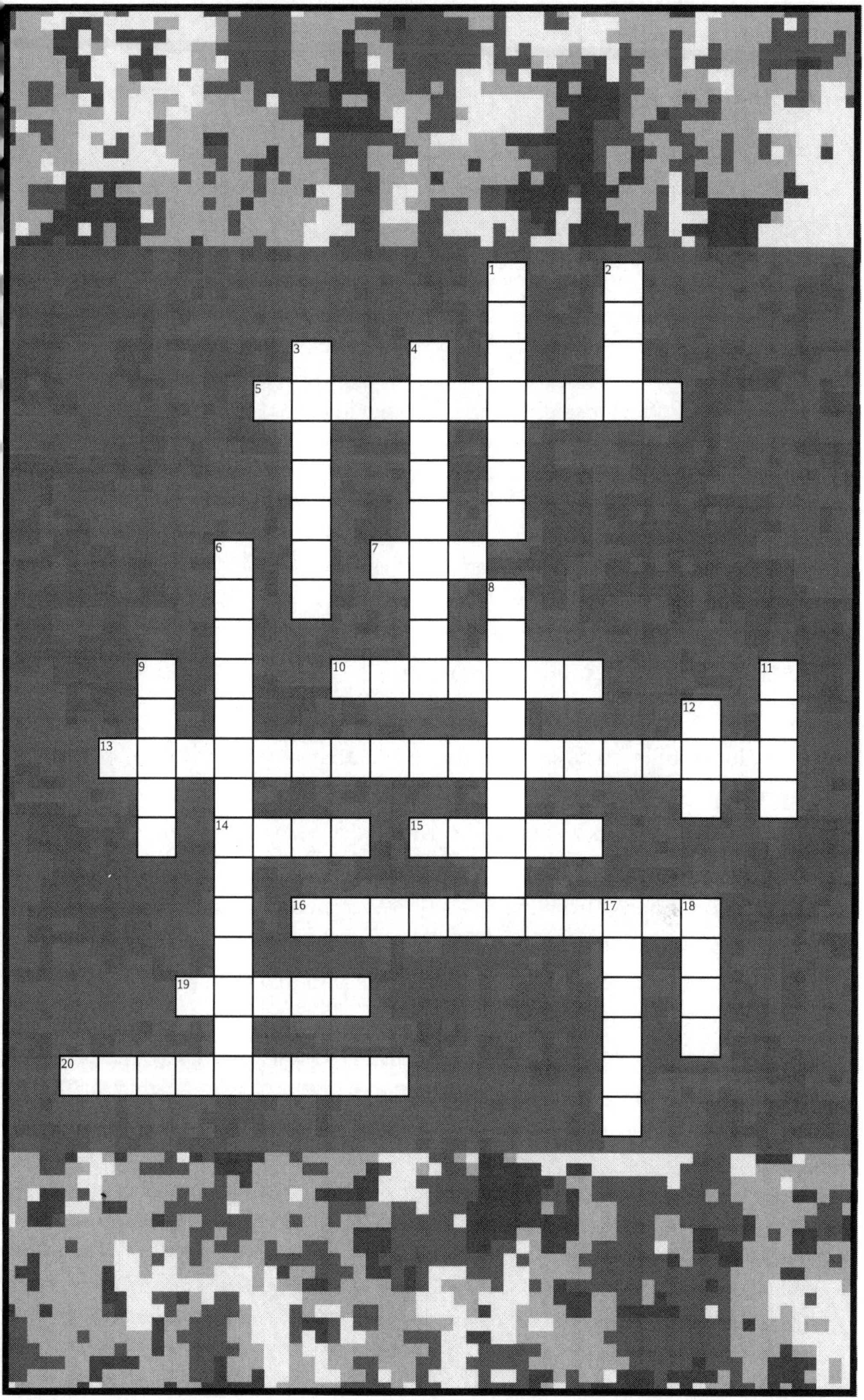
1
2
3
4
5
6
7
8
9
10
11
12
13
14
15
16
17
18
19
20

PUZZLE 20

ACROSS:

3. Shorthand for a chief warrant officer.
8. Often preceded by port or starboard, the ? generally begins abaft the beam on both sides of the ship and extends in an arc aft to the stern.
9. Any Naval personnel that serves aboard a Boomer.
12. Acronym refers to the lower part of a female overlapping stomach stuffed into a pair of utility/dungaree pants.
13. Soft sock brought for personal use.
15. The Pacific Fleet, usually referring to the Seventh Fleet.
16. Officer, usually a LT or LCDR, who is an admiral's aide.
17. Derogatory term for a U.S. Marine.
18. Sailors who work on the flight deck of a carrier.
19. Any decorative metal that must be constantly shined with Brasso or Nevr-Dull to avoid tarnishing. This undesirable duty is often performed by the most junior personnel in the command.
20. Any instrument reading that is all zeros.

DOWN:

1. A sailor of Filipino descent, used affectionately or pejoratively, depending on context.
2. Russian submarines will quickly turn 180 degrees while underway to see whether any American submarines are following.
4. A chain that hangs from the belt of a "short timer" for all to see, with one link representing a day.
5. Roast Beef, or any meat served aboard the ship that even the cooks who prepared it don't know what it is.
6. Slider topped with a fried egg. Also called a "One-Eyed Jack." Named after the first man to receive an artificial heart.
7. Surface Warfare Officer's badge (so named by aviators), a term pridefully used by non-carrier SWOs.
10. A boot camp term for sailors masturbating.
11. The wooden floating structures, at the waterline, that separate ships tied up in a nest.
14. A sailor in the E-1 paygrade who does not have a rating, and who has not yet graduated from Apprentice training..

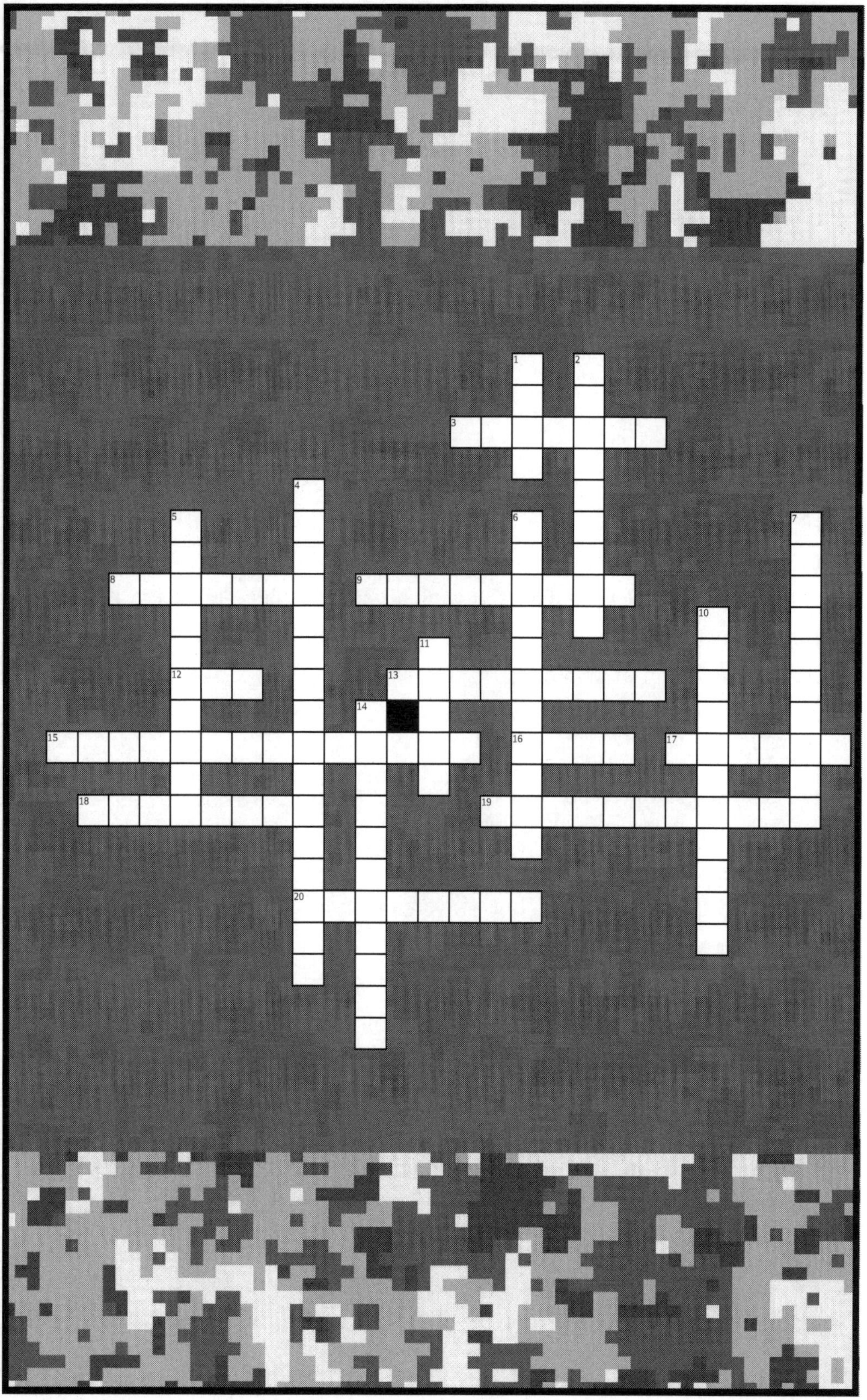
1
2
3
4
5
6
7
8
9
10
11
12
13
14
15
16
17
18
19
20

PUZZLE 21

ACROSS:

3. Watch rotation with five hours on watch and ten hours off.
5. To let go of, give up, or share something.
8. Celebration on the weather decks of a ship.
10. Breast insignia for Naval Aviators, Naval Flight Officers, and Enlisted Aviation Warfare Specialists.
12. A Navy pork chop that is extremely overcooked.
15. To reason out a problem by eliminating obvious wrong answers, encouraging someone to put forth more effort before giving up on a problem.
16. Pejorative term for junior officers, also referring to a sealant device.
18. Slang for Master Chief.
19. Device used in water survival training ("swims") to teach aviators how to get out of the cockpit of a fixed-wing aircraft that has crashed or ditched at sea. Much easier than the dreaded "helo dunker."
20. A single flight of an aircraft.

DOWN:

1. The idea a sailor could walk off the ship and, instead of going into town, step on his crank, throw his wallet into the water and hit himself over the head with a blunt object.
2. Same as a Bosun's Punch, but delivered by a Boiler Technician.
4. Another name for a dirtbag or shitbag
6. Unofficial punishment confining an officer.
7. Similar to "hit" (see below). Also, to cause minor damage to something (Ex. He dinged his aileron when he had a birdstrike on final to the boat.)
9. Enlisted Surface Warfare Specialist.
11. The trim orientation of a submarine (e.g., 5 degree up ???).
13. Over-the-top method of expressing additional items.
14. Usually at least one per ship, a person who mysteriously defecates in inappropriate places onboard.
17. Term referring to smaller class ships, such as destroyers and frigates.

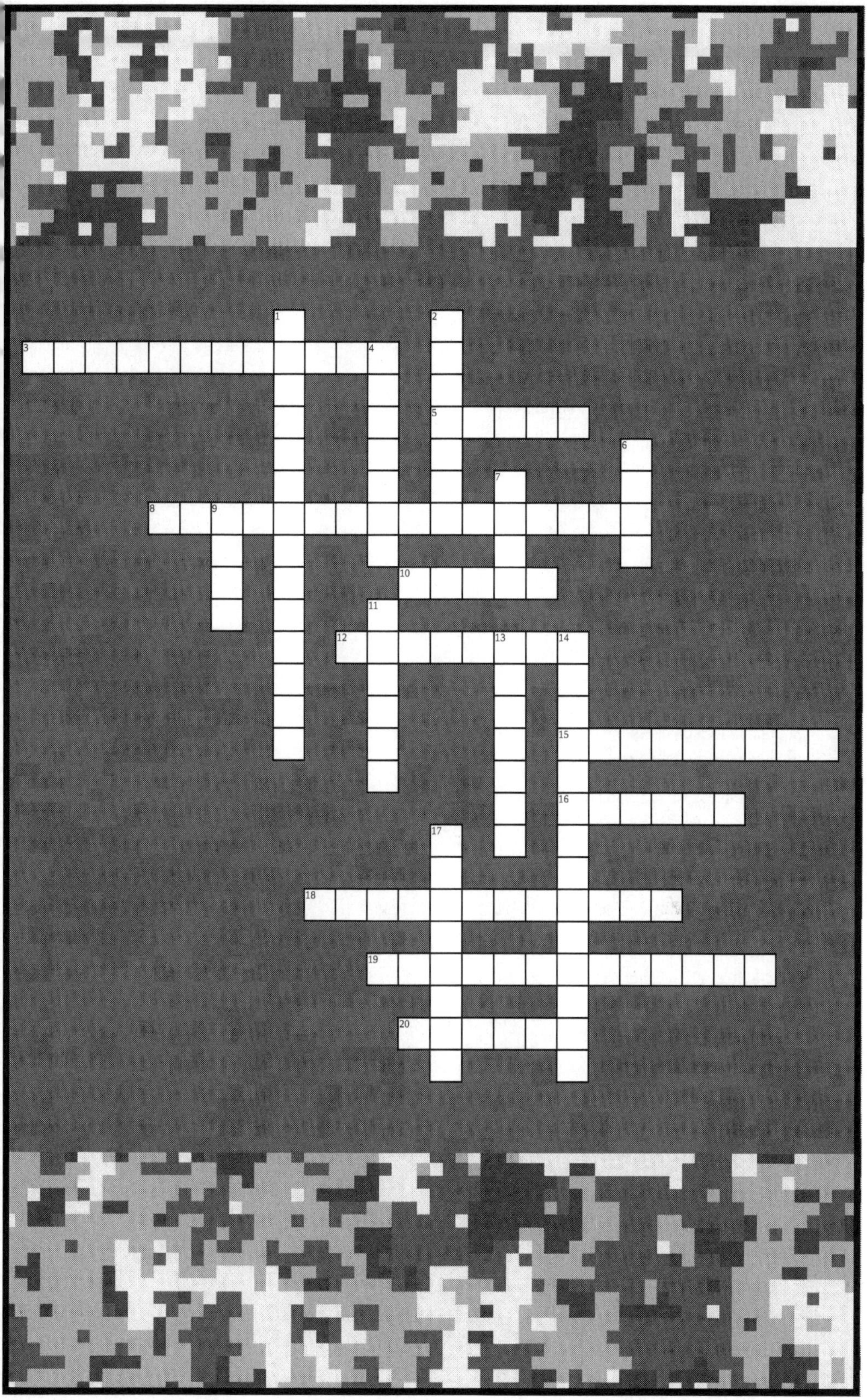
1
2
3
4
5
6
7
8
9
10
11
12
13
14
15
16
17
18
19
20

PUZZLE 22

ACROSS:

3. The creek that divided the base from the civilian side, in the Philippines, Between Olongapo City and Cubi Point Naval Base.
5. Gathering of aviators on a carrier's forecastle.
6. Similar to rimjob but in this case the sailor dunks his nut sack in a beverage of an unliked individual.
8. See Scupper Trout.
11. Radioman or Electrician's Mate.
12. Slang for an officer, referring to their pay grade starting with "O" (O-1, O-2, etc.).
17. Another nickname for the USS "Bonhomme Richard" (LHD-6).
19. Slang for a pile of feces.
20. A turd or other length of feces.

DOWN:

1. Schedules Officer.
2. A pejorative term for a graduate of the U.S. Naval Academy. So named from their large collegiate rings.
4. A term used, usually derisively, when referring to any sailor who has very little time in or a lot less time than the speaker.
7. Navy Filmmakers' acronym for Editorials, Motion Picture, and Television Department.
9. Not paying attention, due to "looking up in the sky" instead of on the assigned task.
10. Rifle, as used in manual-of-arms (rifle drill).
13. A sailor who has failed to qualify in Damage Control in the stipulated time period and has become "Damage Control Delinquent".
14. Junior Staff Instructor.
15. Officer of the Deck.
16. Acronym for Stupid Human Error
18. Aircraft positively identified as hostile.

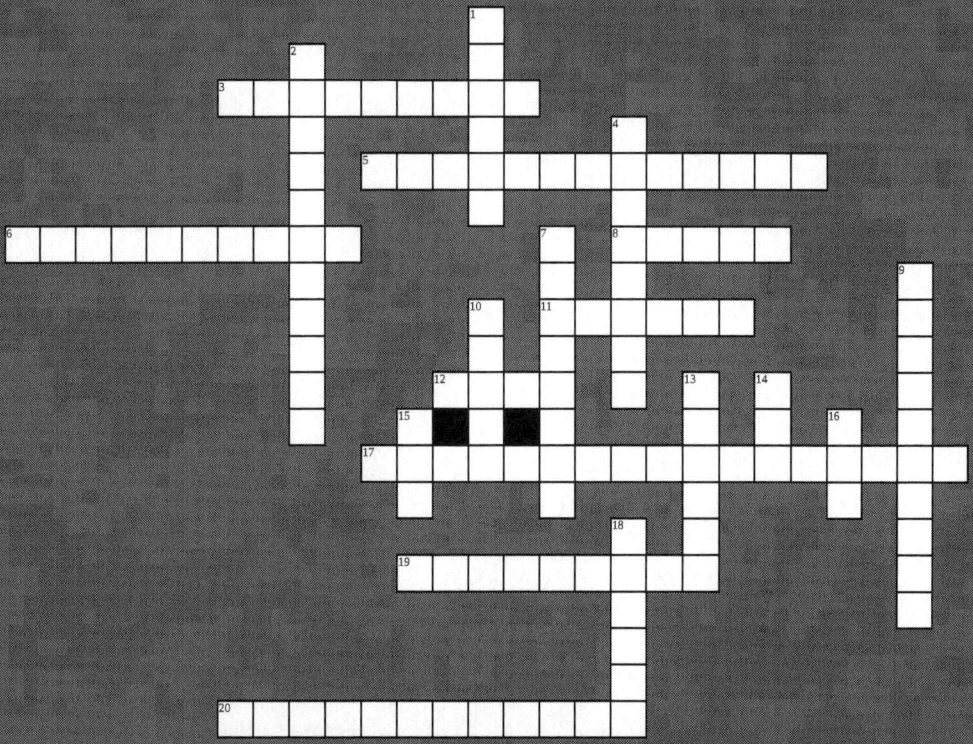

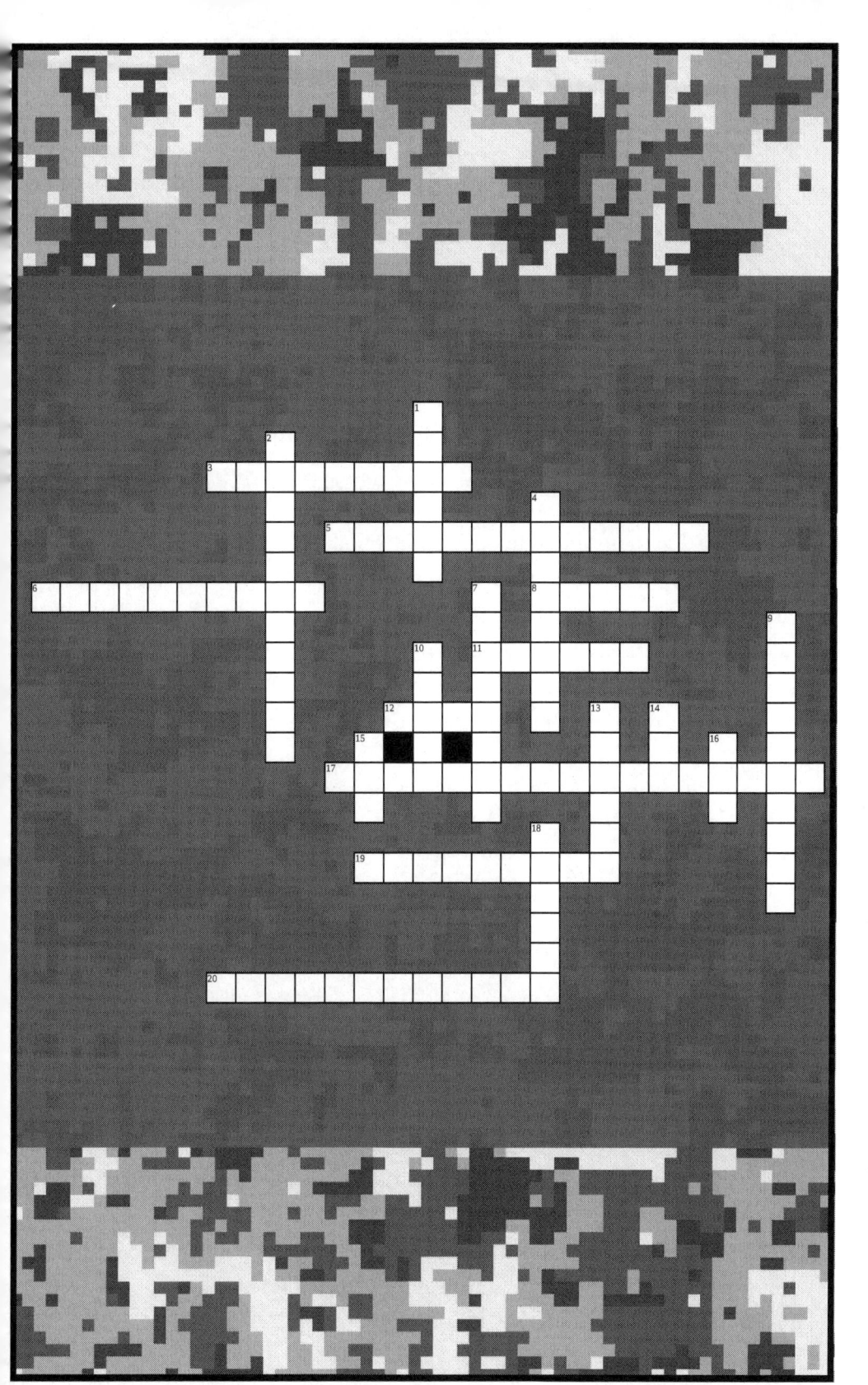

PUZZLE 23

ACROSS:

4. Slang for a Bad Conduct Discharge, which is usually handed out along with an administrative separation (ADSEP) after a sailor pops positive on a "Whiz Quiz."
6. When a pilot loses situational awareness due to task saturation.
8. Prearranged meeting point in-port for carrier pilots.
11. A device on submarines that can shoot countermeasures, flares, and more.
12. Urinalysis for drug testing, commonly referred to as "Piss Test." Failing is known as "popping positive."
14. In naval aviation, to voluntarily discontinue an approach to a landing or a hover due to unsafe or uncomfortable flight conditions.
16. An enlisted sailor below the rank of E-7 (Chief Petty Officer). More modern than the term Bluejacket.
18. Physical exercises as punishment or correctional training.
19. Any fellow sailor. Used as a derogatory term.
20. A saying yelled by the petty officer of the watch to wake everyone up.

DOWN:

1. Metal box used in the Navy for transporting supplies, often difficult to carry.
2. Wiping one's genital organ around the inside of a senior enlisted or officer's coffee cup.
3. An expression voiced (in a very sarcastic cheery manner) on occasions when, in fact, it's not that much of a Fine Navy Day at all.
5. Military creases incorrectly or crookedly ironed into uniforms.
7. Civilian-style shower aboard a ship.
9. 1990s-era Naval Station Norfolk slang for the USS Emory S. Land (AS-39), which during that time period, rarely left port.
10. One half hour after 0'dark hundred. (used in the same context as 0'dark hundred.)
13. Superstructure of an aircraft carrier.
15. Person unwilling to leave a Forward Operating Base.
17. Hamburger Patty

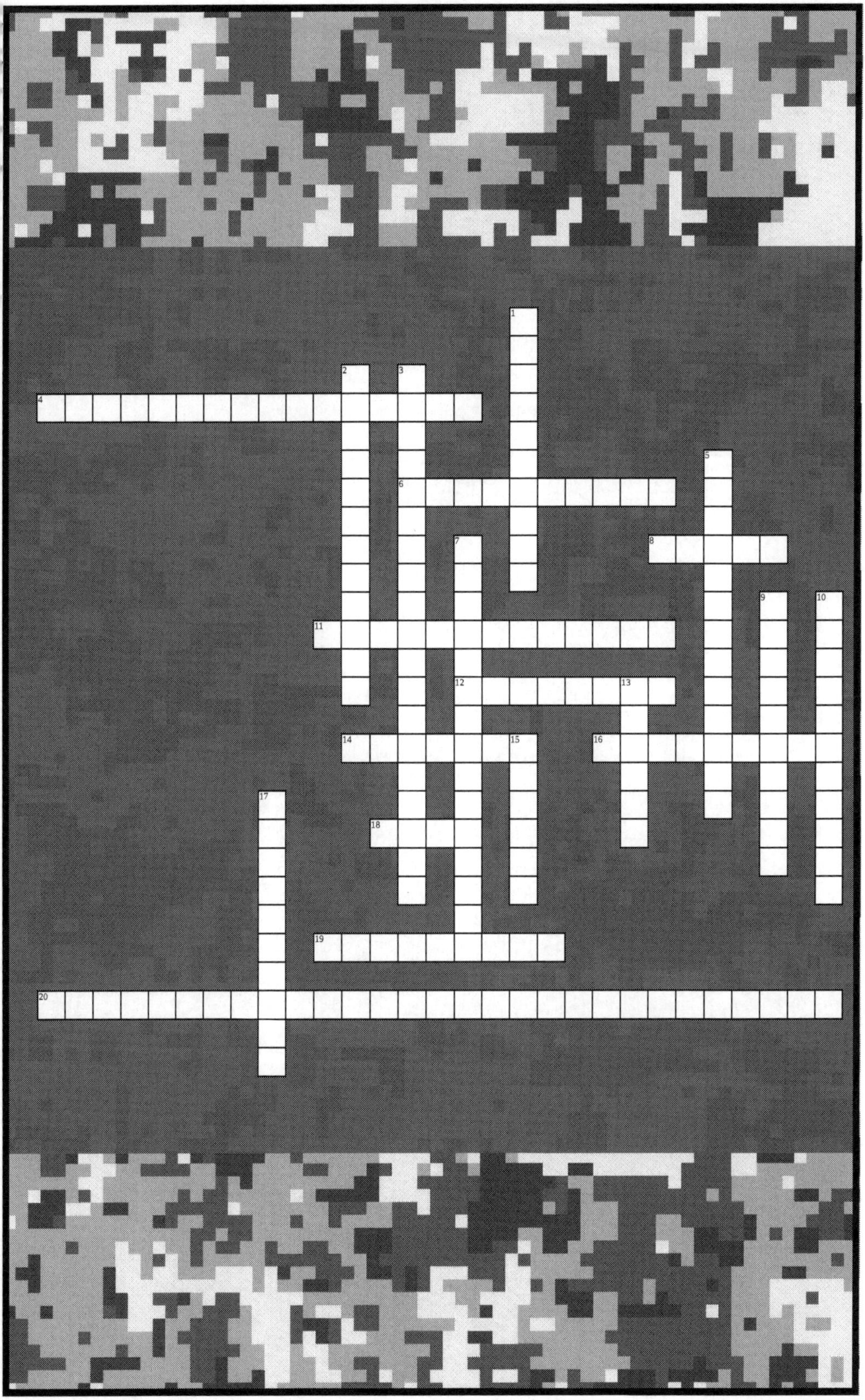
1
2
3
4
5
6
7
8
9
10
11
12
13
14
15
16
17
18
19
20

PUZZLE 24

ACROSS:

1. Dry suit worn by aviators over cold water.
3. To make the best of a bad situation.
9. Sailors assigned mandatory physical training due to being overweight.
11. Big Ol' Standard Navy Issue Ass.
14. Flying in a dangerous manner.
16. Chicken cordon bleu shaped like a hamster.
17. Acronym for "I Hate This Fucking Place," commonly uttered by midshipmen at the Naval Academy.
18. Vertical distance between waterline and gunwale.
19. To scour; generic term for scouring powder.
20. Short for frequency.

DOWN:

2. A long evaluation or training drill onboard a submarine. It normally goes on for hours with no clear ending point.
4. A four hour watch technically spanning from 00:00 to 04:00, though in practice begins at 2345 and ends at 0345. Most commonly seen on a "Dogged Watch" schedule.
5. A Marine (cf. Ground Pounder = soldier).
6. Slang for F/A-18 Hornet aircraft due to its fuel consumption during takeoff.
7. Chicken (food) on the Flight Deck
8. Eating utensils.
10. Term usually applied to personnel in the Aerographer's Mate (AG) Rating.
12. Slang for flight suit.
13. Tripler Army Medical Center, Oahu, scourge of sailors at Pearl Harbor.
15. Fighter Attack Guy, also used derogatorily for Naval Academy graduates or submarine personnel.

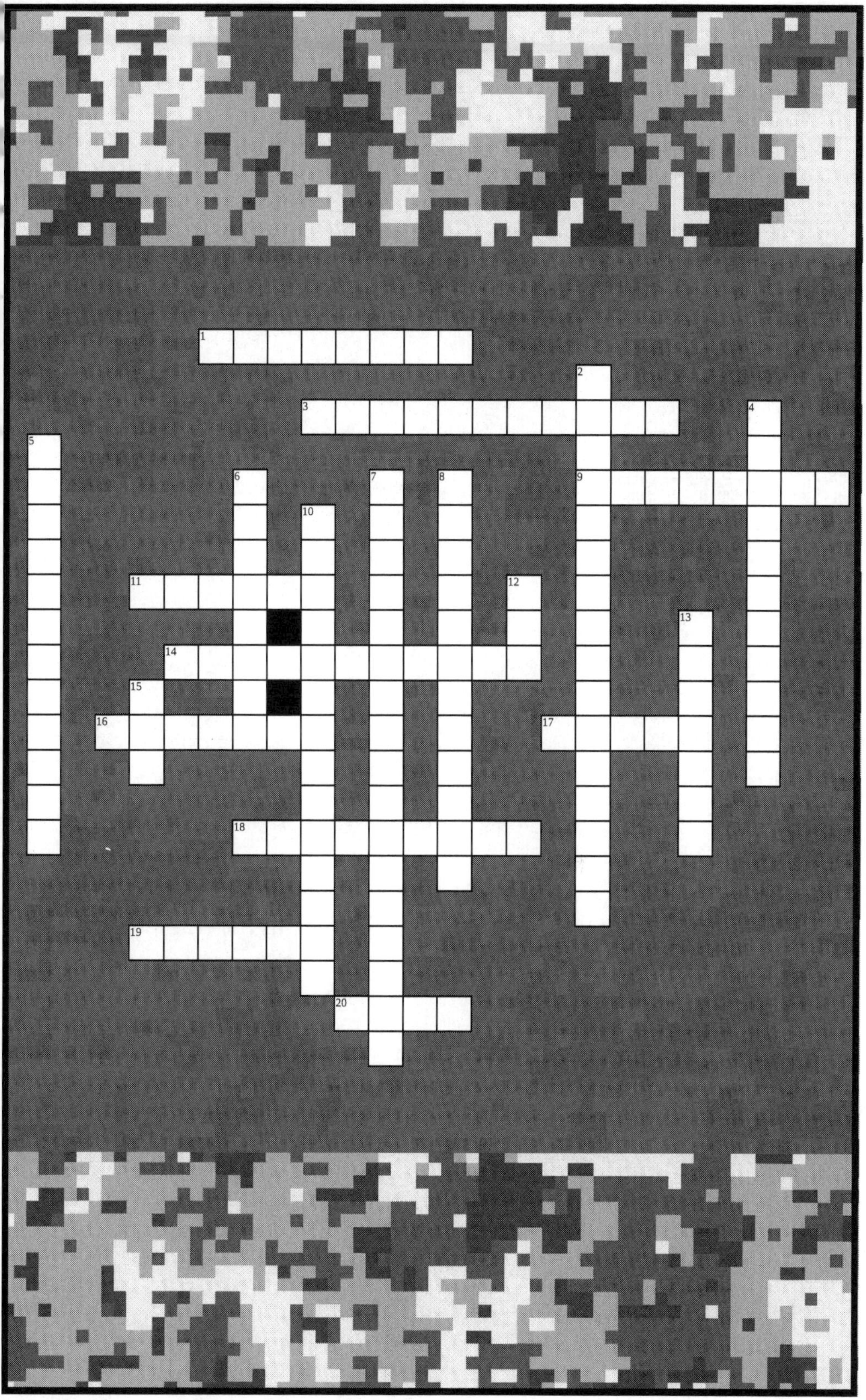
1
2
3
4
5
6
7
8
9
10
11
12
13
14
15
16
17
18
19
20

PUZZLE 25

ACROSS:

4. Diesel submarine or the USS California (CGN-36).
7. A sailor in the Submarine Service.
9. USS Olympia (SSN-717).
10. A civilian in Civil Service positions working for the U.S. Navy. Very derogatory.
13. Slang for masturbating.
15. Any "Surface Navy" officer or CPO, from the dark footwear worn with khaki uniforms.
16. Slang for Yokosuka, Japan.
18. Magical pill dispensed by hospital corpsmen, believed to cure every ailment.
19. Technical term describing malfunctioning or inoperable equipment.

DOWN:

1. A "fun" game in which one or more sailors place a washer or nut around a rod or similar metal device and then hold it to a HP Air hose, 125-700 psi.
2. Refers to the gold-colored bars designating the rank of Ensign
3. Abbreviation for "Friend of Only Black Nuke On Board," referring to a shipmate who is a friend of the only African American nuclear technician onboard a submarine.
5. Phonetic letters C and O. Refers to the Commanding Officer of a unit.
6. Crew-coined term for the USS Juneau. Term could come from the feeling that the Juneau has the homely warmth of a prison cellblock. 10 is the vessel's hull number.
8. Washroom for eating implements such as knives, forks, trays, and cups.
11. Missile Submarine.
12. A form of hazing by taking the round paper cutouts left from a hole punch and putting them in a box or other container rigged to open and rain down on another.
14. A man who was a punk in real life but tries to act tough in the Navy.
17. A lazy and almost useless sailor. Produces substandard work-usually creating extra work for his shipmates.
20. The buoyant dummy used during man-overboard drills.

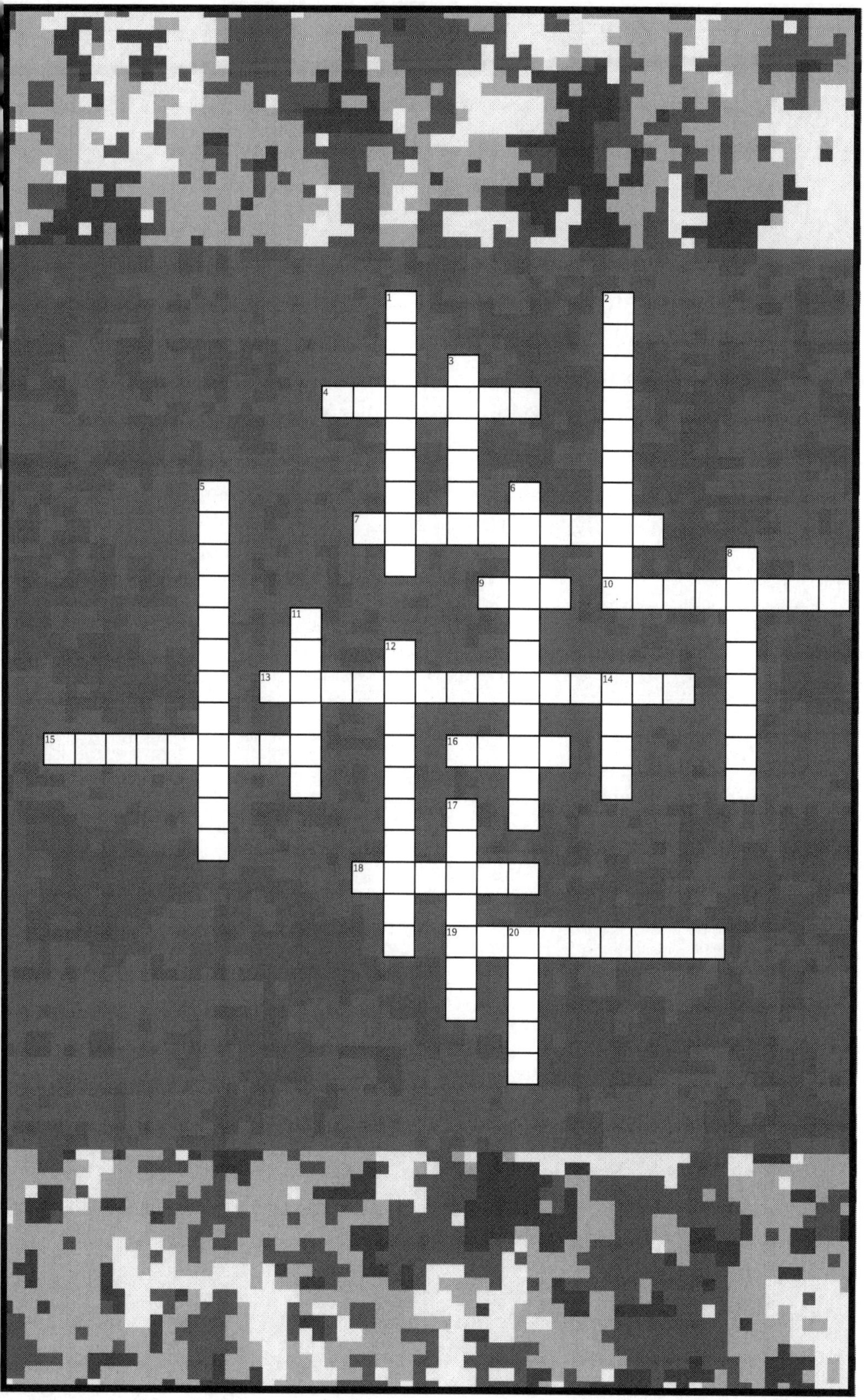
1
2
3
4
5
6
7
8
9
10
11
12
13
14
15
16
17
18
19
20

PUZZLE 26

ACROSS:

4. Sailor wearing the working white uniform.
7. A submarine veteran's previous command.
10. A treat or reward, derived from "Benefit".
12. Refers to when a Submarine orders up All Ahead Flank Cavitate, without rigging for high speed.
15. Carrier Onboard Delivery - the mighty C-2 Greyhound, which ferries people and supplies to and from the carrier on a regular basis.
16. Term used usually by Aviation Boatswains Mates to describe Blue Shirts or Chock Walkers on the flight deck and hangar bay of an aircraft carrier.
17. A mild case of vertigo experienced aboard a ship.
18. Out of commission; hard-down.
19. Long cable containing a sonar array that is trailed out behind a ship or submarine.
20. Using your hands to pick up dustbunnies and dirt from carpet. Similar to Ricky Sweep.

DOWN:

1. A sailor escorting a prisoner to the brig.
2. To overthink an easy task.
3. Term for sailor's trying to tell a story, or give an example of how business was handled at their last command.
5. Condoms
6. The pier liberty facilities at Jebel Ali. Sandbox Liberty means travel outside the port of Jebel Ali is not authorized. All you get is a "beer on the pier". See "Gerbil Alley".
8. Term referring to a subtender comprised primarily of female sailors.
9. Acronym for Delinquent In Qualifications. Ex: "That shitbird is dinq on ship's quals!" Also Delinquent In Nuclear Quals
11. Cancelled Exercise. Used to refer to any event which has been cancelled, not just formal exercises.
13. Naval veteran.
14. Slang for 21 day wine made out of bug juice, sugar and yeast. Tastes like crap but packs a powerful wallop.

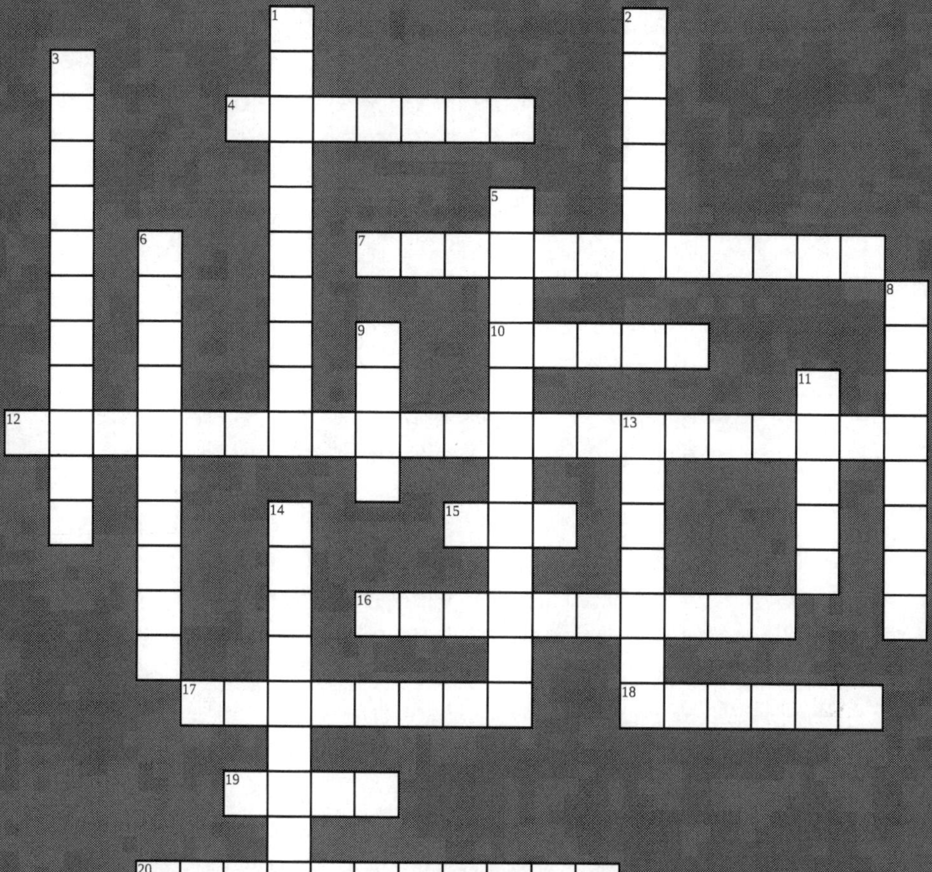
1
2
3
4
5
6
7
8
9
10
11
12
13
14
15
16
17
18
19
20

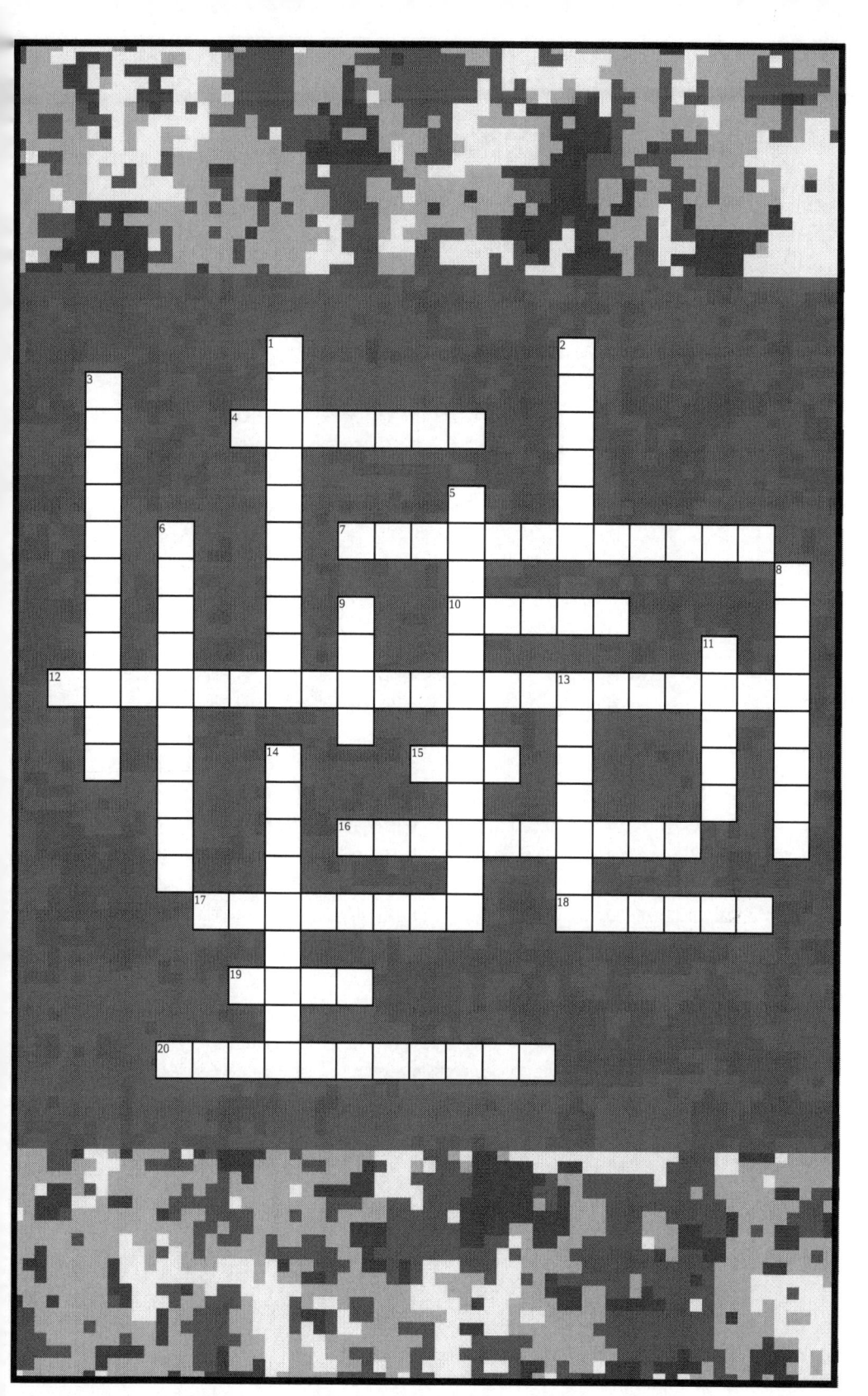

WORD SEARCH 1

```
O H S R E D I L S W I V 9 E O H G K O C W T Y G
R T C C T S O V P D 9 L S T T I G 9 D O G Z W A
L O A N E E M V S M C S D B R Y G N L I U O M N
K L C M G N C Y E C H A R T S R V F N A R G Z I
H C L O D O M A C Z 9 A B U N 9 N S F R O I I E
W E F M I A C G P K R L R C O E F A O C N N K V
F L 9 A M 0 T O T S C 0 M E D O A M 0 T A U W E
E B E N T W A U W B K H 9 L P R O R F A N T O G
T A P D I S T E R W 0 K O F U T M R I L N W D C
F T K P G M U 0 U N I G P V M S E R L O A T I 9
E S 0 O I N N Z W O N D Z A O D A U S 9 C Z W D
L P G P D T B I U O S B U Z N N B I 0 O H V C Z
E R R N O L I R I Y R G U O I T Z 0 F Z A V A L
H O N I W S N T Y T Y H W R E G O N 0 B S D P M
T C K G T U A F C A F Y E R N W E O 0 O U N T P
O E 0 H 0 R B B D D A I I R K R T O U O K A S R
T N D T E N L O D D P P A 9 E T A B A R F L E B
Y I A P O G T T 0 A M N P Y Z S R V E R 0 E W F
S R O A M E S 9 I A F H R Z F P I Z A E Y M D C
S A W Y R E T N V K M D F V T D P Z T O 0 C N D
U M A E T N O I S S E R P P U S Y T I V E L V B
P O H A A I 0 T P K A 0 U D V A Z F I W N 9 I F
V B S E S O O I A G Z P E F N I T V L N G C R R
M E B F M A A C O L B M R W D A P Y F H H V 0 R
```

Vampire
Bull Nuke
Cake Dryer
90-day Wonder
Marine Corps Table Cloth
TAD
Turn 'n Burn

Operation GOLDENFLOW
Pussy to the left
WESTPAC Widow
Levity Suppression Team
Pirate
NFO

Space
Zarf
Mom and Pop night
Here today, GUAM tomorrow
Sliders
Two-Digit Midget

WORD SEARCH 2

```
E N D U U O V B M D D N W W V L S 1 T B P B P N
K S Y M G N V S O P E S O T O I A U U W L Y S N
1 E P A M V G E F M M K N O L T G B F D D A G O
C G L E E B A B R B K A P L U A O V J J R D D V
A P Y Y 1 S B L A H L C S P N H N H B E A S A T
F Y Y K 1 N Y B G V E K K N T D C C V Y L R N A
R R L T 1 U K I I R I A H S O V W E J 1 J E A E
J M O O M K C C K Y E E D 1 L F T O V E S H U M
V T T R F V U L V W M E D R D S O M P P L T J Y
L B V R F C L J E D T J O R C P D O 1 M L A A R
E G R E E N T A B L E T E A P A R T Y S E F L E
M D S S L D T C W S K R H N Y 1 U 1 K E K F U T
A I D L W S A L O P B W L P L F U 1 G P H M H S
C E I S L B M I G E G A P C 1 Y E R U S P H C Y
E I J 1 Y I O I L C N H W M J H O Y S D C M K M
H 1 I 1 U P P O W G K S V B E G A L F A B U W T
T E L Y B T W Y M N 1 M W O R C A T N E R F Y C
S J H U K D C I S 1 D O O C T A S H T T S H D H
S V A D E V T O U S M C L S C J A B Y D G E K B
I 1 D C L W V G F O U G S D S D V B N F F E J N
K H K A S T C C D W K P I W C M J C F N P O U 1
R S U V A L J T L L J V G O K L 1 B O H R Y U J
B W S O B L P D S O T 1 Y O Y G T W P G R T P L
V N C S S H O U O L I B O A S K H S D U S N W C
```

TOD
Below Decks
Pussy Pills
Comshaw
WUBAflage

CIVLANT
Kiss the Camel
Overhead
C-GU11
Rent-A-Crow

Mystery Meat
Chula-juana
JORG
Lucky Bag
NO GAS

Father's Day
Wog
Green Table Tea Party
Voluntold

WORD SEARCH 3

```
G 5 P I W O S J N O I T U L O V E G H R D U V B
W O J 5 X R H O D B B I T C H B O X J U O V D P
S K X W B N E W G W R M 5 W G H T U W O V S I J
N V E J L R F N W D B 5 I L L E W R E D D A L R
I 5 H C J B W P E C E H B F N U D F B H U A S E
K P E 5 A N H S G E X A I E L A S E G K S E K B
S L G L C F T O U U W P T R M S C H N J A F F B
E V U B D R R D T J P T I H B L M P N W K P M U
R H C D A D U U 5 N H H U N P F C V R X I F X R
O R L F O 5 K T S V H R C V J I 5 K P T E B U G
F L A C N O U U A E P V T U U P L E J K G P G N
D K I S 5 J D O V J H L T W A U I L M T I F W I
E F K C O R F H S O L T S J H J O W O T G V C K
M A G R M U X C M K O T N U O M U X J W B A L C
A 5 V F G F M N A M T E D O V D V O W S S C R U
E F C B T P F U W J B K T N E 5 X T X E R E V S
R X 5 L I O T P E F I C B U V M S S S U 5 E C L
C K X G T 5 S H S K 5 I K L F K T G I J G O M G
A H A T I J U B K D D T G L A D C S H E N N U V
F 5 S U V T V V C J E F I T T B E K U E T F P T
B B M E A K C J S T P L E M K C M C R B 5 I C B
W J O C I B C P T F R O P H D G J B P W S G F I
O P G W O L B R 5 N G W S B J R W S F G F C R N
W F A X N L W B K T U N A B O A T M R K W K 5 V
```

Cruise	Bitchbox	Evolution	5MC
Creamed foreskins	Punch Out	Titivaion	Skate
Tweener	Wolf Ticket	Tuna Boat	BCG's
A-Farts	Bust Me on The Surface	Sucking Rubber	Coner
Frock	Death Pillows	JO	Ladderwell

WORD SEARCH 4

```
A R U G J C Q H H G K F R P E O T Z U G H S L
R F V N V A F P J L F C Z A D K Z P A D L S U A
M H P Z E O Q T M R S P K K R A T X K L O C S V
P O A G V R J I U P E N B G G R W A A H I D D E
I C X C E G R L F N U F R U A G T B R K Q W U B
T K K S N Q S S T F R C T O B O S A J E N P F K
O E I E N N A C T I H S E U M R T R B W G I Y O
F Y D W U X W C I V P L D I O A V E C I J L D Q
T P D F M O B F E U R W D T X H G M Z R U S I R
H U I U B F Z R X E E I A T K I S M K K I L F B
E C E L E Y O O X I Q G W F J W D I T I V D F T
N K C S R B V T S K I J W C I A O K V K N L E M
A S R Q E T X E M V M C L I P M B S Q V T L Q U
V J U W D G R X A I K N O R G F L B Q B G E T W
Y R I J C C G N Q P R Z S L X J S H N N V R L Z
Y D S W H Y Z Z U F D N A M R A W M U V A E V G
I O E B I J P L K Y G C O K N D Z J Y W Y Y E K
D U V A E R P X Q L Q T P U U W O C M C Z Z W C
W C B A F W T Q W A E P E Y N J V O S L N X U O
D H M L O O H C S K R O F E F I N K K O Q Z I L
M E H S D T T J C Y K E U A O N D L P U I N L B
X K H Q N W T C F A J Q T L H F K V D J A V E O
P I V B A L L C H H K C L K A U N S W F J R I W
G T I B Z K O R W D E J V H Q M O I X I R H T T
```

SLUF	Warm and Fuzzy	SLURFF	Navigators Balls
Skimmer	"Armpit of the Navy"	Even Numbered Chief	Knife & Fork School
Shit Can	Budweiser	Kiddie Cruise	Hockey pucks
Dink	Gronk	Dixie Cup	Bilge Rat
JO Jungle	LSO	Two-block	Douche Kit

WORD SEARCH 5

```
G Z Y R Y Z R R E T T U C S S I P N D P O F O G
Q Y U V S F G Q B A S C A A F J V L O O V H M O
Y Y X J S W Y O G E D S O K C I C N A L B K K H
Z J D C A P E A Q R I D Z R T A I J W F W S V C
N Y Q Y D F G T A H P Z A G J D N J O F E T H W
S R I F E V I O X H Q C H H Q B M H L M O A S Y
T E Q B R Q B Q Y V K J P I S Z G T V A T C U G
L K C G E R G M E E B D Q F A R L N M N L N R C
O C U G A S Y H R X B J Q N Y O E T A D B B G E
Z E N T S C M J T W I K G M J J Q D O G F N V B
N H S E G M A R V V C I L S S N S V R G O Q G T
N C R W P C O D P U F R W F B E X R C O I T E T
Y R G X K V S O F V Z U O I I B N I V D T P M G
K E A S B N U R R C A R R R N I O U V U M U E Y
Q K C X G M E I C Y M D O N D R E L T N P K C M
S C K X C T G G N Z D T A E K V G O T O S F I W
N E M A S W L H D Y S A K O S R O O T E X R C A
R P G U X E Z A G A Y C E B Y Z J X C S R T J H
T X L S M I W S E M O F M R I O E P M R N T E F
Z C I H H W G S Y S U U L A T M M V O I G U K B
S P M A R I N E S H O W E R Y W C V J N I F G V
V Q K M D O U B L E N U T S T B L N T S Q V E B
T U I Y T P Y T F E I V X A V J U F I K X R A X
H I Q B V G Y Y F E Y K M F D J R C L F U F B V
```

AWOL	Ready Room	O-gang	Bolter	Redass
Piss Cutter	Guns	Form	Marine Shower	Socked-in
Pecker-Checker	Clusterfuck	Bird	Swims	CAG
Cut orders	Sea Stories	Starboard	Cracker Jacks	Double Nuts

WORD SEARCH 6

```
A Y V L A U N D R Y Q U E E N H V M Y D J D H P
D K L M Z R E T S U B E L K C U N K B Z T T P Q
N R I S B M E O I B S D H Z B X E F N G L F C W
H I B D O X T Z B A U C P C O D X X E F X Z M B
U I E I T W R R O H O G V S J I S T B D J Q K A
B W R Z T U N M D Y P A D D W N T W U J P E W Z
Z Z T X S B J G N T A W M Q O I A F R Y M J N H
E E Y N H A F C Q Z H W E I N R P L N Z T R H B
Q B R T M C F L P A X T T G D N E A O X N L M D
Z W I H D H L M B F F A S R P B O T N V Z C A L
T A S B F A R T N A T L O I N N A T E X H D H V
D S K B C R W H R S A O P N E N E O B I R C U K
D N R I I G A G N M B O P L L O P C E D X O W
N Z V P G O W N T V B U A S U V E K D H J U H Q
B A K W G T I E K O O B X T T E E D O X O R G E
E S I H Z N Y M I I K T U N T N L M S J B V W G
S T U M A E D M C L R H S R S L K G V L T M C G
I O M E D C I Z D Z M J G U E F E K G G D C A Q
K K L A H S J X I K V K I B H T E R D U K V O W
T C Y T I C Y T S A N T Z Q R N E S A N N B J I
T T V H W P I B Z L O M T R Z Z R M A C P S M V
E E Y S J L E W H C T O R C Y L O H N Y K A P L
R E T S U B V Q B W B C N K X J U R N U N S H P
K E L D O W B A L D A E T N Z X R Y Q M F X E P
```

WUBA Chariot
Flattop
Fun Meter
Holy Crotch
Knuckle Buster

Wardroom
Chicken Suit
Bug
Laundry Queen
Buster

Liberty Risk
Getting Slant-Eyed
CF
P.C.O.D.
Nasty City

AOM
Burn One
Snuggle Up
Cleaning Stations
Battle Racks

WORD SEARCH 7

```
Z O U S T O H K X E Q F S Z C G N C D G W B O S
I H C Y P O R P X Z I V Y Z V R F I J E P R R A
U B K E I V T Q V T L H Y L E Y J J L P I L G U
F L W B N Q V X V R Y N U K A K H O D W K P X C
L J N I S E Y E G I B Z C U I C A Q F E T G Z T
U I E K E V S A K X M O L O H H Z N C N H K H A
S B I H A Y G I E E L R X E D W L K V N O E I B
W K P N F K Q F C N J D N K F I A N L V B D T U
M I J Z C Q O N I K B G P B J M I P V L O Z W F
F B B G H B D A Z K B A S H T I P J A M U J M G
O P F S T Y R F U G Y A L E E D X C M R I K G L
P B K M L O D V X R M V Y L A B K M Q V N V C N
A O A U T L A R P F K P K C S H T R S K L P L K
V D E P J S A Y P Z W C T E O T T Y Q G F D C F
F T T T L N V B J K O R F L E M H S M B L Z J H
S F S V O J J G N S M A E S W W M I X O L X Q I
F J E U T F M K L O R X U T X D P A R R D X Q L
Z U B F R S O O V Z N O R A Y C B H N T J S G W
G W U I W T R O F K M N E N D X N S Z D Y T S Z
C I T A N T M P K Y Z P A R I N E J D V O K X Q
V T E Z A K L S N C U E I C W S H I T B A G F Z
R F A P Y G P A B H O T P X Z N I A E A D Y R O
V J Z T T L P Z F X U X L A W L M T I J E P I G
R F I N O Y R R A C G F E C N J J J F T D J E S
```

Tube steak	Shitbag	Carry on	CHENG
Balls Thirty	Spook	Sick Bay Commando	EAWS
Rain Locker	IA	Big Eyes	Anymouse
Prop	The Black Hole	Cannon balls	Patrol Sock
NAVY	F.U.B.A.	Haole	

WORD SEARCH 8

```
A W O R H D A H A W I F Y F H A A F E L Q X N Y
G W P D L Z N O V I O N R V H C I N F D G Y U Z
K O B Q W G M F W B S E L P F Z O O I W A T T U
I Z L U S P T Z H F T U L K G T L F G Z C E X G
G L T X O X M J W Q D A C A S T Q O A Y U U H W
H Q S F I S F K G V G K U Y B D A L J X Y H S D
X Q E K U N P M W N T V L K I P D E I Y Q J K U
T J W T V D O Y I X X O D G C S P U U U L L O U
Q N C D J E I M X N H M I D U B B C H D J F B D
P I T E B Q A D V G Z T R E N Q O R M L Z V N V
G M J I N E Z Q L O I Y J G T Y B Q S M K L K S
F E K O R V Q N E T Q B S L A F H B O A F N S Y
G P K C E O N E E T F I F Y H T L I F W Y A T K
M B S I B N F M C P O O Y O A J J Y V B S N B H
W A O K C E A E E V R S Z K T F B V K A Z A O F
H R L N J M I V M S D T P P F N L F T U C L N S
Y Y E M N T S M Y P O Z D E F F U T S X Y W K S
P Z Z F R I C K Y G I R L F R I E N D H T L P Z
F A J W I D E U I I I L L P H V Q Q E M L H J V
E W T P B G C D D Q P N F C G W V L W P B Y W U
O Z J H X L L H I R N W T B H T O T G G E Q G H
J G B K Y F W D Z C L O C C I F E R A M H N S D
D Q Y O S O N C W Z K V L L C Y B R T G P L H Y
M N L J C S T I M E M A C H I N E W D S E X R G
```

MCPOO   TLD   Filthy Fifteen   CUNT
Holy stone   PFM   Ricky Girlfriend   Screaming Alpha
Occifer   Head   Flip me for it   Dig-it
Joe Navy   PQS   Time Machine   Holy Helo
Bonnie Dick   ASWO   Stuffed   RAG

WORD SEARCH 9

```
F F X Q Y O O M R K V M B P B R E M E R L O S O
Q P Y Q P N V U G E O J H O O K E R X V L S N V
V P E Z G W T J D Q K P Q Z Z D E X I D W V Z T
E Q U L C J T L T T V E S T Y W W B A J T U S R
S X D O L H S F S V K L E Q D O I O P I F V E B
P S Y C R P K Y K F N Q U W K X F D O E O W T N
O H I K H G N P A J X F S G T S E A F T O Y P E
R U V K C X D P G B A D M F E K O N J L M U T R
T A L D O V B E D N K Y W Q I V C D B E T U E I
A D F B U L B D S Y M C E M B X E L R E D F V T
N P U D E N O O G U I U I K K E I Q E G F Z D M
D U J O N L O P M Z F F U S C V L L N I D S V O
S S A Z N Y M V X F J N A G E O F O N J O T J L
T X M B R L R W F A Y G O D R B J S W R J K O G
A D E E P S I X E L V Z D C E R Y G R H N J F O
R V O Q L S B D W R M E I E S V O Y N A A K S E
B I S V B Y H L E F R Q N G V M I G C I P Z K C
O D L U U P A I W W J M S I T Q A D V P P W E A
A F A L Y P I F T W Y Q K G U X P S K K E H H N
R F E E O V I E D F N S E I W H K P E J L G V N
D N R T T X X V T T A A T K G U A O H L W D T A
W N S M A H W W J V K C A I Q L T J N M C R V Y
T K B W H R V K C F Q T E Y C Y F X O W T N S G
D G S N U Z W U M A A L P D U H Q O H B P H U P
```

Deep Six
Skivvy Sniffer
Hooker
Fleet Up
Shit-faced

Port and Starboard
Below
Ping Jockey
Uncle Sam's Confused Group
WTFO

Bremerlos
Red Devil Blower
ESFOAD
SNAFU
Sick Bay

Cann
ATFQ
Tweeker
Gooned Up
Sorry I Quit

WORD SEARCH 10

```
H A R C F D K W V M L A U H F N C E Q P Y J G A
Z O X X S Z X V D O H I J W Q D K V E N U D X D
X Y H C Y W S K C I T S S R L P E Y M J D E P R
H X K H D O U B L E D I G I T M I D G E T Q N O
F Z M S W P G D X V B K Z C H M P T B X G Y F K
I W C B G K N I R F L J Z B B K Z E T R R E I E
V L H Y Z Z N O E Q I L E C X I Q M O H P B P Y
Y Q A U H L R S N K E D Y A P P W R P O G W N F
E A R P R R B P N B R G X I A A E I S O O X L K
W P T F P H C A I O Y B T Q B H B M H K S N X B
E O F T T U T I D O S I G B S W Y T Q X T X E D
Y H N F H E X B K T I Q U U K M J Z V C M N U N
N T I E L E W P C E Z B R C Q S L N T M P O K E
G D H P E I B M U R U C S W N O E X C O L J U L
B Y O X Q Y I E D F N Z O O M I E S H C P L M A
H E K E H K E D A O S M J A R Q N C M P B X A F
P B X E U J S D T C A F Y Z E O T U A N U H T X
H A W Q E M F T J U H U X K J U N V O A T T T B
D G T V U A U D I A G V T V O I N E Z Y K P L T
P A X Y M B P Z C E C L S O M G U W B V F X V M
P S B O P L T R F P N K L U A L W H K O B R G N
S S T G S V K K K R R O L O B B N T Z P M V C I
V D I N A V A L A V I A T O R S D I S E A S E G
L R W Z P G L F O H K F U A R R T M X J C F F C
```

The Beach — Out-chop — Naval Aviators' Disease — Sig
Auto — chart — Zoomies — Duck Dinner
Bag Ass — Double-Digit Midget — Blue on Blue — Hook
Button Crusher — FEP — One-eyed Jack — Booter
Aluminum Cloud — People Tank — Bubba — Sticks

WORD SEARCH 11

```
W K W Q L V X V T K W R V H R G U S I H R F Y Z
M N T N N Q L T C M U K D J Z T J E C J B G L D
F R M G R Q Y F S O J G Q X B H G U T L J S G I
A B Z J O E A F H C R V H B R G X S A Z W M U S
S B B I C M T Y B M R P G R F X K U W G T B U N
B Q H J U J P T W K M A S P N Z Y A P I Q R I M
A Q M D T P B Z A X V P M M X K M E R T Z A K F
M V K P A U B Y A P P E I B A T R I G Z O I D W
U G L H W S C B K W E R O P L N C F F C Z L P B
R W S E B B L Y E O E C Y U U E C N Q M Z R C I
R O K G T L X M M G I P N N N I D A L U K O B Z
X X T C W H T D N F Q C O U F R E E N A C A K G
R A M P S T R I K E M L D G O R C J G D N D E E
A Q J G V Q W Z Q U T N A S E B L X B G Y T J R
F A I E U E E Y D U F N I C T Y E Z N F S R F B
U H A O L J H R T J Q V E M V D B U D M L A S I
D V Y D M L O W Y N T J N L A K U A O N H C D L
H Q O P I S S T E S T Q O L A T T I I W M K T A
G O X A M Z U S H H Q Q Z L P T I E P T A S I L
N U L A Z Z Z Y X R V N G L Y R L V G J I P U L
M Z H B K X L L Q S D B C I N G H A W G Z Z W E
I P J A C K O F F C U R T A I N X Q C Z U S Y Y
K N A C O Y O X V N Q D V T R R Q D M O R N D E
O O Z R T S A L T A N D P E P P E R S M L Y V C
```

Local talent
Corpsman Candy
Salt and Peppers
Noodle-winger
Nugget
MTI
Bounce Pattern
Ramp Strike
Scrambled Eggs
Pogey Bait
Vitamin M
FTN
Gerbil Alley
Piss Test
XO's Happy Hour
Jack Off Curtain
Railroad Tracks
TDU

WORD SEARCH 12

```
D D C E F G V K R M V B Z F A D F G A S G Y B
R 3 C L T E U T S E 3 P M Y W F R Y L R V R W Y
S Z A F M W O H T A S B A E L I M V U B D I S D
Z B K U K T Y D M U 3 E T Y D H T K T E L P P T
O 3 E T G A I N P O B F P I C W P 3 N Z M A T N
E V B W 3 V O E M O A E I K G R S D V E Z S T C
L 3 C N I D Y P S M 3 A L F G E U O C P K B C U
B M E S B A O O V L G W H T I R E I N A B I A O
Y P I 3 K Y Y H O B O L O D T F I S S T P G I D
D O L A P T B G O E S A W A Y U V N S E P B S C
N G 3 K H A U L W K W W L F M 3 C E D 3 S B N P
O L C R I O F P F Z E O U S I B T S T E A O A L
T N M T A O B T O Y C O U Z W 3 M W E M R B C F
E I O R Y S R B C L U E W 3 S N O A M M N O 3 K
E L I P C Z P K P V Z P R M Z H Z H S Z C M S 3
O A G N I D N A T S G N I K C U F T U O Y Z U Y
M P H E O M B F M Y P G N R T I H R A O C R E E
M R F U Z W U V M V H F O B H N F O I D N P I N
I G 3 G H M L A G M M B C W F D G G Y I O I M R
T Y C O F Z L T N E A V L K H H G 3 U D N W H S
N R T A U M G T E C T H U Y Y O M D N A N D C R
C U K I B F I V S I K B B H A L B M U 3 R S I O
F L N L N Y G S R E H F L I G H T L I N E D V E
Z O Z M Z E B A L D B L U E A N D G O L D D M W
```

B.B.&G.	F.U.B.Y.O.Y.O.	Blue and Gold	Out-fucking-standing
Bull	3M	Boat	Cruise sock
Division	Goes Away	Flight Line	Tape Zebra
Rhino	Grinder	Scuttlebutt	EOOW
Guard	Dopey	O-Club	

WORD SEARCH 13

```
X D T U R B N O R A U J S K K I D E F E X N L G
D B A A J R A B N K K I S O R L T K C N N R I V
W R R C M V K B W X M V C W P G N O I S M V T Y
O Y H A R I D L R O W E H T F O E L O H S S A R
U A C F H Z I A Y N L K H L M R O M O F D Z B A
X I N D X L D G E R L Y I C U E U L Y U W O L I
W O O G V Z K T V A B Z Z Q G Q V H O S Z N L Z
A L H L F F B Y A O D A R K H U N D R E D T I P
M O X I Z L Q W K X H Y K Q E S Y H O R G Q M R
E K O M O O R D R A W T R I H S Y T R I D U O P
A I A R N Z A X Y P H O K J R C R O N U S K Z G
T X I E K D F T C R L K Q X S M G U R T Y V K P
I T T G P O X Z H B T E C R Z E A H A L F T V B
D E Y G D J D D M W O E H A R Q N N K R J U V Y
E D B A M T V O D O A S T S M G Y X C C K W X
N U O B Q N B W R S M R H D N T U F Q G A Y D Q
T T V N I M L L L R C A T F I E R D H R U X K H
I T U W K X D L X C T A N S A W N A S W F A O V
F N X O W E A C T B O N S D H G T A F M L M P N
I M N R O B Y E R M Z G C M D I I B M T S S I M
E Z T B L R P D Q G J Z W H G A P L T R P H Q L
R G A L F V S Y I I C R R B T M D S L L E J E V
X O A O S K N V Q C J N N N E J P S I I F P D H
B S B D J L A Q U L K K E P G B N B G H D G H J
```

D.I.L.L.I.G.A.F   Twidget   Permanent Help   Meat Identifier
M-Bomb   Donkey-Dick   Athwartships   SPLIB
Roger That   Fart sack   Mom and Dad   Asshole of the World
SNOB   Honch Rat   Mustang   Brown bagger
ALL BALLs   O'dark hundred   Dirty-shirt wardroom   Pit

WORD SEARCH 1-4

```
L W S D D U J T B J F E N N V O E B S O F A J S
H A R P T R F D A P L E O M K N E E P M L O Z P
G P P D O O E L N W T I H A W M A P S J I L U Q
T G L J I H E P A H P W B C M B G R I X O C L U
N K U D H W L M N F O A D C A P E E Q B K E W F
I A K D Q W U L A B C I G G Q R S Y S E T Q B R
L U E F G V J N E E K G F C X O K T R T R Y Z A
J S U W X Q B T A B V Y P T N R E F U G M N J T
X M J H S H O E T D G Q I N Z R A C F Z R W W Z
V B O S N C W K I H B N W X T C E K F H E U F R
N O O F I S P Z N D P O I E T B M O C A S R S I
L W C K K C E A G E R R X O R B L F J T U J N X
S E W A U I K Q C B X B R O G E M S U R O A V P
C E T U M B R I O K A P W R S A Q A G I H R R R
W E I V N S A W N T A N N M I U E S J P K B O R
R D T H J L U Y T Q E G U E A N U S W L C R M R
R Q S M C V J L E R U R E R L T K T W E A R N O
Q W C X J N E Z S S F A E C Z S D F J S R D H O
X Q E E I G U U T S I D R H H C W A O T C F A J
K W U T R S G R U R A S U T R E J H Z I K F I Q
X N U O F Q I I C W T F H H E V C K O C O E M P
L H U O S T T N A R G F G V B R C K K K P D P B
G P N Q S H M Y W P V J W B W B S S P S U Y G Q
W Z T D U R C Y K C I R W D Q P N F J M Y C M U
```

A.J. Squared Away	Crunchies	Crack House	Lobster
T.A.R.F.U.	Lettuce Browner	Package Check	Pucker Factor
FOAD	Smurf Suit	Triple Sticks	OAFO
Ricky Crud	Sea Going Bellhops	Seabag	Banana Eating Contest
Skater	Brown Nose	Sick in Quarters	Battle Group

WORD SEARCH 15

```
E C B V N R K W K H T T Y U N B Q K W Q P J W N
O T Q G Q M T M M V O C R T M B V E H U T H T W
R O I A A E H X N T O R G A B R H L H D I P Q C
H R M P F D O P E T Z S S E T L P V O S M L E X
Z D Z S X H F U N O D I R E U S A U T H I R Z C
A T G Y I O S Y R H L W J F S Y R L J V U W Z B
L M P Z D G Z O X Z G T S U X H I I M G J E D I
I R K J I T K W O K Q R Z Q Z N O O A D J I F T
N U O C M R T M O L E L Q F G P A E O D L I I C
A X R L Z A R W S O K E U S N F B C R B C Y T H
M W V A Y J E L R R T N H T M F K U E F A D S I
E E R K C C W O R M P I O O Y A T R B O A I E N
L U J V A K Q G L E T V G J X E T S Y N J T R G
T R R C F Q M O H C C P J M G P J A W G M T O B
T Y D B I B M O A W R B D L G T S D J D Z A F E
I N J W Y M R N N G D H I D P H O R D W A S D T
L V C O W S O V R S R B S T N S A F R Z F E O T
F P G E V F E O X E T V M T V J P F K O I W O Y
Y H Z D D F X C K I G E R E I O Q U R P D A W R
Z G P E C E P I U V N B R B H R O S K D J N R J
Y T A Y T I R D E R K K U D I R T H M R H C E M
H T P V X T Y E W M E F Y L F D S O H A O G H W
H A E Y S E D D E X J O Z U R R X Z Q F Y W S N
Z S S D F C B L P G R R X G H L H A T W J E C F
```

Sherwood Forest
Secure
Kloosh
Bitching Betty
JARTGO
ROD
Little Manila

Airstart
Whistling Shit Can of Death
Striker
DCA
Dilbert
UNODIR
Horse Shoe

IYAOYAS
Rack Monster
F.U.B.I.J.A.R.
ROTC
Workups
Bilge Turd

WORD SEARCH 16

```
K R Z I G G X S S E X V M Q M L M S S K R G Y G
F A O G R M E G C H V X Y E L O L Q S R R W J F
V I V A F W Q V R E K E D M I X V P H Z H J G D
Z L D C M P N N L B O E W W D O R K P H F N I I
X I P S G W J A C F V S U W E O J M O K R O D V
L G T E J R S C V A R C W Q G H O N F K R I Y R
L Z N Y I B I S C J Y W U D U L J H L W W T O J
L Q F U G U A A M A R I N E O B N J F H O I R R
M S R E K N U D O L E H P U G W B L N V S S S X
U K T N U O C T F I R D A U I Z F D Y U O I Q U
K E C S W O B L E D N A S E L O H S S A N U E D
C E U U E H E T I M E O N T H E P O N D U Q P W
E V C I C T T F F N Y N Z P G V H P G P B E O J
H Y Q V D D R I T Z I P S S Q S H I T T E R Q O
C S W O C N U C L E A R W A S T E P Y N V T R A
Y T B C A P T A I N S M A S T P L G F Z L H M X
T A H S Z G T N D D B Q Q T K X O J L Z B G W L
I C A X U M M O J M R E V O C T N U C S C I Y T
L K C J B I H S O N U E G V B R N M D L J N V F
A E M G F A K L C A E H T V O X O O A W B D N F
E R I T E O D X H E O N B O C T E F O M V I F W
R Z T P J M K N Q D N I K D O J S R U N X M O Z
A D D J A Y L I S E A D D O D W D S W K E S I O
R C X N U Q I M H R C I S G N W O Q Z H O R S M
```

Assholes and elbows	Reality Check	Helo Dunker	CIC
Midnight Requisition	Gouge	Nooner	Captain's Mast
Cunt Cover	Old Man	MARINE	MEDEVAC
Canoe U	Nuclear Waste	B.O.C.O.D	Skeevy Stacker
Shitter	BUNO	Time On The Pond	Drift Count

WORD SEARCH 17

```
B W V K E O C M O F T A D E N I P E B R N L G A
K 2 O N B E Y H A 2 O E D O A S D F F G C Y E P
P U D D L E P I R A T E S P L D O L P E D G 2 M
F 2 J W I T 2 B O C P N K I T T O H B A A V H O
L H U B A L S B P 2 O E N V I E M R M T Y J B B
M 2 O N A L V H V P T G A R M 2 A D L R M 2 L I
B B Q R T R K F S D I R P X M H R X P V C D U L
T C W I S L C G W N A R P X Y A S J Y L S Y E E
Y G G Y P E N E G Y E D N V E W N T J I K A J C
H P 2 H F I C G H K S 2 J P L D M N H J P W A H
H G T S K C A O C E F C S H S A E A D G Y Y C E
D E M O W M B O C U W C D O J G N R T T Q C K R
W E M Y E J L C P K U J S F G G O P J E B D E N
E S V O G T J N L X K F H P A D B L I X F F T O
D A B I A L Q Q K C E G W R O V N P G W Y L G B
W W O O L H I H A C J R Q E V K K A Y N K F Q Y
A E G S 2 D F B Q K H U C A Y L C L H B I D V L
J F G S L E O 2 R G E X O V A V M A I C R X J T
Y B V B U S S C O E L V 2 D M N Y A R A U X O Y
R L F T O T O F N C G I D F I U C N N N O O U X
S D F O A A V Q C U K U H G B I D C F 2 P U T X
A M B S E N D O F T H E W O R L D P A R T Y E Q
M F I C G F Y Y Q W A N W R C C I Q A N H 2 G B
K H R X O X P D P R 2 X S L X B 2 T H G U Q L K
```

Xoxing Logs
End-of-the-World Party
Hangar Queen
Devil Doc
Puddle Pirate

EAOS
Gerbil Gym
Rack Ops
Horse Cock
2JV

Bluejacket
Slinging Game
Timmy
Goat locker
Mobile Chernobyl

P.D.O.O.M.A.
Touch and Go's
Crab
Smoking Sponson
PRT

WORD SEARCH 18

```
F O Y 0 F G U A N 2 E T T K P H M D A C B R D E
W S L W W Z 0 M 2 S Z I D Z E K M P N I W 0 0 W
M M S 0 G B T A H A G 2 D N P T I K R B N B Y N
R 0 C E U R T H E Z 0 O T I G P B D H S Y 2 K D
A G R A R T E E L S A O F G L F F S H T Y 2 C
U F B F W T P E F W W Y E T 2 A E L 0 2 R W E A
R N A M F O S B N S Y R Y H R H M G N C A F B S
S O I Y M Z T I L S B F I M Z Z R U T L P E D R
R C P M E S S Y M I C N M B L N Y S I D E E Z E
A K M K G N T E L Y W R N A A K T S N E G K I P
B U S B O W S N B F K N U D W B A C K A L L E Y
L I T B L B O K S C U C A B E K 0 I O P I D U I
2 G A G B G U B N F G K I D B R D U G I B C O B
C Y R 0 N P B I 0 B C H Z R 2 Y F D U K Z O O G
E T M 0 H C 2 T L E B S Z M F K T R B F I T N 0
S S A N O O B A B D P B A F F L E S A M P L E G
D N Y R D Y U M P T I O R M A F D K 0 W 0 2 W H
S B L P N E E T D L R N R P M T S Z A Z B R P O
D K O W 0 W T S D S H A G T W Y R Y A F T H A K
C Z F Y H U I O O C E G D 2 A L U P K Z E B A C
F L W E E M C G B T H Y D K 0 O W S T Y L T K U
B N T R N O K E A B K S R W 0 2 G D W Z N L B F
W O H C G Z E U N C H R O M E D O M E B E K H N
T S H Y A G T S G A B A E S T R O H S R Y 0 A U
```

The Zoo	Back Alley	Baffle Sample	Chow	Short Seabag
Ricky Mistress	Birdfarm	FRED	Goatrope	'Rats
Gerbil	Building 20	Baboon Ass	CASREP	Chrome Dome
Bilge Party	Green Scrubby	S.N.O.B.	Un-Fuck	E-ticket

WORD SEARCH 19

```
O R Y C J M E A T G A Z E R Q P C N H R M D R R
H J U L U P N W U X F A T O Z U T Y P A O R H Z
H E Z I K W D G Z D G T O V S O B R E S H N H V
G Y T O M X E I E W C G F P J R R Y U N R K L Q
D V Y Q F F R T O Z V L M O C G Y Z V C Y A D A
V F H O P B G H I S S M I S W E G O G G L E S U
K C J H G A G Z W D B K T I L K U E H F F N F L
O V F T S O L R F E K A B X N I D X W L K S R V
L W G P T O N T T E Z H A T P R N R Z Q W R B P
P W U O E C G L Q I O D R K J T I J A Y T J P O
E X M S L R I H R F B B R S D S A J N O T M P P
L I F S J D T Q J Y Q O I X W R C A B J B V G K
Z J O Z X B E R H D U A C R B E P P L K M B Z M
E Y I M I P Z N E F D T A B N I I O Z S U M X E
D Q B W R U K B R V Y S D G R R L J U N E M D A
I A T N Z G I X U I Z B E O L R U Z N I E O U O
Z D K F U N C H X K V N O H N A V Y D B I K O G
I B R J W O Y K A P Y E I L H C T H Q G N Y T I
Y Q U E W L U W L B P A T W Z U H V J A D J Q C
A O G O L O H U M A H W F W B T Y L R K T F K R
R I L X U A U I C U I B Z E L O I C P V F J P U
G I S U E D U S T C W P O O P I E P A N T S K N
O M S P J P O O E C Y T R E B I L E R I P M A V
L C S W U F Q K B J O Q P O D B N W C N G N O Q
```

Boats	DITE	Vampire Liberty	Board
Barricade	Carrier Strike Group	POD	IYARGOL
Bunny Tube	Crank	LOST	Poopie Pants
SAR	No Load	Sims	Meat Gazer
VERTREP	Golden rivet	JOPA	Goggles

WORD SEARCH 20

```
Y R S O D R C F V R K P Q D T N P Z G E M O K F
S J A V E B H A X O I A Q P M V L X E N D U R N
O M W D C W X O Z I S R L S Q E E G O E K O I W
E D U Z B K K N W G L T Q L M L T N B R I Q T R
O N S C B X X R T E O X D A B O E X C Y D Q S W
X U D X B U F Z R H O S C G N A E R G G K N K T
S H O R T T I M E R S C H A I N L G A D A Y I Q
B B L U G O Y L W N K D C A E B F L G C E C T P
Q Q Y C P A S I A F E R P J A W E M S Y T K T B
H U I X H J L V T G D W A T I Y L N T H H V L R
D M H R R B I K E M V V L L O D P K W I O G E I
X M F V Q Y C N R E Y I M M C H P F Y K Y F S G
F I C Z Z T K X W G D L R E B Y A Y Q F Z B N H
K X P A L M S G I C N D W G D G E E U W N T M T
C R R T Q Q L M N R S I O W A O N N A P Q P Z W
O C S R D B E A G A O B X F Z I I J R H R F N O
S C R G N Y E X S W L A R O Z U P I T A T W O R
Y Z Q U T A V V A F D E S T B S U F E E B F Q K
P W Y U X C E R Y S M F Z T Q Y K L R R X Y Y S
P G H V L T R Y V O G A Z O B K K B S A H M M Z
A V Y R C A O W O P P A T B M E Y C S P H R Y K
H D I J N Z J B L O Y D V S R N A Y I U G X F Q
X S I T Q S Y Z O F J S P S E Y X S I R X K K V
W F L G Q S P L A P W H X O R M D N T V D Y B B
```

Barney Clark
Pare
Water wings
Ricky Boxing
Camel
BUF
Happy Sock

Slick Sleeve
Gyrene
Pineapple Fleet
Boomer Fag
Roast Beast
Crazy Ivan
Quarter

Skittles
Short Timer's Chain
Warrant
All Balls
Loop
Brightworks

WORD SEARCH 21

```
O N B J P U V U Z A B F Y S F L Q H S N F F R U
U G T S L D V A U F J R M Z J U O E O I E H B E
B N H U Z Q Y Y P B H A G U O U M A P I C C T E
J L A H T V Z D G J L I S O H I D K H I R R L I
O S C S Z Q Z Y S L H W C E D V D C T Q E Y U T
K T F H S Y C W B N P N M D A G D X L R C U N R
G E M H V N S O P E F U N J K R D A F Q E N U O
W E N F N E Y K Q X A A I E A A L O Z N W W K S
I L R V F I A T I Z E U S T H C N U P T B D E M
T B Y G Q C R R R V S X S G Y A Y C C U L T I D
R E D G P W H Y I A S A L W H W L V U J U Q T F
G A S M O T I F T S B P J H T Y F B A L X I O C
I C S B H I T D G R E K N U D T R E B L I D U K
P H O G C P Y N F S E A H B H N S G G H H X T C
B P N S K X I M M U J B C P E H O W E V E R U A
C I F G C W H X D C H M I K J R B P B U Y E X H
D C M N U D U C Y K S W G L Z X W W M A O L B K
S N H I P Q Y J G B V B H H L K G B G U K N N A
O I R R J P Z B H A V E F B B A E B X V T J J Z
K C E O I L A Y O G J D R C U J U A U Z A W F N
O K X G V D X A L C K V A B B W K T Z B L K Y I
P H A N T O M S H I T T E R M Z N M R Y B H H F
M R Z M D F F G L A W X F O T F R Q P I W L L G
X Y N R M G O Y T N P Q Q Y X Y B Y B R V H E T
```

ESWS
Ding
However
Hack
Steel Beach Picnic
Dilbert Dunker
Small Boy
Bastard Chief
Un-ass
BT Punch
Nuke It Out
Virtual Liberty
Five and Dimes
Bubble
Puck Chop
Wings
Suckbag
Phantom Shitter
O-Rings
Sortie

WORD SEARCH 22

```
L V U M P T U J O T G F S R W G L V N R S L N Q
X D V N M G U D Y O Y K S K H X V E W H M F D S
S I G B Z O O O R J Y H U H I W R D W Z S O F T
B O U M B D O E R L E T O M S D E K X T D C N S
Y K S O M C Z D A T R T S H I T R I V E R S C W
P Y S D S L D R B G R X F N U F L I T A H L A F
V S V G K Y K R L E U E S A T C Z P U P P E X S
U V Z Z C I I V A W T A P S L A D F O Z W F I T
V K B I N N P D K H J J L P C A X T R V S O Z F
H W C G S K D Z I C C J K A U S E U T H G L Z B
D O U A V G I P F S F I P U B C H U Z P R L O L
T B F Z S J E N P S K I R O Q M S E A I N I W L
C L Q E Z H S J U H E V O D H M P T N M C E I J
R I S J S J T X Y C C T I A R K L G K K S S F Y
H D J E J I Y R E V C R B V B A K O Z N Y B K N
H K L O D Y M G A A J N A H Q N H J T U N B Z G
F D H N O E A C M E O X J G O O H E M V I A R K
Y O A Z J B W P Y I J N K C Q S O O M A H K X T
A B D T P S K E D S O J K O P R Z Z Y E D X L I
H W G V F P X V J O S E N A C Q Q S K F N T E K
Y C P R F V N H W J R L R K N M Q H W A O O V A
R N R D H G B F E G K K M K N I D C D W E X B W
O N I Q U I P Z V O Y Z V X T C N P Y O A T G W
T B C G N I G G A B A E T F D P H U N C T S H Z
```

Trout
Earth Sack
JSI
Zero
OOD

Bandit
Shit River
Piece
Ed's Motel
Bootcamp

Skeds-O
Scupper Trout
Bone Me Hard Richard
Sparky
Skylarking

Ring Knocker
Fo'c's'le Follies
Tea Bagging
S.H.E.
D.C. Dink

WORD SEARCH 23

```
F R O V E Q R Q S ! X B E 0 W Y S ! J Q V Y D N
F G F G M V 0 V O O L E I D J 9 V W C J G N G C
I B 0 0 Z X L Q B N 9 X J X M B D R 9 Y E I 9 0
! I E R O T C E J E L A N G I S M 3 J B K M 3 3
J G O P F R L I G V J C V V L 9 H O X T J D Z F
F C A A P K X T R U M U M W H I Z Q U I Z A Q Q
M H 9 N C F W R L P D Q H S V B W T W 0 K T U F
M I J U O Q 9 I U M Z Q V U ! D V W D 9 V S O K
3 C N X Z T Z H 9 Z U F E P I O U J K L I B Y C
D K E G A L H S Y 3 ! M X C Y K I F 3 B B J Q E
L E U S ! T C E J F G 9 X D L 0 Y A Y I F C L R
0 N A H U 0 J U R B G N I K C I D Y T R I D N W
D D ! T E M Z L I F C S I D N A L S I P N Z E P
A I R Z H L M B C W I O J D X T M G J S O O K I
R N W H C P M E F 3 J N 9 3 L J I I 3 V E W U H
K N Z 9 L 9 U E R W B F E Y N I C R ! S I Z X S
T E E T L W P C T C M 0 E N Q X U S F I R N L V
H R H J Z E ! G K F R T F L A W C B S K J A M S
I 3 0 I C 0 T P 9 S I E J F 3 V H T J M D B A Y
R Q V A F J V 9 Q P R R A M O E Y I W Q J L S G
T Y Z ! I I C P A D F 9 E S M E N D E X S K H H
Y H O L L Y W O O D S H O W E R V K A O A ! O 3
! F Q G L C D Z T 3 Z Y F P M S Y A 3 Y 3 W F 3
B O H I F D T Y W C F U E S U W D J W I ! Y H Z
```

Dirty-dicking
Island
Helmet Fire
Signal Ejector
Hollywood Shower

Fobbit
Death Pucks
Whiz Quiz
Summer creases
Shipwreck

Blue Shirt
Mash
Knuckle Box
"Another Fine Navy Day!"
Big Chicken Dinner

Building 39
O'dark thirty
Wave-off
Admin

WORD SEARCH 24

```
I N A M A T W E A T H E R G U E S S E R Q B R N
I E C W E N D R K J F P P S O N I I L U H U I D
M B Q I M Q P C E T T V D G U M J F V C A L A E
R X P E O B Z X P B W Z X Y W X S W T I H C Y J
H E X E F V Y O S O O R U U K A U A H V A B F V
D X D H T Z U X V L T Q E R F P W T F Y M U L C
D X V N N N T A T U U V F H O H F S M W S H I A
V V G I U A W Y A W W A Z L T P C N N B T C G Q
S U D B D O D Z U K R P I A N F B Z F O E C H M
L J N Y D V P L A T E S E Q U B C U P K R C T H
B A W G U P B H S C H D C B D A D V E R Q O D P
F H Q Q H Q L U C A N A Y Q W L R C Y C B Y E Q
V A O K S C I T T A B N Y P H L A J Z Q Y Z C B
F R G V C T J U C W E S U X R S O F L O H Z K V
L B D F R A R L E S K B P I O T B N M F K B B S
A A I E I D U F U M O S E U M O E G P G G U U F
T N B E P V F N J G B U C V C F E A T D K C Z B
H L G U L T J T V B O J G K M O R B R W S M Z Q
A M B U E K S G C S S K M E J U F E P U L O A M
T B Z I R H M V P R N I T C E R O D Q G X Q R P
T E K Y M C A G N O I X Y R V W U K S S L L D Z
I X Z Q F X S L H G A U K H T R A D N W A L C G
N R K X F I G H T I N G E A R F Z R P M K F A
G P X J N H G O A L N R B J K B X Q X B B V X K
```

Freeboard
Chub Club
Lawn Dart
Balls to Four
Cripler

Weather Guesser
IHTFP
Bag
Polish a Turd
Beach Pounder

Fighting gear
B.O.S.N.I.A.
Freq
Flight Deck Buzzard
Flathatting

Fart Suit
Hamster
Vulcan Death Watch
FAG
Sougee

WORD SEARCH 25

```
U S 0 H D K M K D S R A C S O E I L R A H C O L
S P M M P I S U R B O 0 1 U S M N E E B C A C 0
L R O T B H R A U K S G I M V B 1 1 K A H O H M
O Y P V P 1 B T D B 1 0 V H D Y E R M 1 B 1 N S
K K D M I R 1 A B R V K T N O E A M O T F P 0 A
L I E T E I N E V A U F F O P E O G T M Y U M N
H S O T D G S H S A G C R O S F P C R H L P G D
S N T 1 E P H P Y K F D S D E C I G I U O R Y C
K U 1 R A I B M O B T O D T I D A D N O G U H R
B C N D F E D G F I U K P I N Y F R V D T O V A
S U I N A V K V 1 D 0 L U A R 0 Y O K O I Y P B
T O G D P E 0 1 H B 0 O F L G E A F V K 0 G T F
P F S L E L H Y S G G G B 0 G O M T N S P N Y L
S 1 C T R K D E P K V V A P S U 1 O H Y C I C L
F C E O 1 L O O L G D L B C Y T P I O T F P D N
U E L L 1 L F R Y B F S U 1 O M B L E B B P G K
L T L 0 O H 1 E B E B L O D F O B N O B O O F G
N A B Y Y I Y K C H L U B L A C K S H O E P E B
G O L F G C O 0 O E 1 M B V L P Y M I T 1 P V H
N B O D 0 S R I R C 0 P O L F A N 1 V Y T E L S
B G C B L T M Y E P A U T U R K G C U Y D D Y O
K I K M K L 1 B I B L G T U I R E H K U P D O R
B P 1 N O P H U C P A V Y S 1 G D L E G C B E O
A U 0 N O G U D V 0 N V U S P V H 0 E T V V E I
```

Pavy	Broke-dick	Scullery	Black Shoe
Oly	Yoko	Dit Dot Bomb	Boomer
Motrin	Pig boat	Oscar	FOBNOB
Cellblock 10	Bubblehead	Charlie Oscar	Popping Your Pup
Sand Crab	Butter Bars	Danger Nut	Dirtbag

WORD SEARCH 26

```
D J Z R S Z D S S P K K G Q F S E W C J J P R F
J I H B R D U Y Y O I W X N G N I Y K V A B V M
U O N K F H N S S D U Y T M U M W I I H B J N N
L J E Q T P U W M G W B T A Y K F N E J T U F I
R E S A H C E R I T Y H E F I V E A E K H K G D
N N R P A A N A U Z D Q L N E L D I V E E A N M
O R E K H K C A J E L P P A N F W A T R L H J Y
P U S T I T K J E F P B N O R Y N E S P E L D J
S H A M T I P J D P P V S A R H Y D Y Q A N Y F
C S H J S A O M K I D M N J Q D S A C A N X L U
T N C I V C X O X A K K C O Z Y N T U S S L R O
K U G R O I L J G L C G C U E P K R S T Y C Q T
Q L I K I U B X R R S B N O I X K Q S X O U U S
W P R E J C A Y A S Q F O H L I N C U D B D H J
V Y B U X M K P V N V H S H O Y A G S M I I I M
D I E P I O O Y Z Z R T R N V Z M R E G P Y O X
M J H B A N Q L V E S O W S E I K Z T B X O L B
S O H H P B L Y B A O G H X B P L B A Y X H D M
T J D L K C O B L X C F M N O B I Z F L K P S X
Q I A J W E U S T Y L U J X A M M W I E O P A I
G T I L U R S K W Z H O U R T H A T S Z T S L G
E W M H X U Y P H H G S E M A N X M H O Z K T I
N W P Q I U I X T H E S A N D B O X F E N J V N
C R H S W Z F D C A N E X V J P Y N K K L G V B
```

Old Salt
Tits-up
Tire Chaser
Dinq
USS LASTSHIP
Ricky Vacuum
Tail
CANEX
Brigchaser
Milkman
The Leans
Love Boat
Ahead Frank Crap on Plate
Benny
The Sandbox
USS Usetafish
Apple Jack
Rubber Hooeys
COD
Nuke It

1

Across:
5. SPACE
8. HERE TODAY, GUAM TOMORROW
9. ZARF
12. BULL NUKE
13. VAMPIRE
14. NFO
15. WESTPAC WIDOW
16. MOM AND POP NIGHT
17. PUSSY TO THE LEFT
19. TWO DIGIT MIDGET

Down:
1. OPERATING GOLDEN FLOW
2. MARINE CRP STABLE CLOTH
3. 90 DAY WONDER
4. LEVITT
6. CAKDY
7. PIRATE
10. TURN BURR
11. TD
18. SLIDERS

2

Across:
4. VOLUNTOLD
6. OVERHEAD
9. CHULA JUANA
10. MYSTERY MEAT
13. WUBAFLAGE
16. BELOW DECKS
18. RENT A CROW
19. FATHERS DAY

Down:
1. CIVILANT
2. WG
3. LCKYBG
5. GREEN TABLET
7. KISS THE CAMEL
8. PSSPID
11. TOD
12. CU11
14. JOG
15. NGAS
17. COOMSHW

3

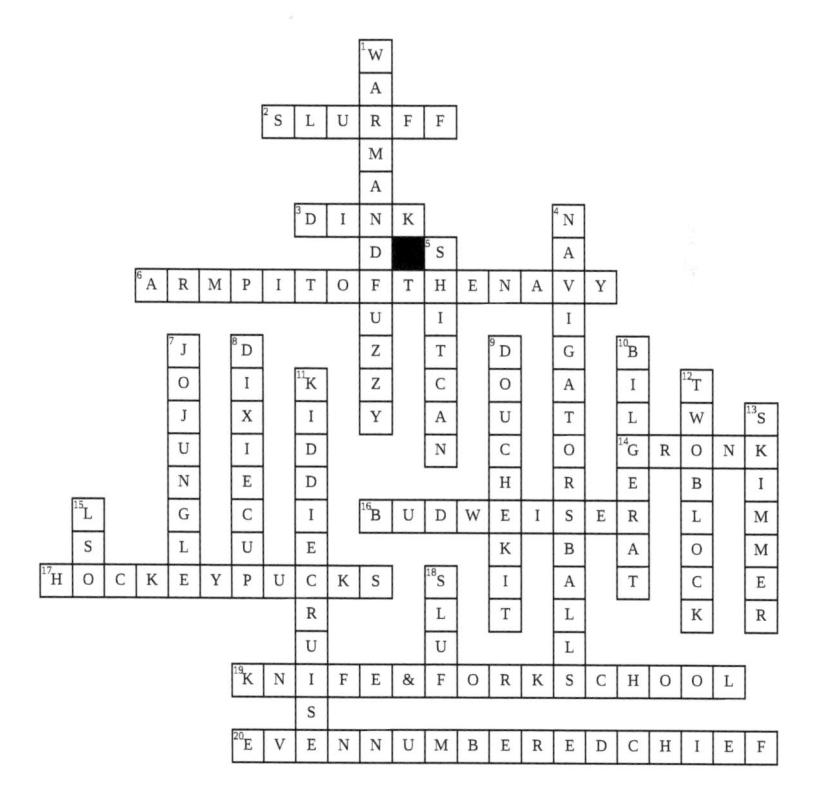

Across:
- 3: AFARTS
- 4: TUNABOAT
- 5: LADDERWELL
- 10: TWEENER
- 11: JO
- 13: PUNCHOUT
- 16: TITIVATION
- 18: BCGS
- 19: WOLFTICKET
- 20: SKATE

Down:
- 1: BUSTMEONTHESURFACEPILLOW
- 2: CREAMDFOESK
- 6: SUCKINGRUBBER
- 7: EVOLKSKTNBOX
- 8: 5MC
- 9: DEARFAILLW
- 12: FRCHEKER
- 14: COCKER
- 15: BTTHBOX
- 17: CRUSR

4

Across:
- 2: SLURFF
- 3: DINK
- 6: ARMPITOFTHENAVY
- 14: GRONK
- 16: BUDWEISER
- 17: HOCKEYPUCKS
- 19: KNIFE&FORKSCHOOL
- 20: EVENNUMBEREDCHIEF

Down:
- 1: WARMAA
- 4: NAVIGATOR
- 5: SITCAN
- 7: JOJUNGL
- 8: DIXIECUP
- 9: DOUCHKIBALL
- 10: BILGE
- 11: KIDDIE
- 12: TWBLOCK
- 13: SKIMMER
- 15: LS
- 18: SLULL

5

Across
- 6. REDASS
- 7. CLUSTERFUCK
- 12. FORM
- 13. CRACKERJACKS
- 15. STARBOARD
- 16. CUTORDER
- 18. READYROOM
- 20. SEASTORIES

Down
- 1. AWOL
- 2. GUN
- 3. DOUBLENUTS
- 4. MARINASSHOWER
- 5. PECKERCHECKER
- 8. PISSCUTTER
- 9. BLE
- 10. BIDAG
- 11. OGGINSG
- 14. CAG
- 17. SWIMS
- 19. SOCKEDIN

6

Across
- 2. WUBACHARIOT
- 4. BURNONE
- 5. LIBERTYRISK
- 8. BUSTER
- 10. CF
- 11. BUG
- 13. GETTINGSLANTEYED
- 14. SNUGGLEUP
- 15. FUNMETER
- 16. AOM
- 17. BATTLERACKS
- 19. CLEANINGSTATIONS
- 20. HOLYCROTCH

Down
- 1. LAUNDRYQUEUE
- 3. KNUCKLER
- 6. CHICKENSUIT
- 7. FLATTOP
- 9. WARROOM
- 12. NSE
- 18. PCD

7

Across:
- 3. RAINLOCKER
- 5. CARRYON
- 8. CHENG
- 10. IA
- 12. FUBA
- 14. CANNONBALLS
- 15. BIGEYES
- 17. SPOOK
- 18. THEBLACKHOLE
- 19. NAVY

Down:
- 1. HALE
- 2. AYMUSE
- 4. PATROLS
- 6. SICKMMANDO
- 7. SHITBAG
- 9. EAW
- 11. TUBESTEAK
- 13. BALLS / THIRT
- 16. PREP

8

Across:
- 2. FLIPMEFORIT
- 3. JOENAVY
- 7. SCREAMINGALPHA
- 10. PQS
- 11. RAG
- 12. DIGIT
- 14. HOLYHELO
- 15. TLD
- 17. HEAD
- 18. OCCIFER
- 19. CUNT
- 20. PFM

Down:
- 1. RCKYGILR
- 4. FILTYFF
- 5. TIEM
- 6. HOLYSTON
- 8. STUFFE
- 9. AWC
- 13. BONNIEDICK
- 16. MPOO

9

Across:
- 2. ESFOAD
- 9. BELOW
- 10. WTF
- 14. SHITFACED
- 15. UNCLESAMSCONFUSEDGROUP
- 16. PORTANDSTARBOARD
- 17. HOOKER
- 18. TWEEKER
- 19. SICKBAY

Down:
- 1. R...
- 3. FIDDLEVILBOWER
- 4. ATFQUP
- 5. DEPSIX
- 6. SKIVVYS
- 7. SORRYIQ
- 8. GONEDUP
- 11. SNF
- 12. BREESELS
- 13. PINJCE
- 20. CANN

10

Across:
- 3. DUCKDINNER
- 4. ONEEYEDJACK
- 8. BUTTONCRUSHER
- 11. BUBBA
- 13. NAVALAVIATORSDISEASE
- 14. AUTO
- 15. HOOK
- 18. OUTCHOP
- 19. DOUBLEDIGITMIDGET
- 20. SIG

Down:
- 1. BLUEOBL
- 2. BOTTEE
- 5. TEE
- 6. BAGAS
- 7. PEOPLETEP
- 9. ALUMNUMCL
- 10. CHR
- 12. FEP
- 16. ZOOMIES
- 17. STCK

11

Across:
- 4. VITAMIN M
- 10. CORPSMAN CANDY
- 11. PISS TEST
- 13. TDU
- 15. GERBIL ALLEY
- 16. NUGGET
- 17. RAILROAD TRACKS
- 18. POGEY BAIT

Down:
- 1. XOSH
- 2. MT
- 3. FT
- 5. SALT AND PEPPER
- 6. BOUNCE PATTERN
- 7. RAPPS
- 8. LOCAL
- 9. NOODLE WINGER
- 12. SCRAMBLED EGGS
- 14. JACK OFF CURTAIN

12

Across:
- 4. EOOW
- 6. OUT FUCKING STANDING
- 12. FUBYOYO
- 13. RHINO
- 14. BOAT
- 15. BB & G
- 17. O CLUB
- 18. DIVISION
- 19. TAPE ZEBRA

Down:
- 1. FLIGHT LINE
- 2. BLUE ADGER
- 3. SCUTTLE BUTT
- 5. BLL
- 7. GUARD
- 8. CRUSSES OOK
- 9. 3M
- 10. GOES AWAY
- 11. DOPEY
- 15. BRIND R
- 16. GRINDR

13

Across:
2. ASSHOLEOFTHEWORLD
4. DONKEYDICK
13. MEATIDENTIFIER
14. FARTSACK
16. ROGERTHAT
18. SNOB
19. MBOMB
20. ODARKHUNDRED

Down:
1. MUSTANG
3. DIRTY
5. ATHWARTSHIPS
6. PERMANENTHELP
7. BROWBEATER (BROWN...)
8. DILF (DI...)
9. TWDGET (TWDGGER)
10. SPLIB
11. ALLBALLS
12. HONCHRT
15. PI
17. MOMANDAD

14

Across:
5. PACKAGECHECK
8. CRACKHOUSE
9. FOAD
10. SMURFSUIT
13. SEABAG
14. BATTLEGROUP
16. TRIPLESTICKS
17. BROWNNOSE
19. LOBSTER
20. LETTUCEBROWNER

Down:
1. BANANAEATINGCONTEST
2. TRF
3. STATER
4. SAGIN
6. AJQUARED
7. CUNTHAIRIDAWAY
11. OAF
12. SICKINQUARTERS
13. (SEABAG)
15. PUKES
18. BICKYRUD
19. (LOBSTER)
— FUCKERFACTOR

15

Across:
- 6. SECURE
- 12. AIRSTART
- 13. BITCHINGBETTY
- 14. ROT C
- 16. HORSESHOE
- 18. ROD
- 20. SHERWOODFOREST

Down:
1. UNOD
2. WHISTLINGS
3. LITTLEMAILER... (LITTLEMAILAT)
4. RAIKMOINSERT...
5. BILGEBURRD...
7. IYOYEARS...
8. WOKUPS...
9. JATGO
10. FUBIJAR
11. DINLERT
15. KLOOSH
17. STICKAE
19. DCHA

16

Across:
- 2. NUCLEARWASTE
- 6. OLDMAN
- 7. CIC
- 8. BUNO
- 11. ASSHOLESANDELBOWS
- 13. NOONE
- 15. DRIFTCOUNT
- 16. GOUGER
- 17. MIDNIGHTREQUISITION
- 18. MEDEVAC
- 19. TIMEONTHEPOND
- 20. SKEEVYSTACKER

Down:
1. CPTAIN...
3. SHITT...
4. CUTCVER...
5. HELO
9. BMAAS...
10. CRNEKA...
12. MARINE
14. REEALIYCH...

17

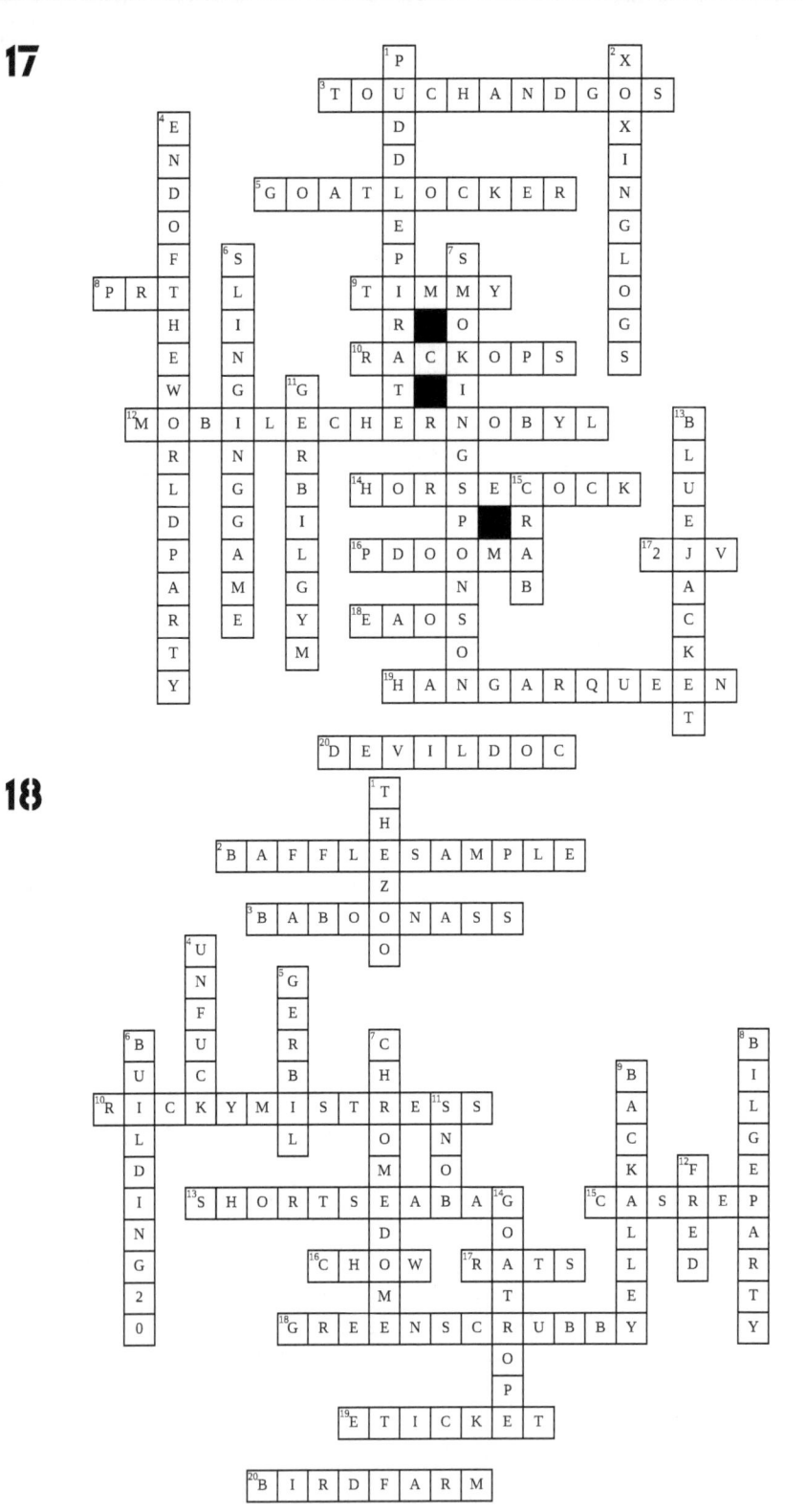

Across:
- 3: TOUCHANDGOS
- 5: GOATLOCKER
- 8: PRT
- 9: TIMMY
- 10: RACKOPS
- 12: MOBILECHERNOBYL
- 14: HORSE
- 15: COCK
- 16: PDOOMA
- 17: 2JV
- 18: EAOS
- 19: HANGARQUEEN
- 20: DEVILDOC

Down:
- 1: PDDEP
- 2: XXINGLOGS
- 4: ENDOFTHEWORLDPARTY
- 6: SLINGINGGAME
- 7: SOOIGNONSO
- 11: GRBILGYM
- 13: BLUEJACKET

18

Across:
- 2: BAFFLESAMPLE
- 3: BABOONASS
- 10: RICKYMISTRESS
- 13: SHORTSEABAG
- 15: CASREP
- 16: CHOW
- 17: RATS
- 18: GREENSCRUBBY
- 19: ETICKET
- 20: BIRDFARM

Down:
- 1: THZO
- 4: UNFUCL
- 5: GERB
- 6: BUILDING20
- 7: CHOMMDM
- 8: BILGEPARTY
- 9: BACKLLE
- 11: SNO
- 12: FED
- 14: GODMTOOP

19

1 IYARGOL
2 DIT
3 GOGGLES
4 MEATGAZE
5 GOLDENRIVET
6 VAMPIRELIBERTY
7 SAR
8 BARRICADE
9 BOARD
10 VERTREP
11 JOPA
12 POD
13 CARRIERSTRIKEGROUP
14 LOST
15 BOATS
16 POOPIEPANTS
17 NOLOAD
18 SIMS
19 CRANK
20 BUNNYTUBE

20

1 PARE
2 CRAZYIVAN
3 WARRANT
4 SHORTTIMERSCHAIN
5 ROASTBEAST
6 BARNEYCLARK
7 WATERWINGS
8 QUARTER
9 BOOMERFAG
10 RICKYBOXING
11 CAMEL
12 BUF
13 HAPPYSOCK
14 SLICKSLEEVE
15 PINEAPPLEFLEET
16 LOOP
17 GYRENE
18 SKITTLES
19 BRIGHTWORKS
20 ALLBALLS

21

Across:
3. FIVEANDDIMES
5. UNASS
8. STEELBEACHPICNIC
10. WINGS
12. PUCKCHO
15. NUKEITOUT
16. ORINGS
18. BASTARDCHIEF
19. DILBERTDUNKER
20. SORTIE

Down:
1. VIRTUAL
2. BTP
4. SUCKBAG
6. HACK
7. DNC
9. ELIBERTYSWS
11. BBBLE
13. HOWEVER
14. PHANTMS
17. SMLBY

22

Across:
3. SHITRIVER
5. FOCSLEFOLLIES
6. TEABAGGING
8. TROUT
11. SPARKY
12. ZERO
17. BONEMEHARDRICHARD
19. EARTHSACK
20. SCUPPERTROUT

Down:
1. SKD
2. RNGKOCKER
4. BO
7. EDC
9. SKYLARKING
10. PIM
13. DCIN
14. JS
15. OCT
16. SE
18. BKNDI

23

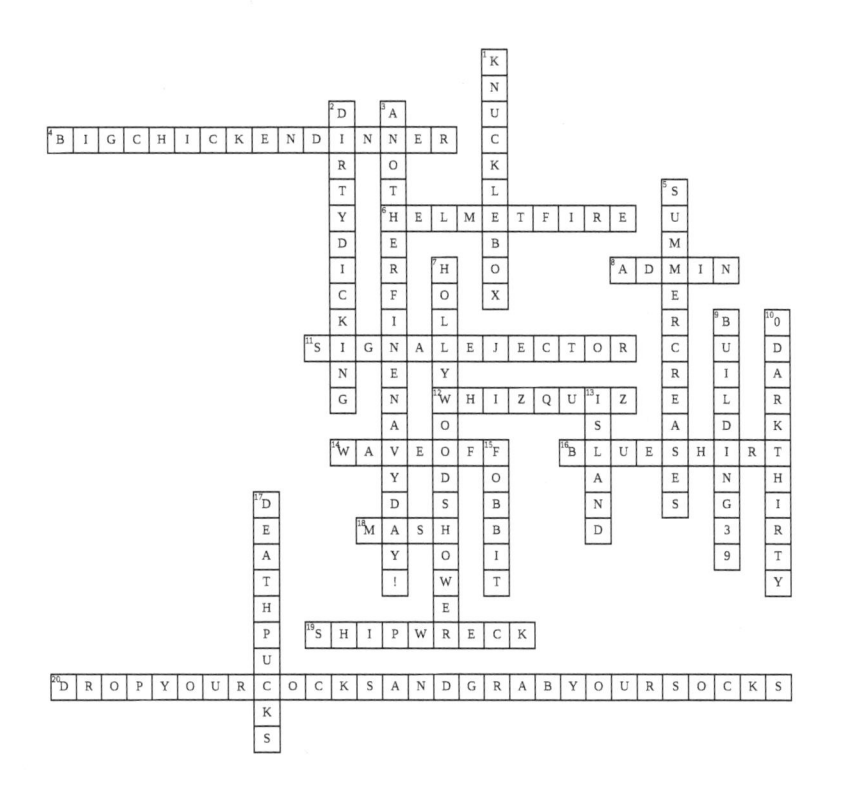

Across
4. BIGCHICKENDINNER
6. HELMETFIRE
7. HOX
8. ADMIN
11. SIGNALEJECTOR
12. WHIZQUIZ
14. WAVEOF
16. BLUESHIRT
18. MASH
19. SHIPWRECK
20. DROPYOURCOCKSANDGRABYOURSOCKS

Down
1. KNUCKLE
2. DIRTYDICK
3. AOTHERFILENAME
5. SUMER
6. HEYYDDY!
7. HOLYBOXWET
9. BUILDINGS39
10. ODARKTHIRTY
11. SIGNAG
13. IZO
15. FOSBBIT
17. DEATHPUCKS

24

Across
1. FARTSUIT
3. POLISHATURD
9. CHUBCLUB
11. BOSNIA
14. FLATHATTING
16. HAMSTER
17. IHTFP
18. FREEBOARD
19. SOUGEE
20. FREQ

Down
2. VLAD
4. BALLSTOFOUR
5. BEACHPOUNDER
6. LAW
7. FLIGHHGUSS
8. FIGHTINGGEAR
10. WEIGHTDECK
11. BANDEAT
12. BAR
13. CRIPLER
14. FTR
15. FG

25

Crossword puzzle grid with the following filled entries:

Across:
- 4: PIGBOAT
- 7: BUBBLEHEAD
- 9: OLY
- 10: SANDCRAB
- 13: POPPINGYOUR
- 14: PUP
- 15: BLACKSHOE
- 16: YOKO
- 18: MOTRIN
- 19: BR
- (continued): OKEDICK

Down:
- 1: DANENRNT
- 2: BUTTERBAR
- 3: FBNO
- 5: CHARLIEOSCAR
- 6: CLBLCY
- 8: SULLERY
- 11: BOOMER
- 12: DITDOTBAG
- 14: PAVVY
- 17: DIT
- 20: OSCAR

Notable words visible: DAN, FERN, BUBBLEHEAD, CHARLIEOSCAR, BUTTERBAR, SANDCRAB, SULLERY, OLY, POPPINGYOURCHERRY, BOOMER, PUPPY, BLACKSHOE, YOKO, DITDOTBAG, MOTRIN, BROKEDICK, OSCAR

26

Crossword puzzle grid with the following filled entries:

Across:
- 4: MILKMAN
- 7: USSUSETAFISH
- 10: BENNY
- 12: AHEADFRANKCRAPONPLATE
- 15: COD
- 16: TIRECHASER
- 17: THELEANS
- 18: TITSUP
- 19: TAIL
- 20: RICKYVACUUM

Down:
- 1: BRIGCHASER
- 2: NUKE
- 3: USSLASTSSIP / USSLASTSSIPBOX (visible: U,S,S,L,A,S,T,S,S,I,P,B,O,X)
- 5: RB (REBEHOLDSL visible)
- 6: THESNDBO
- 8: LOVEBOAT
- 9: DIQ
- 11: CNEXT
- 13: OLDSL
- 14: APPLJC

1

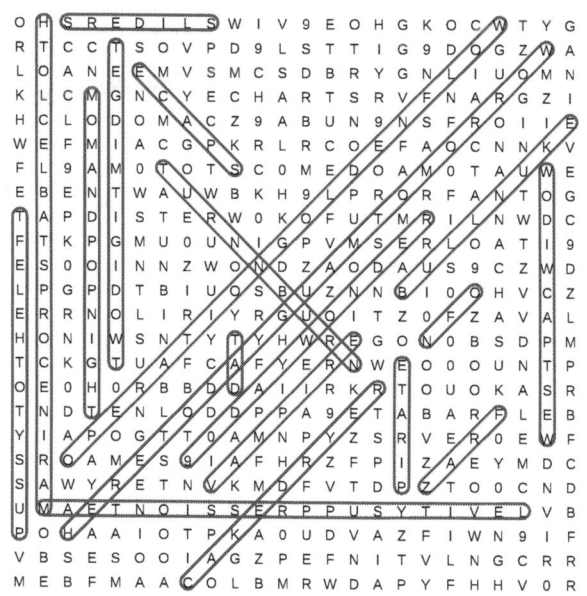

Vampire
Bull Nuke
Cake Dryer
90-day Wonder
Marine Corps Table Cloth
TAD
Turn 'n Burn

Operation GOLDENFLOW
Pussy to the left
WESTPAC Widow
Levity Suppression Team
Pirate
NFO

Space
Zarf
Mom and Pop night
Here today, GUAM tomorrow
Sliders
Two-Digit Midget

2

TOD
Below Decks
Pussy Pills
Comshaw
WUBAflage

CIVLANT
Kiss the Camel
Overhead
C-GU11
Rent-A-Crow

Mystery Meat
Chula-juana
JORG
Lucky Bag
NO GAS

Father's Day
Wog
Green Table Tea Party
Voluntold

3

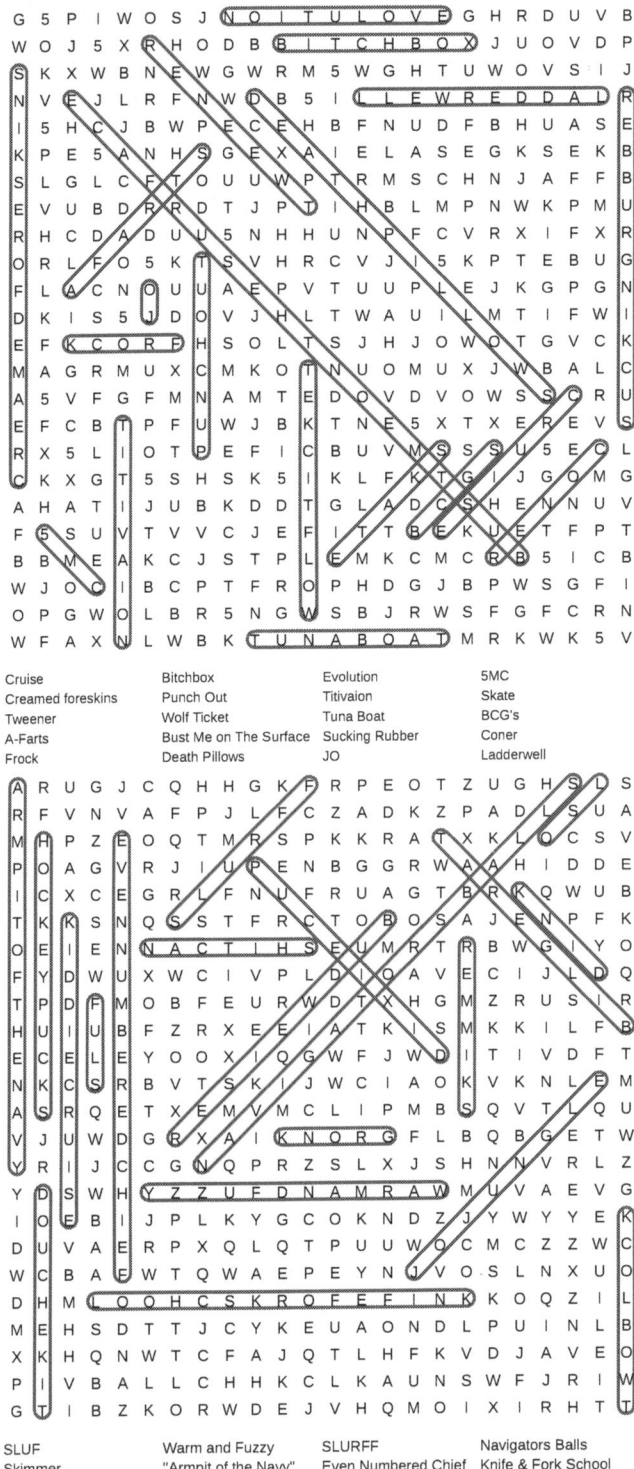

Cruise
Creamed foreskins
Tweener
A-Farts
Frock

Bitchbox
Punch Out
Wolf Ticket
Bust Me on The Surface
Death Pillows

Evolution
Titivaion
Tuna Boat
Sucking Rubber
JO

5MC
Skate
BCG's
Coner
Ladderwell

4

SLUF
Skimmer
Shit Can
Dink
JO Jungle

Warm and Fuzzy
"Armpit of the Navy"
Budweiser
Gronk
LSO

SLURFF
Even Numbered Chief
Kiddie Cruise
Dixie Cup
Two-block

Navigators Balls
Knife & Fork School
Hockey pucks
Bilge Rat
Douche Kit

5

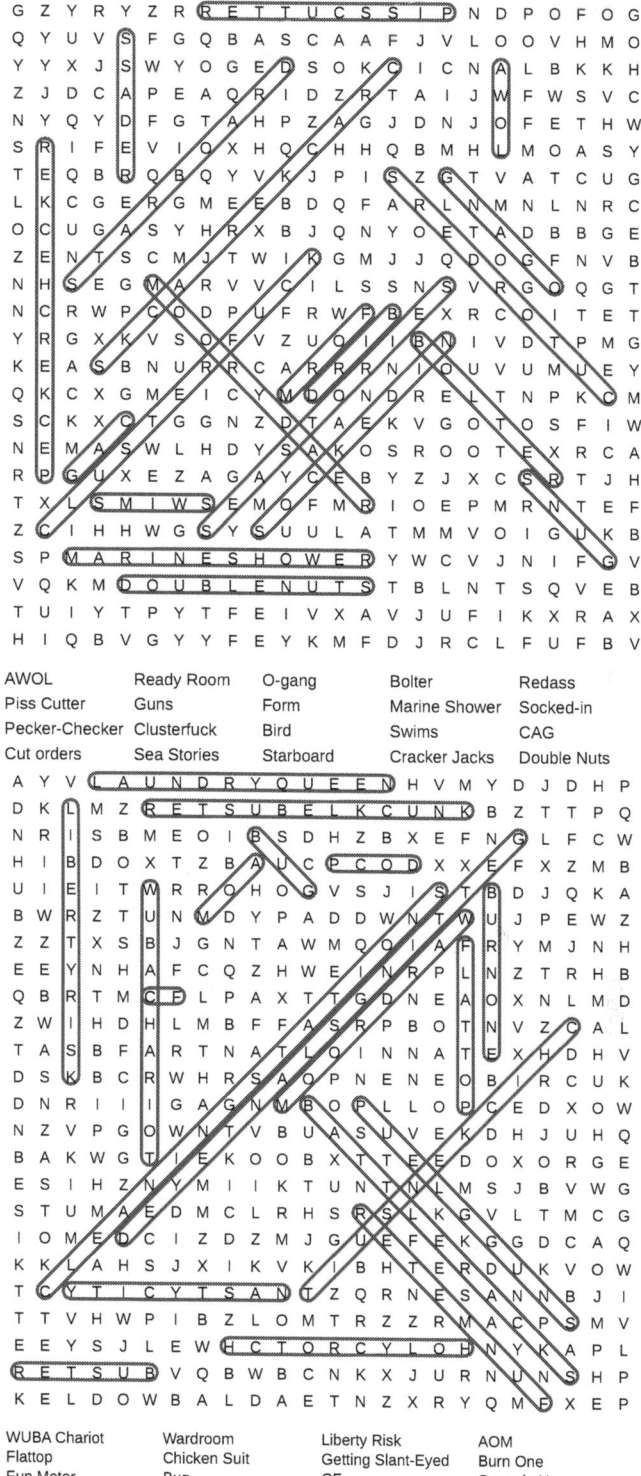

G	Z	Y	R	Y	Z	R	R	E	T	T	U	C	S	S	I	P	N	D	P	O	F	O	G
Q	Y	U	V	S	F	G	Q	B	A	S	C	A	A	F	J	V	L	O	O	V	H	M	O
Y	Y	X	J	S	W	Y	O	G	E	D	S	O	K	C	I	C	N	A	L	B	K	K	H
Z	J	D	C	A	P	E	A	Q	R	I	D	Z	R	T	A	I	J	W	F	W	S	V	C
N	Y	Q	Y	D	F	G	T	A	H	P	Z	A	G	J	D	N	J	O	F	E	T	H	W
S	R	I	F	E	V	I	O	X	H	Q	C	H	H	Q	B	M	H	U	M	O	A	S	Y
T	E	Q	B	R	O	B	Q	Y	V	K	J	P	I	S	Z	G	T	V	A	T	C	U	G
L	K	C	G	E	R	G	M	E	E	B	D	Q	F	A	R	L	N	M	N	L	N	R	C
O	C	U	G	A	S	Y	H	R	X	B	J	Q	N	Y	O	E	T	A	D	B	B	G	E
Z	E	N	T	S	C	M	J	T	W	I	K	G	M	J	J	Q	D	O	G	F	N	V	B
N	H	S	E	G	M	A	R	V	V	C	I	L	S	S	N	S	V	R	G	O	Q	G	T
N	C	R	W	P	C	O	D	P	U	F	R	W	F	B	E	X	R	C	O	I	T	E	T
Y	R	G	X	K	S	O	F	V	Z	U	Q	I	I	B	N	I	V	D	T	P	M	G
K	E	A	S	B	N	U	R	R	C	A	R	R	R	N	I	O	U	V	M	U	E	Y
Q	K	C	X	G	M	E	I	C	Y	M	D	O	N	D	R	E	L	T	N	P	K	C	M
S	C	K	X	C	T	G	G	N	Z	D	T	A	E	K	V	G	O	T	O	S	F	I	W
N	E	M	A	S	W	L	H	D	Y	S	A	K	O	S	R	O	O	T	E	X	R	C	A
R	P	G	U	X	E	Z	A	G	A	Y	C	E	B	Y	Z	J	X	C	S	R	T	J	H
T	X	L	S	M	I	W	S	E	M	O	F	M	R	I	O	E	P	M	R	N	T	E	F
Z	C	I	H	H	W	G	S	Y	S	U	U	L	A	T	M	M	V	O	I	G	U	K	B
S	P	M	A	R	I	N	E	S	H	O	W	E	R	Y	W	C	V	J	N	I	F	G	Y
V	Q	K	M	D	O	U	B	L	E	N	U	T	S	T	B	L	N	T	S	Q	V	E	B
T	U	I	Y	T	P	Y	T	F	E	I	V	X	A	V	J	U	F	I	K	X	R	A	X
H	I	Q	B	V	G	Y	Y	F	E	Y	K	M	F	D	J	R	C	L	F	U	F	B	V

AWOL   Ready Room   O-gang   Bolter   Redass
Piss Cutter   Guns   Form   Marine Shower   Socked-in
Pecker-Checker   Clusterfuck   Bird   Swims   CAG
Cut orders   Sea Stories   Starboard   Cracker Jacks   Double Nuts

6

A	Y	V	L	A	U	N	D	R	Y	Q	U	E	E	N	H	V	M	Y	D	J	D	H	P
D	K	L	M	Z	R	E	T	S	U	B	E	L	K	C	U	N	K	B	Z	T	T	P	Q
N	R	I	S	B	M	E	O	I	B	S	D	H	Z	B	X	E	F	N	G	L	F	C	W
H	I	B	D	O	X	T	Z	B	A	U	C	P	C	O	D	X	X	F	X	Z	M	B
U	I	E	T	W	R	R	O	H	O	G	V	S	J	I	S	T	B	D	J	Q	K	A
B	W	R	Z	T	U	N	M	D	Y	P	A	D	D	W	N	T	W	U	J	P	E	W	Z
Z	Z	T	X	S	B	J	G	N	T	A	W	M	Q	O	I	A	F	R	Y	M	J	N	H
E	E	Y	N	H	A	F	C	Q	Z	H	W	E	N	R	P	L	N	Z	T	R	H	B
Q	B	R	T	M	C	E	L	P	A	X	T	T	G	D	N	E	A	O	X	N	L	M	D
Z	W	I	H	D	H	L	M	B	F	F	A	S	R	P	B	O	T	N	V	Z	C	A	L
T	A	S	B	F	A	R	T	N	A	T	L	O	I	N	N	A	T	E	X	H	D	H	V
D	S	K	B	C	R	W	H	R	S	A	O	P	N	E	N	E	O	B	I	R	C	U	K
D	N	R	I	I	G	A	G	N	M	B	O	L	L	O	P	C	E	D	X	O	W
N	Z	V	P	G	O	W	N	T	V	B	U	A	S	U	V	E	K	D	H	J	U	H	Q
B	A	K	W	G	T	I	E	K	O	O	B	X	T	T	E	E	D	O	X	O	R	G	E
E	S	I	H	Z	N	Y	M	I	I	K	T	U	N	T	N	L	M	S	J	B	V	W	G
S	T	U	M	A	E	D	M	C	L	R	H	S	R	S	L	G	V	L	T	M	C	G
I	O	M	E	D	C	I	Z	D	Z	M	J	G	U	E	F	K	G	G	D	C	A	Q
K	K	L	A	H	S	J	X	I	K	V	K	B	H	T	E	R	D	U	K	V	O	W
T	C	Y	T	I	C	Y	T	S	A	N	T	Z	Q	R	N	E	S	A	N	N	B	J	I
T	T	V	H	W	P	I	B	Z	L	O	M	T	R	Z	Z	R	M	A	C	P	S	M	V
E	E	Y	S	J	L	E	W	H	C	T	O	R	C	Y	L	O	H	N	Y	K	A	P	L
R	E	T	S	U	B	V	Q	B	W	B	C	N	K	X	J	U	R	N	U	N	S	H	P
K	E	L	D	O	W	B	A	L	D	A	E	T	N	Z	X	R	Y	Q	M	E	X	E	P

WUBA Chariot   Wardroom   Liberty Risk   AOM
Flattop   Chicken Suit   Getting Slant-Eyed   Burn One
Fun Meter   Bug   CF   Snuggle Up
Holy Crotch   Laundry Queen   P.C.O.D.   Cleaning Stations
Knuckle Buster   Buster   Nasty City   Battle Racks

7

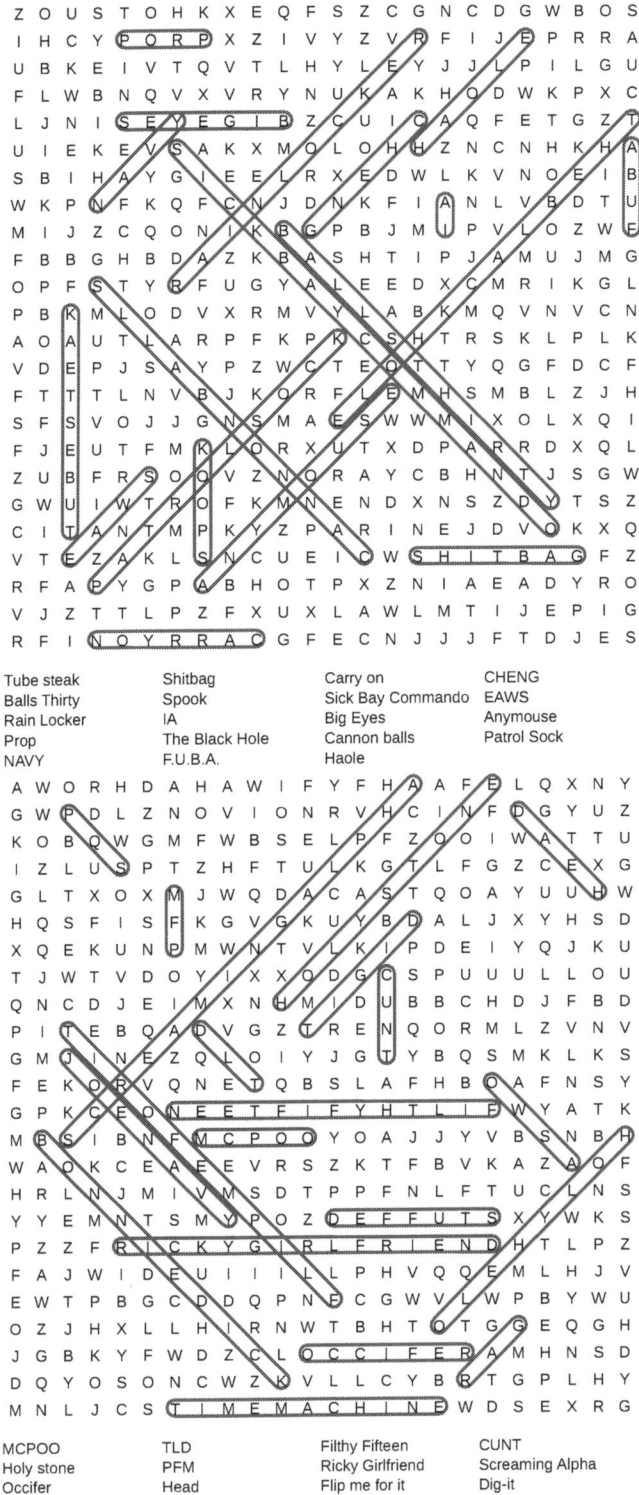

```
Z O U S T O H K X E Q F S Z C G N C D G W B O S
I H C Y P O R P X Z I V Y Z V R F I J E P R R A
U B K E I V T Q V T L H Y L E Y J J L P I L G U
F L W B N Q V X V R Y N U K A K H O D W K P X C
L J N I S E Y E G I B Z C U I C A Q F E T G Z T
U I E K E V S A K X M O L O H H Z N C N H K H A
S B I H A Y G I E E L R X E D W L K V N O E I B
W K P N F K Q F C N J D N K F I A N L V B D T U
M I J Z C Q O N I K B G P B J M P V L O Z W E
F B B G H B D A Z K B A S H T I P J A M U J M G
O P F S T Y R F U G Y A E E D X C M R I K G L
P B K M L O D V X R M V Y L A B K M O V N V C N
A O A U T L A R P F K P K C S H T R S K L P L A
V D E P J S A Y P Z W C T E O T Y Q G F D C F
F T T T L N V B J K O R F L E M H S M B L Z Q I
S F S V O J J G N S M A E S W W M I X O L X Q I
F J E U T F M K L O R X U T X D P A R R D X Q L
Z U B F R S O O V Z N O R A Y C B N T J S G W
G W U I W T R O F K M N E N D X N S Z D Y T S Z
C I T A N T M P K Y Z P A R I N E J D V O K X Q
V T E Z A K L S N C U E I O W S H I T B A G F Z
R F A P Y G P A B H O T P X Z N I A E A D Y R O
V J Z T T L P Z F X U X L A W L M T I J E P I G
R F I N O Y R R A C G F E C N J J J F T D J E S
```

Tube steak — Shitbag — Carry on — CHENG
Balls Thirty — Spook — Sick Bay Commando — EAWS
Rain Locker — IA — Big Eyes — Anymouse
Prop — The Black Hole — Cannon balls — Patrol Sock
NAVY — F.U.B.A. — Haole

8

```
A W O R H D A H A W I F Y F H A A F E L Q X N Y
G W P D L Z N O V I O N R V H C I N F D G Y U Z
K O B O W G M F W B S E L P F Z Q O I W A T T U
I Z L U S P T Z H F T U L K G T L F G Z C E X G
G L T X O X M J W Q D A C A S T Q O A Y U U H W
H Q S F I S F K G V G K U Y B D A L J X Y H S D
X Q E K U N P M W N T V L K I P D E I Y Q J K U
T J W T V D O Y I X X O D G C S P U U U L L O U
Q N C D J E I M X N H M I D U B B C H D J F B D
P I T E B Q A D V G Z T R E N Q O R M L Z V N V
G M O I N E Z Q L O I Y J G T Y B Q S M K L K S
F E K O R V Q N E T Q B S L A F H B O A F N S Y
G P K C E O N E E T F I F Y H T L I F W Y A T K
M B S I B N F M C P O O Y O A J J Y V B S N B H
W A O K C E A E E V R S Z K T F B V K A Z A O F
H R L N J M I V M S D T P P F N L F T U C L N S
Y Y E M N T S M Y P O Z D E F F U T S X Y W K S
P Z Z F R I C K Y G I R L F R I E N D H T L P Z
F A J W I D E U I I L L P H V Q Q E M L H J V
E W T P B G C D D Q P N E C G W V L W P B Y W U
O Z J H X L L H I R N W T B H T O T G G E Q G H
J G B K Y F W D Z C L O C C I F E R A M H N S D
D Q Y O S O N C W Z K V L L C Y B R T G P L H Y
M N L J C S T I M E M A C H I N E W D S E X R G
```

MCPOO — TLD — Filthy Fifteen — CUNT
Holy stone — PFM — Ricky Girlfriend — Screaming Alpha
Occifer — Head — Flip me for it — Dig-it
Joe Navy — PQS — Time Machine — Holy Helo
Bonnie Dick — ASWO — Stuffed — RAG

9

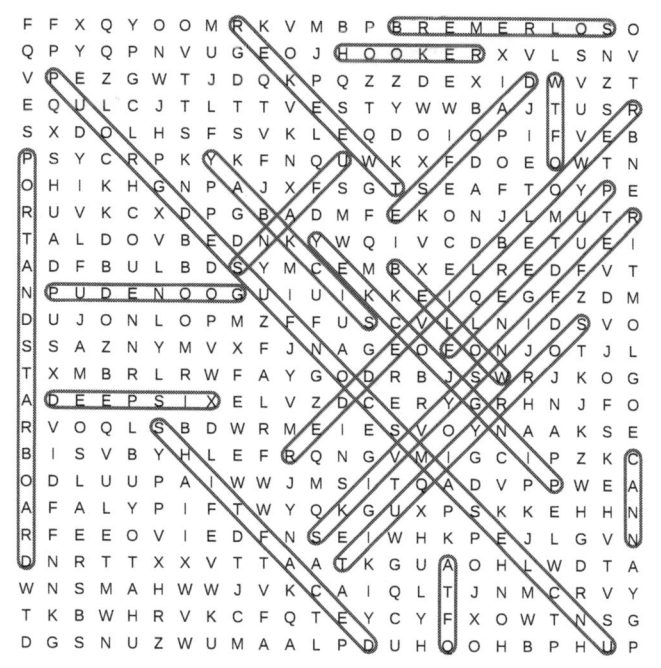

[word search grid]

- Deep Six
- Skivvy Sniffer
- Hooker
- Fleet Up
- Shit-faced
- Port and Starboard
- Below
- Ping Jockey
- Uncle Sam's Confused Group
- WTFO
- Bremerlos
- Red Devil Blower
- ESFOAD
- SNAFU
- Sick Bay
- Cann
- ATFQ
- Tweeker
- Gooned Up
- Sorry I Quit

10

[word search grid]

- The Beach
- Auto
- Bag Ass
- Button Crusher
- Aluminum Cloud
- Out-chop
- chart
- Double-Digit Midget
- FEP
- People Tank
- Naval Aviators' Disease
- Zoomies
- Blue on Blue
- One-eyed Jack
- Bubba
- Sig
- Duck Dinner
- Hook
- Booter
- Sticks

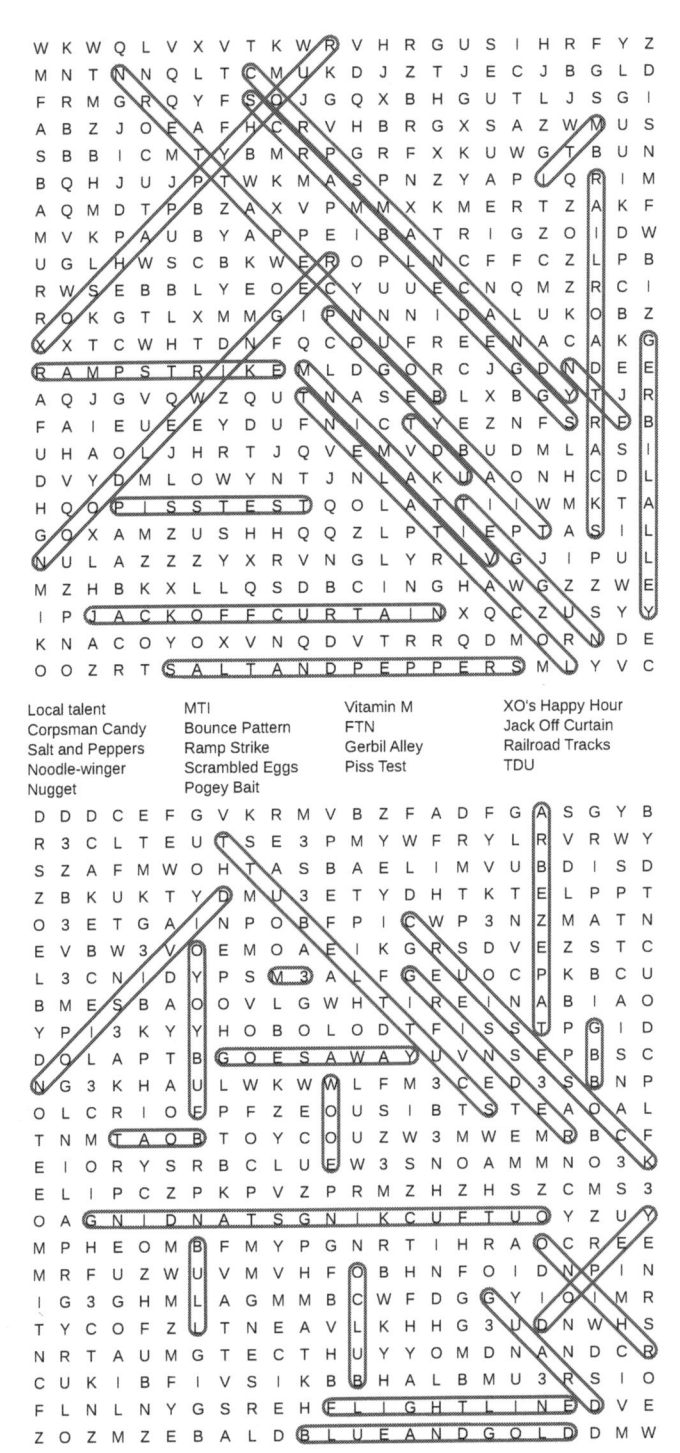

11

```
W K W Q L V X V T K W R V H R G U S I H R F Y Z
M N T N Q L T C M U K D J Z T J E C J B G L D
F R M G R Q Y F S O J G Q X B H G U T L J S G I
A B Z J O E A F H C R V H B R G X S A Z W M U S
S B B I C M T Y B M R P G R F X K U W G T B U N
B Q H J U J P T W K M A S P N Z Y A P U Q R I M
A Q M D T P B Z A X V P M M X K M E R T Z A K F
M V K P A U B Y A P P E I B A T R I G Z O I D W
U G L H W S C B K W E R O P L N C F F C Z L P B
R W S E B B L Y E O E C Y U U E C N Q M Z R C I
R O K G T L X M M G I N N N I D A L U K O B Z
X X T C W H T D N F Q C O U F R E E N A C A K G
R A M P S T R I K E M L D G O R C J D N D E E
A Q J G V Q W Z Q U T N A S E B L X G Y T J R
F A I E U E E Y D U F N I C T Y E Z N F S R E B
U H A O L J H R T J Q V E M V G D M L A S I
D V B H F M L O W Y N T J N L A K U O N H C D L
H Q X A M Z U S H H Q Q Z L P T I E V A S I L
G O U L A Z Z Z Y X R V N G L Y R L V G J I P U L
M Z H B K X L L Q S D B C I N G H A W G Z Z W E
I P J A C K O F F C U R T A I N X Q C Z U S Y V
K N A C O Y O X V N Q D V T R R Q D M R N D E
O O Z R T S A L T A N D P E P P E R S M Y V C
```

Local talent   MTI   Vitamin M   XO's Happy Hour
Corpsman Candy   Bounce Pattern   FTN   Jack Off Curtain
Salt and Peppers   Ramp Strike   Gerbil Alley   Railroad Tracks
Noodle-winger   Scrambled Eggs   Piss Test   TDU
Nugget   Pogey Bait

12

```
D D D C E F G V K R M V B Z F A D F G A S G Y B
R 3 C L T E U T S E 3 P M Y W F R Y L R V R W Y
S Z A F M W O H T A S B A E L I M V U B D I S O
Z B K U F X Y D M U 3 E T Y D H T K T E L P P T
O 3 E T G A I N P O B F P I C W P 3 N Z M A T N
E V B W 3 V O E M O A E I K G R S D V E Z S T C
L 3 C N I D Y P S M 3 A L F G E U O C P K B C U
B M E S B A O O V L G W H T I R E N A B I A O
Y P I 3 K Y Y H O B O L O D T F I S S T P G I D
D O L A P T B G O E S A W A Y U V N S E P B S C
N G 3 K H A U L W K W L F M 3 C E D 3 S B N P
O L C R I O F P F Z E O U S I B T S T E A O A L
T N M T A O B T O Y C O U Z W 3 M W E M R B C F
E I O R Y S R B C L U E W 3 S N O A M M N O 3 K
E L I P C Z P K P V Z P R M Z H Z H S Z C M S 3
O A G N I D N A T S G N I K C U F T U O Y Z U Y
M P H E O M B F M Y P G N R T I H R A O C R E E
M R F U Z W U V M V H F O B H N F O I D N P I N
I G 3 G H M L A G M M B C W F D G G Y I O I M R
T Y C O F Z U T N E A V L K H H G 3 U D N W H S
N R T A U M G T E C T H U Y Y O M D N A N D C R
C U K I B F I V S I K B B H A L B M U 3 R S I O
F L N L N Y G S R E H F L I G H T L I N E D V E
Z O Z M Z E B A L D B L U E A N D G O L D D M W
```

B.B.&G.   F.U.B.Y.O.Y.O.   Blue and Gold   Out-fucking-standing
Bull   3M   Boat   Cruise sock
Division   Goes Away   Flight Line   Tape Zebra
Rhino   Grinder   Scuttlebutt   EOOW
Guard   Dopey   O-Club

13

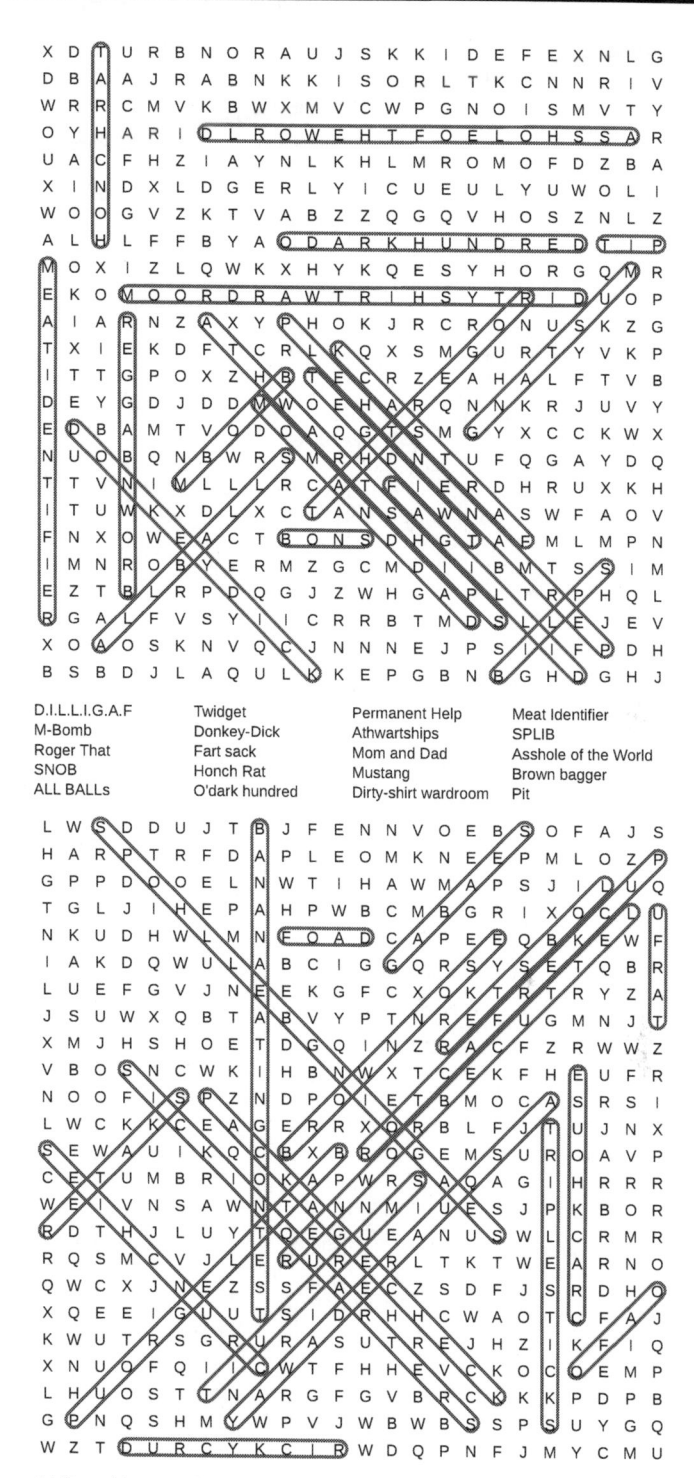

[word search grid]

D.I.L.L.I.G.A.F	Twidget	Permanent Help	Meat Identifier
M-Bomb	Donkey-Dick	Athwartships	SPLIB
Roger That	Fart sack	Mom and Dad	Asshole of the World
SNOB	Honch Rat	Mustang	Brown bagger
ALL BALLs	O'dark hundred	Dirty-shirt wardroom	Pit

14

[word search grid]

A.J. Squared Away	Crunchies	Crack House	Lobster
T.A.R.F.U.	Lettuce Browner	Package Check	Pucker Factor
FOAD	Smurf Suit	Triple Sticks	OAFO
Ricky Crud	Sea Going Bellhops	Seabag	Banana Eating Contest
Skater	Brown Nose	Sick in Quarters	Battle Group

15

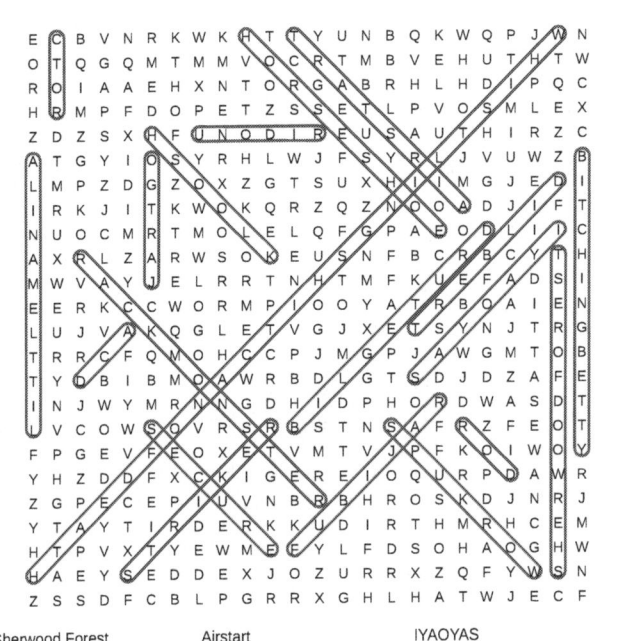

Sherwood Forest
Secure
Kloosh
Bitching Betty
JARTGO
ROD
Little Manila

Airstart
Whistling Shit Can of Death
Striker
DCA
Dilbert
UNODIR
Horse Shoe

IYAOYAS
Rack Monster
F.U.B.I.J.A.R.
ROTC
Workups
Bilge Turd

16

Assholes and elbows
Midnight Requisition
Cunt Cover
Canoe U
Shitter

Reality Check
Gouge
Old Man
Nuclear Waste
BUNO

Helo Dunker
Nooner
MARINE
B.O.C.O.D
Time On The Pond

CIC
Captain's Mast
MEDEVAC
Skeevy Stacker
Drift Count

17

```
B W V K E O C M O F T A D E N I P E B R N L G A
K 2 O N B E Y H A 2 O E D O A S D F F G C Y E P
P U D D L E P I R A T E S P L D O L P E D G 2 M
F 2 J W I T 2 B O C P N K I T T O H B A A V H O
L H U B A L S B P 2 O E N V I E M R M T Y J B B
M 2 O N A L V H V P T G A R M 2 A D L R M 2 L I
B B Q R T R K F S D I R P X M H R X P V C D U L
T C W I S L G W N A R D X Y A S J Y L S Y E E
Y G G Y P E N E G Y E D N V E W N T J I K A J C
H P 2 H F I C G H K S 2 J P L D M N H J P W A H
H G T S K C A O C E F C S H S A E A D G Y Y C E
D E M O W M B O C U W C D O J G N R T T Q C K R
W E M Y E J L C P K U J S F G G O P J E B D E N
E S V O G T J N L X K F H P A D B L I X F F T O
D A B I A L Q Q K C E G W R O V N P G W Y L G B
W W O L H I H A C J R Q E V K K A Y N K F Q Y
A E G S 2 D F B Q K H U C A Y L C L H B I D V
J F G S L E O 2 R G E X O V A V M A I C R X J T
Y B V B U S S O E L V 2 D M N Y A R A U X O Y
R L F T O T O F N C G I D F I U C N N N O O U X
S D F O A A V Q C U K U H G B I D C F 2 P U T X
A M B S E N D O F T H E W O R L D P A R T Y E Q
M F I C G F Y Y Q W A N W R C C I Q A N H 2 G B
K H R X O X P D P R 2 X S L X B 2 T H G U Q L K
```

Xoxing Logs	EAOS	Bluejacket	P.D.O.O.M.A.
End-of-the-World Party	Gerbil Gym	Slinging Game	Touch and Go's
Hangar Queen	Rack Ops	Timmy	Crab
Devil Doc	Horse Cock	Goat locker	Smoking Sponson
Puddle Pirate	2JV	Mobile Chernobyl	PRT

18

```
F O Y 0 F G U A N 2 E T T K P H M D A C B R D E
W S L W W Z 0 M 2 S Z I D Z E K M P N W O 0 W
M M S 0 G B T A H A G 2 D N P T I K R B N B Y N
R 0 C E U R T H E Z O O T I G P B D H S Y 2 K D
A G R A R T E E L S A O F G L F F S H T Y 2 C
U F B F W T P E F W W Y E T 2 A E L 0 2 R W E A
R N A M F O S B N S Y R Y H R H M G N C A F S N
S O I Y M Z T I L S B F I M Z Z R U T L P E E
R C P M E S S Y M I C N M B L N Y S I D E E Z E
A K M K G N T E L Y W R N A A K T S N E G K I P
B U S B O W S N B F K N U D W B A C K A L L E Y
L I T B L B O K S C U C A B E K 0 I 0 P I D U I
2 G A G B G U B N F G K I D B R D U G I B C O B
C Y R 0 N P B 0 B C H Z R 2 V P D U K Z O 0 G
E T M 0 H C 2 T L B S Z M F K T R B F I T N 0
S S A N O O B A B D P B A F F L E S A M P L E G
D N Y R D Y U M P T I O R M A F D K 0 W 0 2 W H
S B L P N E E T D L R N R P M T S Z A Z B R P O
D K O W 0 W T S D S H A G T W Y R Y A F T H A K
C Z F Y H U I O O C E G D 2 A L U P K Z E B A C
F L W E E M C G B T H Y D K O O W S T Y L T K U
B N T R N O K E A B K S R W 0 2 G D W Z N L B F
W O H C G Z E U N C H R O M E D O M E B E K H 2
T S H Y A G T S G A B A E S T R O H S R Y 0 A U
```

The Zoo	Back Alley	Baffle Sample	Chow	Short Seabag
Ricky Mistress	Birdfarm	FRED	Goatrope	'Rats
Gerbil	Building 20	Baboon Ass	CASREP	Chrome Dome
Bilge Party	Green Scrubby	S.N.O.B.	Un-Fuck	E-ticket

19

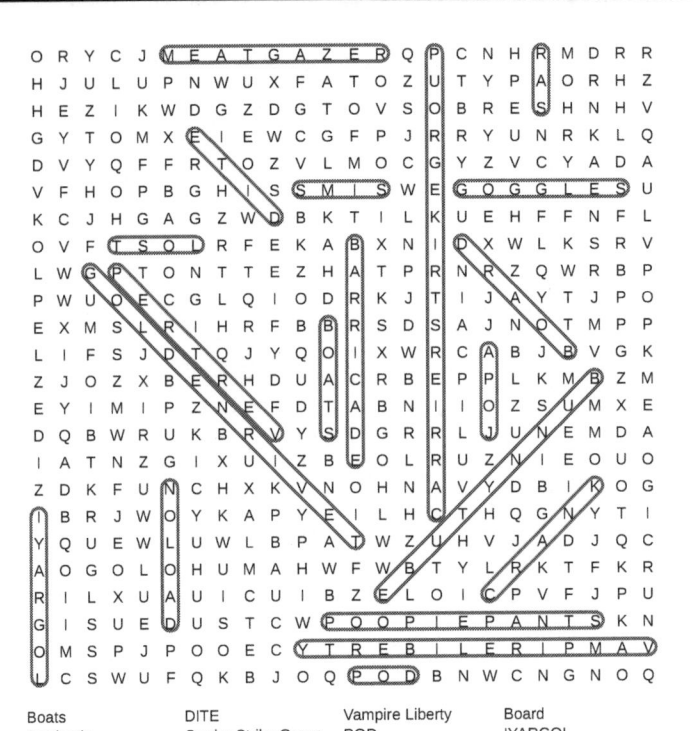

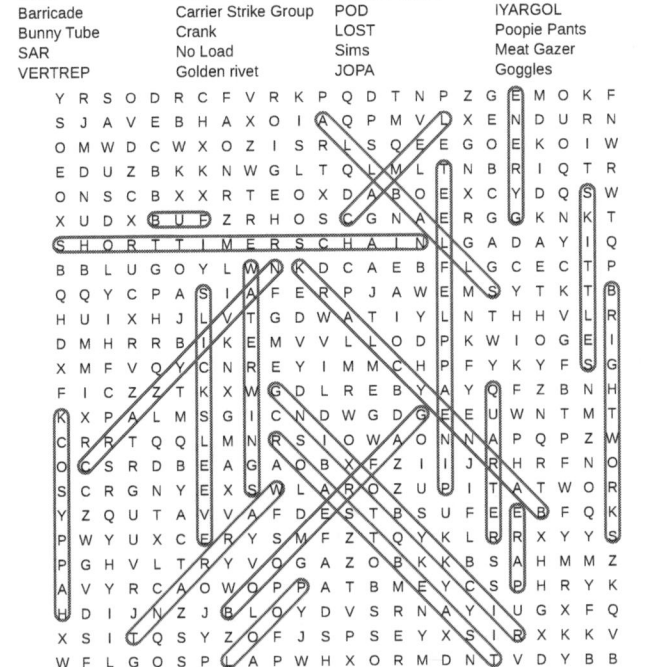

Boats
Barricade
Bunny Tube
SAR
VERTREP

DITE
Carrier Strike Group
Crank
No Load
Golden rivet

Vampire Liberty
POD
LOST
Sims
JOPA

Board
IYARGOL
Poopie Pants
Meat Gazer
Goggles

20

Barney Clark
Pare
Water wings
Ricky Boxing
Camel
BUF
Happy Sock

Slick Sleeve
Gyrene
Pineapple Fleet
Boomer Fag
Roast Beast
Crazy Ivan
Quarter

Skittles
Short Timer's Chain
Warrant
All Balls
Loop
Brightworks

21

ESWS
Ding
However
Hack
Steel Beach Picnic

Dilbert Dunker
Small Boy
Bastard Chief
Un-ass
BT Punch

Nuke It Out
Virtual Liberty
Five and Dimes
Bubble
Puck Chop

Wings
Suckbag
Phantom Shitter
O-Rings
Sortie

22

Trout
Earth Sack
JSI
Zero
OOD

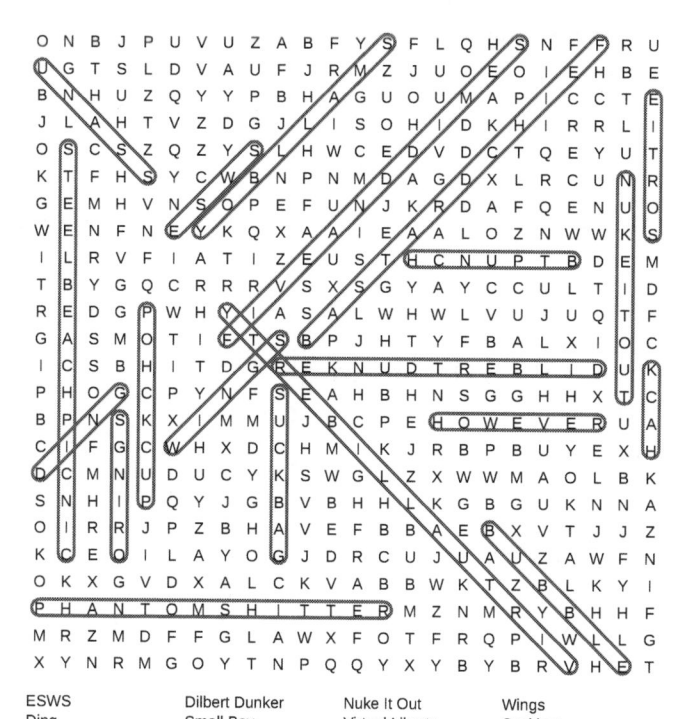

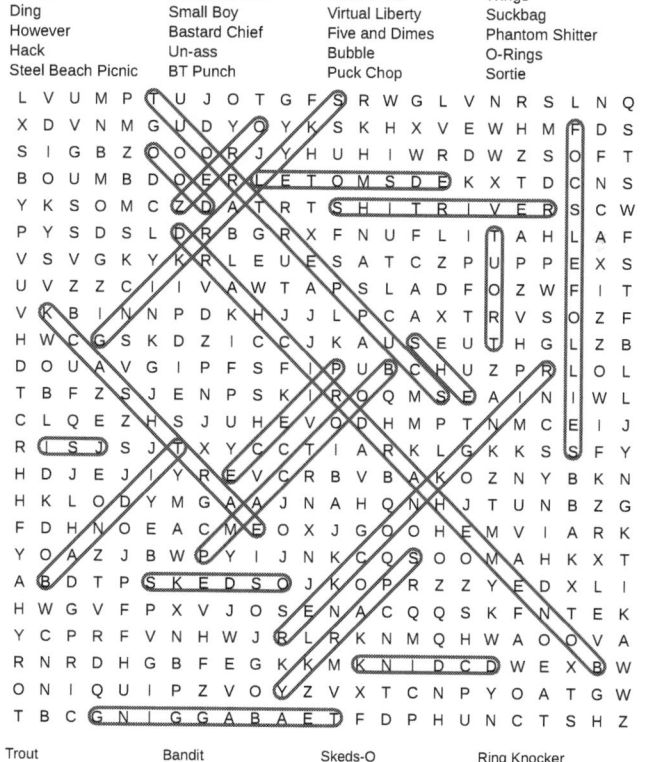

Bandit
Shit River
Piece
Ed's Motel
Bootcamp

Skeds-O
Scupper Trout
Bone Me Hard Richard
Sparky
Skylarking

Ring Knocker
Fo'c's'le Follies
Tea Bagging
S.H.E.
D.C. Dink

23

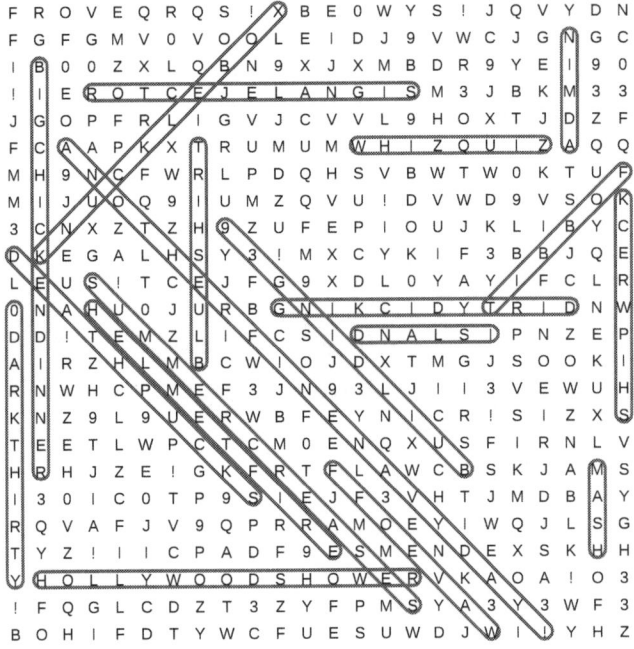

Dirty-dicking
Island
Helmet Fire
Signal Ejector
Hollywood Shower
Fobbit
Death Pucks
Whiz Quiz
Summer creases
Shipwreck
Blue Shirt
Mash
Knuckle Box
"Another Fine Navy Day!"
Big Chicken Dinner
Building 39
O'dark thirty
Wave-off
Admin

24

Freeboard
Chub Club
Lawn Dart
Balls to Four
Cripler
Weather Guesser
IHTFP
Bag
Polish a Turd
Beach Pounder
Fighting gear
B.O.S.N.I.A.
Freq
Flight Deck Buzzard
Flathatting
Fart Suit
Hamster
Vulcan Death Watch
FAG
Sougee

25

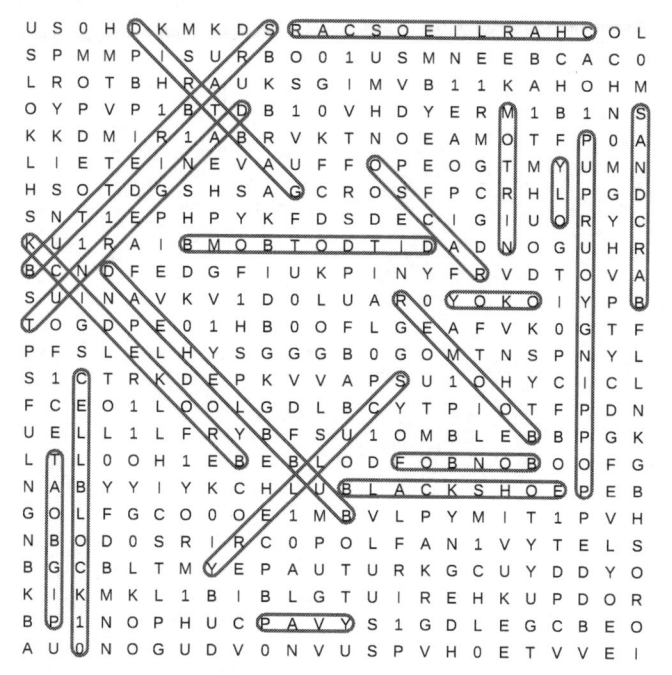

Pavy
Oly
Motrin
Cellblock 10
Sand Crab

Broke-dick
Yoko
Pig boat
Bubblehead
Butter Bars

Scullery
Dit Dot Bomb
Oscar
Charlie Oscar
Danger Nut

Black Shoe
Boomer
FOBNOB
Popping Your Pup
Dirtbag

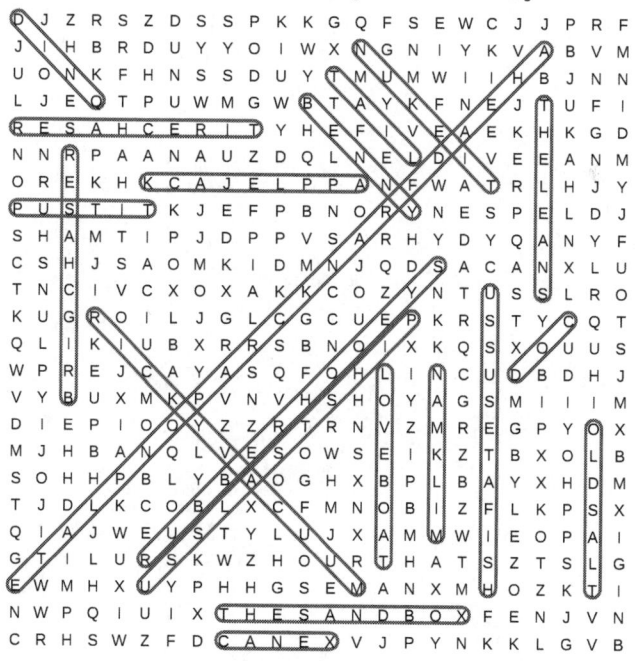

26

Old Salt
Tits-up
Tire Chaser
Dinq
USS LASTSHIP

Ricky Vacuum
Tail
CANEX
Brigchaser
Milkman

The Leans
Love Boat
Ahead Frank Crap on Plate
Benny
The Sandbox

USS Usetafish
Apple Jack
Rubber Hooeys
COD
Nuke It

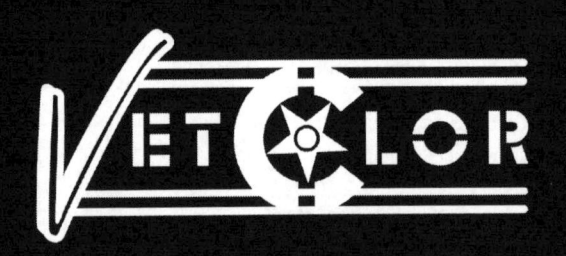

VETCOLOR.COM

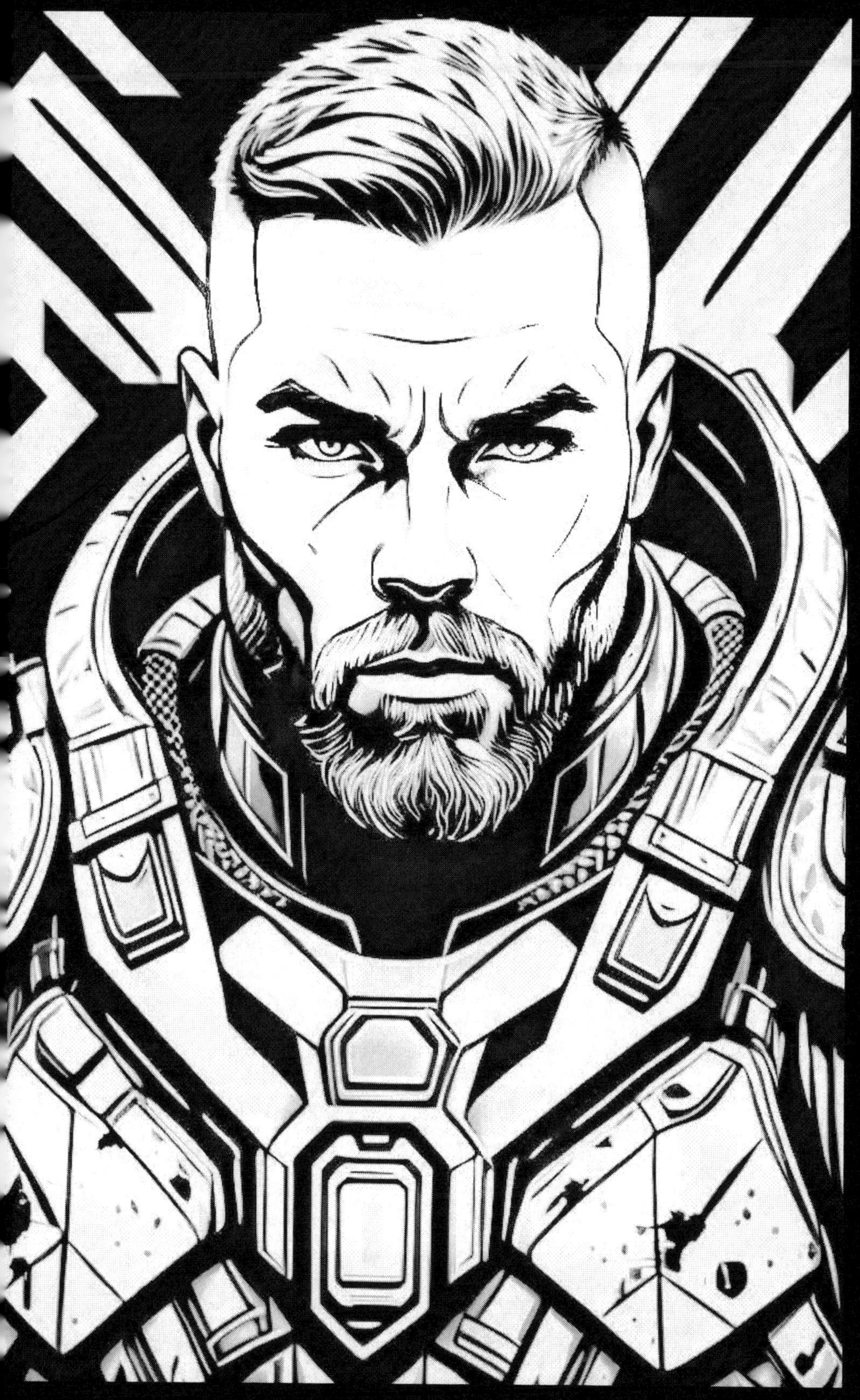

VETCOLOR.COM

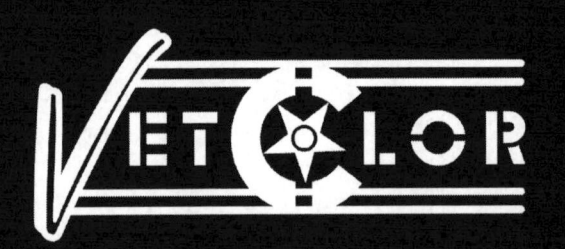

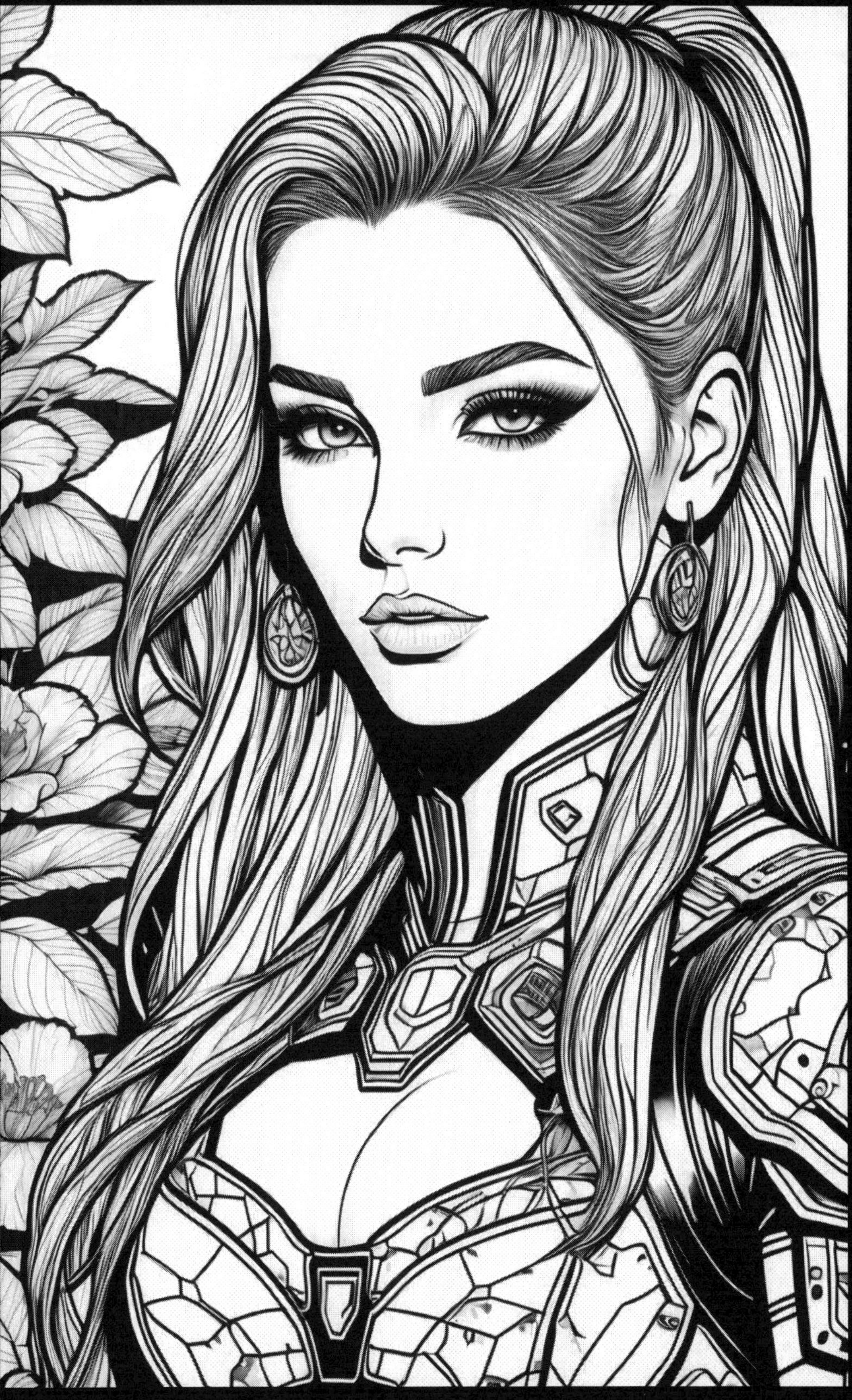

VETCOLOR

VETCOLOR.COM

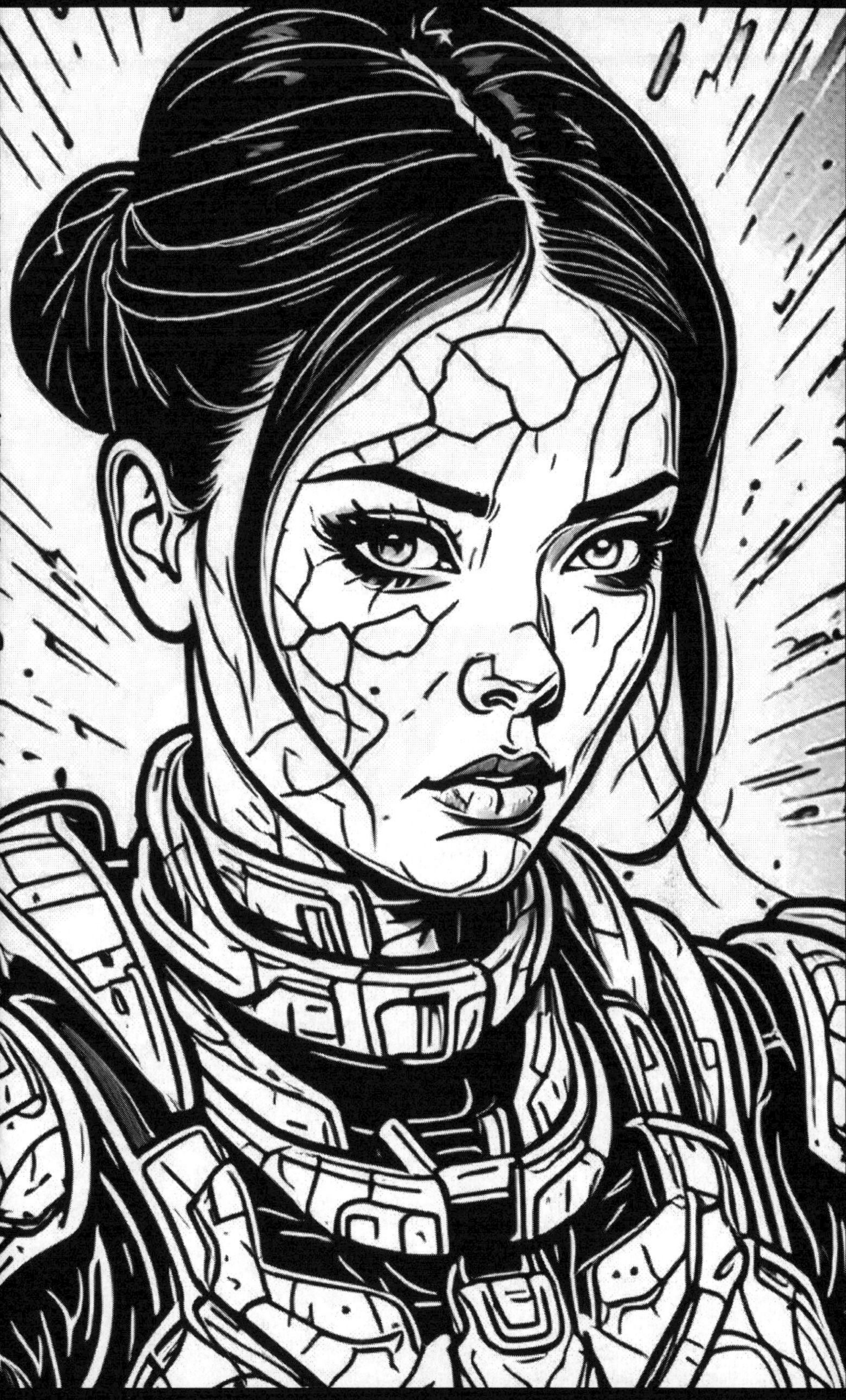

VETCOLOR.COM

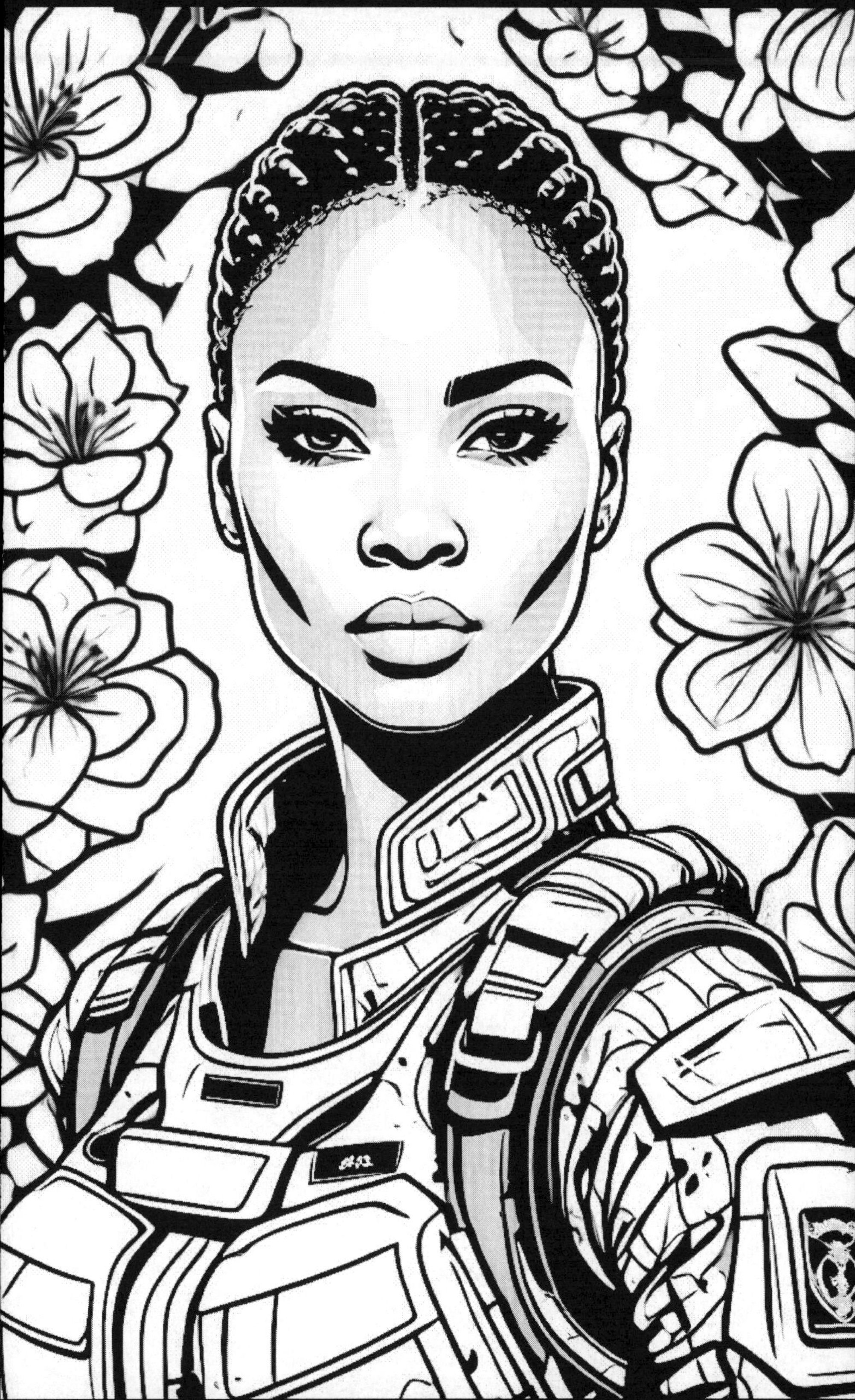

VETCOLOR.COM

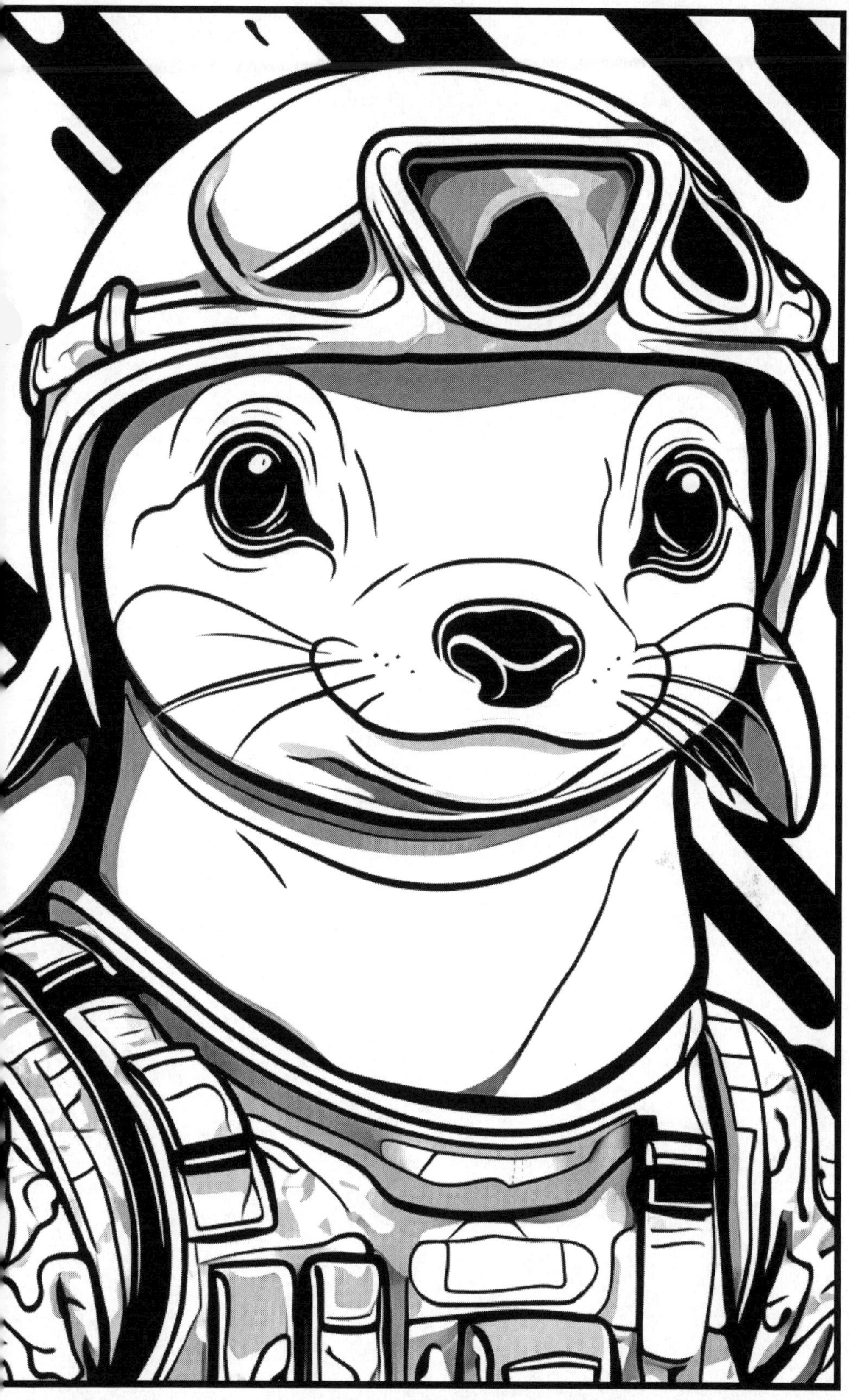

VETCOLOR

VETCOLOR.COM

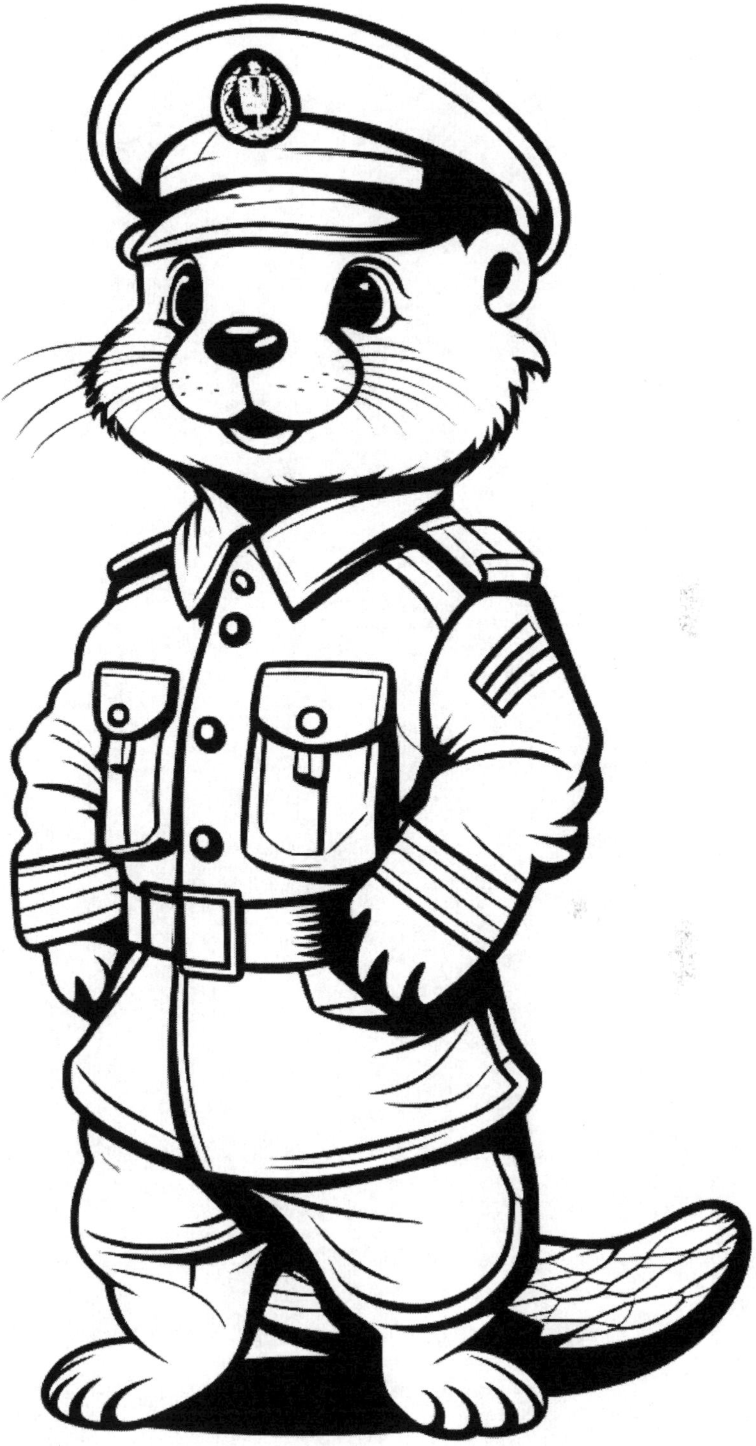

VETCOLOR.COM

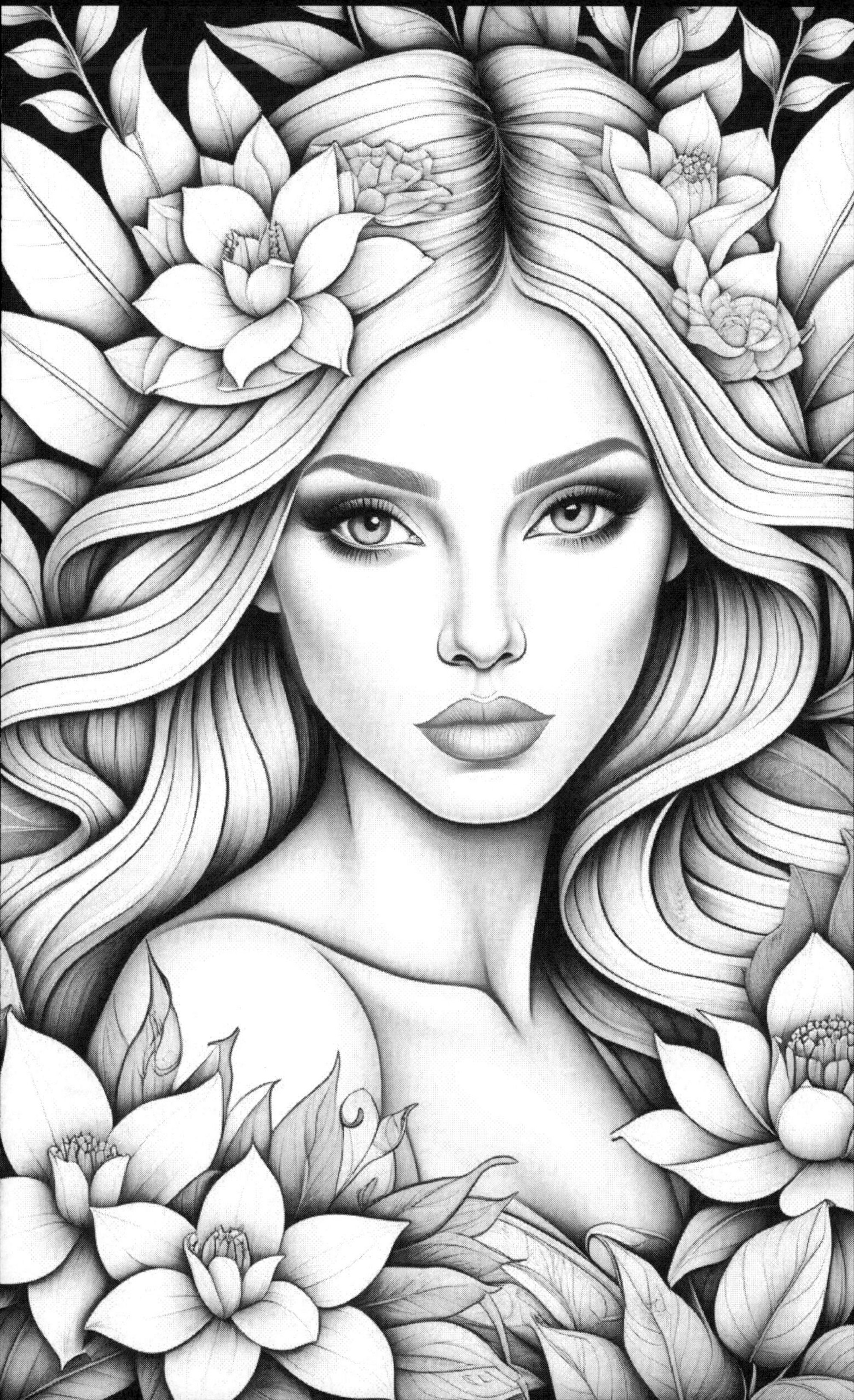

VETCOLOR.COM

13	Intership navigation (bridge-to-bridge); 156.650 MHz.
16	International VHF hailing/distress channel for marine communications; frequency is 156.8 MHz (FM).
688	Often used when referring to Los Angeles class fast-attack nuclear submarines, is the hull number for the lead ship in the class.
ANOTHER FINE NAVY DAY!	An expression voiced (in a very sarcastic cheery manner) on occasions when, in fact, it's not that much of a Fine Navy Day at all.
ARMPIT OF THE NAVY	Slang for NAS Lemoore, so named because of the smell and air quality of the San Joaquin Valley.
ASSHOLES AND ELBOWS	In days of old, a deck hand on his hands and knees holystoning a wooden deck. Now it just means to work hard without rest.
O'DARK THIRTY	One half hour after O'dark hundred. (used in the same context as O'dark hundred.)
1JV	Sound-powered circuit used between the bridge, lookouts, and main control.
1MC	One of many communication circuits aboard a ship, this is probably the most widely recognized. When used, it is heard on every external speaker but is not always heard by every crew member.

1ST LIEUTENANT	Division found in most aviation and afloat commands that is responsible for the material condition and cleanliness of the ship or the spaces occupied by the Airedales.
2JV	Engineering sound-powered circuit.
2MC	Engineering loudspeaker circuit.
3/4 MILE ISLAND	USS Enterprise (CVN-65)
3M	Maintenance and Material Management.
4 BALLS	Midnight or 0000Hrs (See 'All Balls' below)
4MC	Emergency circuit, goes straight to the control room of a submarine, or bridge of a ship.
50/50/90	Used to describe the phenomenon whereby a question that statistically has a 50/50 chance of being answered correctly is actually answered incorrectly 90% of the time.
5MC	Similar to the 1MC, except that it is only heard on the flight deck of an air-capable ship.
90-DAY WONDER	An Officers Candidate School graduate.
99 (PRON. NINER NINER)	When "99" is heard on the radio following a unit's call sign, it means that the transmission is for all of the aircraft in that unit.

A.J. SQUARED AWAY	A term used to describe a sailor who is always on point with hair cut and grooming.
ABAFT THE BEAM	On a ship, this refers to anything aft of the 090/270 degree relative beam of the ship, which is perpendicular to the bow/stern axis.
ABOVEDECKS	A direction: Navy for "up." If you ascend to a higher deck on a Navy ship (using a ladder), you go "above."
ABU DHABI (ADJ.)	Refers to any product labelled in Arabic aboard a ship, particularly soda cans. Also referred to as "Haji Pop".
ADMIN	Prearranged meeting point in-port for carrier pilots.
ADMIN WARFARE SPECIALIST	Joking, sometimes derisive term for Yeomen, Personnelmen or other Navy administrative ratings.
ADSEP	Administrative Separation - Involuntary separation from the armed services due to circumstances which are not deemed dishonorable.
A-FARTS	Slang for Armed Forces Radio & Television Service.
AFT	Towards the stern of the ship. Aft is always a direction, never a place.
A-GANG	The Auxiliary Division of the Engineering Department. Members known as "A-Gangers."

AHEAD FRANK CRAP ON PLATE	Refers to when a Submarine orders up All Ahead Flank Cavitate, without rigging for high speed.
AIR BOSS	Air Officer. His assistant is the "Mini Boss".
AIR FORCE COMMON	Sarcastic term for the Guard frequencies. These are supposed to be used only in the case of an emergency, however, sailors perceive the Air Force using the frequencies far too often for routine communications.
AIRDALE	A naval aviator. A sailor who works on or around aircraft.
AIRDALE TUCK	The act of folding and one's garrison cover (piss cutter) so as to have the rear end kick up vertically.
AIRSTART	Any attempt to restart an aircraft's engine(s) after in-flight failure.
AIRWING	All of the squadrons aboard an aircraft carrier make up the airwing.
ALL BALLS	Midnight or 0000Hrs.
ALL BALLS	Any instrument reading that is all zeros.
ALL BALLS	Refers to a crew or unit that is all male.
ALOFT	A location above the weather decks, such as the rigging or antenna farm. Usually heard in word passed every 15-minutes when personnel are working on radars aboard ship.
ALUMINUM CLOUD	Slang for the F-14 Tomcat.

ANCHORS AND SPURS	Famous dance club at NAVSTA San Diego where many-a lonely Navy wife has broken the seventh commandment. Many sailors find this amusing until it happens to them.
ANGLES AND DANGLES	Placing the boat in extreme angles (also known as 'up and down bubbles') soon after leaving port, to see whether anything breaks loose.
ANTI-SMACK OR ANTI-SMASH	Anti-collision strobe light on an aircraft. Also called simply "Smacks."
ANYMOUSE	Slang for anonymous. Safety system where sailors can drop an anonymous recommendation into a locked box.
AOL	Navyspeak for AWOL.
AOM	All Officers Meeting, held for a variety of reasons like training, port calls, mess issues, etc.
APE	Slang for an Auxiliary Power Unit, or APU.
APPLE JACK	Slang for 21 day wine made out of bug juice, sugar and yeast. Tastes like crap but packs a powerful wallop.
APPLEJACKED	Extremely intoxicated. Refers to a sailor who is so piss-drunk on liberty that his shipmates actually notice it.
ASSHOLE OF THE NAVY	Slang for Norfolk, Virginia, home of the fabled "DOGS AND SAILORS KEEP OFF THE GRASS!" sign.

ASSHOLE OF THE WORLD	Tijuana, Mexico. It is thus labeled because it is dirty, smells like shit, has high crime and drugs, corrupt police officials, and has few redeeming qualities.
ASWO	Anti-Submarine Warfare Officers
ATFQ	Answer The Fucking Question. This grading remark often appears on nuke-school exams.
ATHWARTSHIPS	A direction perpendicular to the bow-stern axis of the ship. That is, moving port-to-starboard or starboard-to-port.
AUTEC	Atlantic Undersea Test and Evaluation Center
AUTO	Short for autorotation.
AUTO DOG	Self-serve ice cream dispensed from a machine in wardrooms and mess decks throughout the navy. Resembles a pile of dog poop.
AWOL	Absent Without Official Leave
AYE	Yes (I understand).
AYE, AYE	Yes (I heard the order, I understand the order, and I intend to obey the order).
B.B.&G.	Buffarilla Bar and Grill (Club outside the Ingalls shipyard in Pascagoula, MS.).
B.O.C.O.D	Acronym for the date before returning home from a deployment to stop masturbating in order to save it up for your wife or girlfriend.
B.O.H.I.C.A.	Bend Over, Here It Comes Again.

B.O.S.N.I.A.	Big Ol' Standard Navy Issue Ass.
BABOON ASS	Nickname for corned beef, based on color and flavor.
BABY BIRDFARM	An Iwo Jima-class helicopter carrier.
BACK ALLEY	Card game of trump played by 2 to 4 players (mostly "snipes"). A player unable to make their bid goes set 3 X the bid. Game can be played by partners.
BAFFLE SAMPLE	(Submarines) A prank, similar to the Portable Air Sample snipe hunt, conducted on a NQP that, played correctly, can involve several departments including sonar, engineering, and weapons.
BAFFLES	The area directly aft of a submarine in which she cannot hear because of the screw's turbulence in the water and the lack of ship mounted hydrophones in that immediate area.
BAG	Slang light suit.
BAG ASS	Leave a place of duty (go on liberty)
BAG IT OUT	Fill an aircraft with its max fuel load.
BAG NASTY	A pre-packaged bag lunch usually consisting of a cold cut sandwich, piece of fruit, and juice box or can of soda. Served at galleys in lieu of regular chow for sailors on the go.
BALLS THIRTY	A term used to indicate the time of the 0030 security sweep on some bases.

BALLS TO FOUR	A four hour watch technically spanning from 00:00 to 04:00, though in practice begins at 2345 and ends at 0345. Most commonly seen on a "Dogged Watch" schedule.
BALLS TO THE WALL (SUBMARINE SERVICE)	Main propulsion plant dialed up to 11 for maximum speed.
BALLS TO THE WALLS	Extremely fast, hurry up.
BALLS TO TWO	A short watch stood from. Not generally seen outside of training commands.
BANDIT	Aircraft positively identified as hostile.
BARNEY CLARK	Slider topped with a fried egg. Also called a "One-Eyed Jack." Named after the first man to receive an artificial heart.
BARRICADE	Also called the barrier, this is a huge nylon net strung across the landing area of a carrier to arrest the landing of an aircraft with damaged gear or a damaged tailhook.
BASE BUNNY	Slutty woman who hangs around in front of the entrance to a base, hoping to pick up a Sailor.

BASKET LEAVE	Highly illegal free time off. When a sailor who takes leave has his leave chit destroyed after he's returned, thereby not charging the liberty against his leave balance without the command's knowledge.
BASTARD CHIEF	Slang for Master Chief.
BATTLE GROUP	A group of warships and supply ships centered around a large deck aircraft carrier and its airwing.
BATTLE RACKS	When mission-exhausted aviators are allowed to sleep through General Quarters drills.
BATTLE WAGON	Battleship (Note: While the Navy still owns the four remaining Iowa-class battleships, they are no longer in active duty - in fact most now serve as public museums).
BCG'S	Birth Control Glasses. Standard Navy-issue corrective eyewear.
BEACH POUNDER	A Marine (cf. Ground Pounder = soldier).
BEAM	The width of a naval vessel. Also refers to any contact close to 90 degrees off the fore/aft axis of the ship.
BEER DAY	On many Navy ships, even in the present day, all hands are given 2 beers if they are underway without a port call for a given period of time - generally 45 days.

BEER TICKETS	Foreign currency - so called because a sailor has no idea how much the bills and coins are worth. All he wants to know is how many are needed to buy drinks while in port.
BELLS	Naval way of announcing the time of day aboard ship, usually over the 1MC.
BELOW	The interior of a submarine.
BELOW	Navy for "down."
BELOW DECKS	The watch responsible for monitoring the forward spaces of a submarine while in port.
BENNY	A treat or reward, derived from "Benefit".
BENNY SUGGS	The Navy's Beneficial Suggestions program, a method where DON employees, and Navy and Marine personnel can make suggestions to improve various programs and operations.
BENT SHITCAN	Someone below Naval standards.
BERTHING	Living quarters for enlisted personnel. Aboard ship berthing is usually a relatively large space filled with three-deep racks, lockers, a couple of TV's, minimal furniture, and an attached head.

BIG CHICKEN DINNER	Slang for a Bad Conduct Discharge, which is usually handed out along with an administrative separation (ADSEP) after a sailor pops positive on a "Whiz Quiz."
BIG EYES	Large mounted binoculars normally found on or near the Signal Shack.
BILGE PARTY	The cleaning of the bilges in Machinery Rooms, generally performed by younger sailors while supervisors poke fun.
BILGE RAT	Someone who works in the engineering spaces.
BILGE TURD	Derogatory term for "Boiler Technician," typically from Machinist Mates who attend the identical A school.
BINGO	Minimum fuel needed to return to base (RTB).
BINNACLE LIST	The daily list of ship's crew who are sick in quarters. So called because in the old days of sailing, this list was posted on the binnacle, the casing that housed the ship's compass.
BIRD	Aircraft.
BIRDFARM	Aircraft carrier.
BITCHBOX	Intercom or amplified circuit used to communicate between spaces of a ship.
BITCHING BETTY	The computer generated female voice heard in an aviator's earpiece when something is not as it should be.

BLACK HOLE	An extremely dangerous situation encountered by naval aviators when landing aboard a ship on a very dark night.
BLACK SHOE	Any "Surface Navy" officer or CPO, from the dark footwear worn with khaki uniforms.
BLOW THE DCA	A task made up by more senior enlisted, which sends an inexperienced junior sailor looking for an imaginary DCA horn.
BLOWING A SHITTER	Accidentally flushing a toilet while San Tanks are being vented overboard, despite the posted warning signs. Also refers to losing one's composure, adapted from first definition.
BLUE AND GOLD	Alternating crews for the same ship - usually applied to submarines, but recently applied to forward deployed "small boys" in the "Sea Swap" program.
BLUE ON BLUE	Fratricide or friendly fire. Named for the color associated with friendly forces during "workups" and exercises.
BLUE SHIRT	An enlisted sailor below the rank of E-7 (Chief Petty Officer). More modern than the term Bluejacket.
BLUE TILE	An area of the carrier on the starboard main passageway, O-3 level, where the Battle Group (now called Carrier Strike Group) admiral and his staff live and work.

BLUE WATER	Deep water far from land. Only larger, self-sufficient ships can operate on these waters.
BLUEJACKET	An enlisted sailor below the rank of E-7 (Chief Petty Officer).
BLUENOSE	An individual who has crossed the Arctic Circle.
BOARD	To land a fixed-wing aircraft successfully aboard an aircraft carrier via the tailhook and arresting wires.
BOAT	Water craft small enough to be carried on a ship, unless a submarine, which is always called "a boat" or "the boat" when referring to the actual vessel.
BOAT CUTIE	Applied to female sailors who would not be attractive on the beach, but who become extremely attractive after being underway for a prolonged period of time.
BOAT GOAT	Usually refers to females aboard ship that are unattractive.
BOAT HO	Usually refers to females aboard ship that are assumed to be promiscuous.
BOATS	A sailor in the Boatswain's Mate rating. Nickname for a Boatswains Mate.
BOGEY	Unknown aircraft which could be friendly, hostile, or neutral.

BOLTER	Failed attempt at an arrested landing on a carrier by a fixed-wing aircraft. Usually caused by a poor approach or a hook bounce on the deck.
BONE ME HARD RICHARD	Another nickname for the USS "Bonhomme Richard" (LHD-6).
BONNIE DICK	Nickname for USS Bonhomme Richard (LHD-6)
BOOMER	Missile Submarine.
BOOMER FAG	Any Naval personnel that serves aboard a Boomer.
BOONDOCKERS	Navy issue work boots. They are made out of black leather with black rubber sole, come up to your ankle and have steel toes.
BOONDOGGLE	Any unorganized, inefficient evolution, usually grand in scale and involving many confused participants.
BOOPDIDDLEY	All-inclusive word usually pertaining to something ridiculous.
BOOTCAMP	A term used, usually derisively, when referring to any sailor who has very little time in or a lot less time than the speaker.
BOOTER	A Sailor that has just reported to his first duty assignment after completing Recruit Training.

BOSUN'S PUNCH	New sailors on ship are sometimes assigned to find this mythical tool in the office of one of the ship's Bosuns. The sailor is then typically punched very hard in the shoulder by the Bosun in question.
BOUNCE PATTERN	When several aircraft are practicing touch and go landings at the same airfield or ship.
BOW	The front of the ship. When used by lookouts, it may be preceded by port or starboard when a contact is slightly to the left or right of the bow.
BRAIN FART	A condition when, under stress, one cannot recall or perform something that would normally be easy or second nature.
BRANCH	Lowest organizational level in most naval commands. Below department and division.
BRAVO FOXTROT	Buddy Fucker - someone who will make himself look good at the expense of his shipmates.
BRAVO ZULU	Originally "BZ" was a signal meaning "Well Done." It is sometimes co-opted by seniors praising subordinates in one form or another.
BREAKAWAY MUSIC	Music played over the 1MC at the conclusion of an underway replenishment evolution, used to motivate the crew, but regularly fails.

BREMERLOS	Large civilian women who prey on the sexual needs of unwary junior enlisted personnel.
BRIG	Jail.
BRIGCHASER	A sailor escorting a prisoner to the brig.
BRIGHTWORKS	Any decorative metal that must be constantly shined with Brasso or Nevr-Dull to avoid tarnishing. This undesirable duty is often performed by the most junior personnel in the command.
BROKE-DICK	Technical term describing malfunctioning or inoperable equipment.
BROWN BAGGER	Married sailor who brings his lunch from home in a paper bag (because he is receiving a Commuted Rations or COMRATS cash allowance for his meals).
BROWN NOSE	Sailor trying a "little too hard" to make rate by sucking up to superiors.
BROWN SHOE	An officer or CPO in the Naval Aviation community.
BROWN TROUT	Part of what comes out when there's a sewage spill. As the ship heaves to and fro, brown trout can actually "swim" on the deck.
BROWN WATER	Shallow water close to land. Also called the littorals. Smaller ships can operate in these waters.
BT PUNCH	Same as a Bosun's Punch, but delivered by a Boiler Technician.

BUBBA	Affectionate term for someone who does what you do. In aviation, someone who flies the same type of aircraft as you.
BUBBLE	The trim orientation of a submarine (e.g., 5 degree up bubble).
BUBBLEHEAD	A sailor in the Submarine Service.
BUDWEISER	A SEAL Special Warfare insignia. Consists of a pistol, trident, and eagle.
BUF	Acronym refers to the lower part of a female overlapping stomach stuffed into a pair of utility/dungaree pants.
BUFFARILLA	Mixture of Buffalo and Gorilla. Result of many years of female inbreeding practiced by multiple heavyset inhabitants of the Southern United States.
BUG	Seabee Combat Warfare insignia. Consists of a 1903 Springfield rifle, officer's sword, Banana leaves, anchor, and the Seabee "???" in the middle.
BUG JUICE	Kool-Aid-like beverage in dispensers on the messdeck.
BUG JUICE SUNRISE	Orange with a splash of Red.
BUILDING 20	Slang for the USS Mount Whitney (LCC-20), which rarely leaves port.
BUILDING 39	1990s-era Naval Station Norfolk slang for the USS Emory S. Land (AS-39), which during that time period, rarely left port.

BULKHEAD	Wall.
BULL	The senior-most Ensign onboard a surface ship. In charge of various wardroom duties.
BULL NUKE	The most senior nuke onboard a nuclear-powered vessel.
BULLET SPONGE	U.S. Marine.
BUNNY TUBE	Pneumatic tube system used for sending documents such as hard copies of radio messages to and from the radio room to other areas of the ship.
BUNO	Short for Bureau Number - this is a 6-digit serial number assigned to every naval aircraft when it is accepted into service. In no way related to an aircraft's 3-digit "side number."
BURN A COPY	Make a Xerox copy of a document or sheet of paper. (Probably goes back to Thermofax copiers.)
BURN A FLICK	Watch a Movie.
BURN BAG	Trash bag for outdated or no longer needed classified materials.
BURN ONE	Taking a smoke break. To smoke a cigarette.
BUS DRIVER UNIFORM	The unpopular uniform, based on an officer's dress blues, which was briefly issued to recruits in the 1970s.

BUST ME ON THE SURFACE	An expression voiced when a subordinate strongly disagrees with a superior's order and the subordinate takes actions he knows to be the correct procedure, counter to the order.
BUSTER	Proceed at max possible speed.
BUTT KIT	Ash tray. Aboard ship it is a can with a hole in the lid, usually hung from the bulkhead near watch stations.
BUTTER BARS	Refers to the gold-colored bars designating the rank of Ensign (the lowest rank for commissioned officers).
BUTTON CRUSHER	Imaginary machine used by a ship's laundry to pulverize buttons.
CAG	Title used when addressing the airwing commander.
CAKE DRYER	Imaginary appliance in a ship's galley used to dry (like toast) otherwise good pieces of cake.
CAMEL	The wooden floating structures, at the waterline, that separate ships tied up in a nest.
CANDY-O	Candidate Officer, a trainee of Navy Officer Candidate School upon reaching the final two weeks of training.
CANEX	Cancelled Exercise. Used to refer to any event which has been cancelled, not just formal exercises.

CANN	Short for cannibalize, which is the practice of using one or more of a unit's aircraft strictly for parts to keep the rest of the aircraft flying.
CANNON BALLS	Baked, candied apples served to midshipmen at the Naval Academy on special occasions.
CANOE CLUB	The United States Navy.
CANOE U	United States Naval Academy.
CAPTAIN'S MAST	Navy term for Nonjudicial punishment under Article 15 of the Uniform Code of Military Justice.
CARRIER STRIKE GROUP	Another name for a Battle Group.
CARRY ON	An officers reply to a junior person's call to "attention on deck".
CASREP	Inoperative, casualty reported; casually, OOC (out of commission). Often jocularly applied to broken minor items not requiring any report, or to personnel on the binnacle list.
CAVU	Ceiling and Visibility Unlimited - perfect flying weather. Pronounced as "Ka-Voo".
CB	Construction Battalion (pronounced Seabees).
CBC	Clean Bitches Clean. A term used to order junior sailors to clean so they can to secure for the day, or to commence field day.

CELLBLOCK 10	Crew-coined term for the USS Juneau. Term could come from the feeling that the Juneau has the homely warmth of a prison cellblock. 10 is the vessel's hull number.
CF	Acronym meaning completely screwed up.
CFIT	(pron. see-fit): Controlled Flight into Terrain - When a pilot flies a perfectly good airplane into the ground or the water. Often fatal if unanticipated.
C-GU11	Seagull. Pronounced "See-Gee-Yuu-Eleven." Similar to "bulkhead remover," an inexpensive way to derive enjoyment from inexperienced personnel on watch.
CHANNEL FEVER	Said if a sailor is anxious when approaching port to get leave.
CHARLES COUNTY CRAB	The term refers to the "crab" insignia worn by graduates of Naval School Explosive Ordnance Disposal, who attended when it was based at Naval Ordnance Station, Indian Head, Charles County Maryland.
CHARLIE FOXTROT	see "clusterfuck".
CHARLIE NOBLE	The stove pipe from the mess deck, the cleaning of which is a major chore.
CHARLIE OSCAR	Phonetic letters C and O. Refers to the Commanding Officer of a unit.
CHART	What landlubbers call a "map".

CHARTING	A practice peculiar to Operations Specialists in which they take any personal gear left unstowed by the previous watch section and fling them overboard, marking the location on the chart.
CHENG	Chief Engineer.
CHICKEN SUIT	Is a yellow cloth suit that is worn from head-to-toe by navy "Nukes".
CHIT	Name given to the document a sailor fills out to make various types of special request.
THE CHOP	Supply Officer. Taken from the Supply Corps' porkchop-shaped insignia.
CHOW	Food.
CHROME DOME	Bright silver helmet worn by officer candidates as part of the "poopie suit" during the first week of OCS.
CHUB CLUB	Sailors assigned mandatory physical training due to being overweight.
CHULA-JUANA	Derisive term for the city of Chula Vista, CA.
CIC	Combat Information Center - see "Combat" below.
CINDERELLA LIBERTY	Liberty that expires at midnight.
CIVLANT	Form DD-214 transfers you from COMSUBLANT to CIVLANT.

CIWS	Close in Weapon System, or Phalanx gun, is intended to shoot down incoming missiles, but is frequently under repair.
CLEANING STATIONS	Hour-long field day evolution where everyone drops what they're doing and cleans their spaces.
CLINOMETER	An instrument for measuring angles of slope (or tilt), elevation or inclination of an object with respect to gravity.
CLOBBERED	When the landing pattern or the comms frequency at a field or ship is filled to capacity and you can't get an aircraft or a word in.
CLUSTERFUCK	Term used to describe an evolution that has gone awry.
COASTIE	A Coast Guardsman.
COB	(Submarine Service) Chief of the Boat; a chief (generally a Master or Senior Chief) specifically assigned to the submarine to liaise between the CO and the crew of the boat.
COD	Carrier Onboard Delivery - the mighty C-2 Greyhound, which ferries people and supplies to and from the carrier on a regular basis.
COFFIN LOCKER	A personal storage area located underneath a sailor's rack.

COLD SHOT	A catapult launch from a carrier in which insufficient speed is attained to generate lift. Often fatal for the aircrew if they do not eject in time.
COMBAT	Short for Combat Information Center.
COMBAT DUMP	Evacuating the bowels right before a flight or a mission.
COMBO COVER	A short form for a type of hat worn by chiefs and officers. It is circular on top and covered with white or khaki fabric.
COMMODORE	Title of the Captain (O-6) in charge of a squadron of ships or submarines or a wing of the same type of aircraft.
COMP TIME	Compensation Time, time/days off during the week for shore-based sailors who had weekend assignments, above and beyond mere watch-standing.
COMSHAW	Other than ethical means of procurement.
CONER	A submarine crewman who is not part of the engineering department.
CORPSMAN CANDY	Sore-throat lozenges handed out at sick bay in lieu of any substantive treatment. Sometimes accompanied by two aspirin.
COUNTERSUNK SAILOR	Female sailor.
COVER	Hat

CRAB	Affectionate slang term for the warfare insignia/badge worn by special operations personnel qualified in Explosive Ordnance Disposal (BOMB SQUAD).
CRACK HOUSE	Designated smoking area aboard ship that is not a weatherdeck space. Quickly fills with a haze of smoke. Also called "Crack shack".
CRACKER JACKS	Slang for the dress blue uniforms worn by sailors E-6 and below. (see Marine Corps Table Cloth).
CRANK	See "Mess Crank".
CRASH & SMASH	Permanently assigned flight deck firefighting personnel.
CRAZY IVAN	(Submarine Service), demonstrated in the movie The Hunt for Red October. Russian submarines would quickly turn 180 degrees while underway to see whether any American submarines were following.
CREAMED FORESKINS	Creamed chipped beef.
CRIPLER	Tripler Army Medical Center, Oahu, scourge of sailors at Pearl Harbor.
CROTCH CRICKETS	Pubic lice, a/k/a Crabs.
CROW	Black eagle for petty officer rank used on a white uniform.

CROW FEVER	A term when a sailor reaches E-4 and lets the limited authority of the rank go to his head, causing him to go mad with petty power.
CRUISE	A 6-month (or longer) deployment on a ship. Work-ups precede cruise.
CRUISE SOCK	A sock that is sacrificed early in a deployment and used to clean up after masturbating. It is usually kept under the mattress and can stand up on its own by the end of cruise.
CRUNCH	Aircraft handling mishap that results in structural damage to one or more aircraft.
CRUNCHIES	Marines or soldiers. Derived from the sound they make when tanks roll over them.
CRUSTY	A term applied to an old, seasoned sailor when he is beyond salty.
CRYPPY/CRYPPY CRITTER	Cryptographer, also seen on a highway near the Cryptography School in San Angelo, Texas without vowels, as CRYPPY CRTTR.
CUM DUMPSTER	A derogatory term for a woman, used by sailors who are looking for a quick sexual release after an extended period of celibacy.
CUNT	Civilian Under Naval Training.
CUNT COVER	See "Piss Cutter".

CUT ORDERS	Before photocopiers were common, such were prepared by typing a mimeo or ditto master, due to the number of copies required.
CVIC	Acronym for a centrally located space on an aircraft carrier occupied by intelligence officers and IS's.
D.B.F.	(Diesel Boats Forever) unauthorized pin showing a non-nuclear submarine.
D.C. DINK	A sailor who has failed to qualify in Damage Control in the stipulated time period and has become "Damage Control Delinquent".
D.I.L.L.I.G.A.F	(Do I Look Like I Give A Fuck?), A term indicating supreme indifference; "Gaffer".
DANGER NUT	A "fun" game in which one or more sailors place a washer or nut around a rod or similar metal device and then hold it to a HP Air hose, 125-700 psi.
DCA	Damage Control Assistant, usually is a junior officer.
DDA	Acronym in naval aviation for a very enjoyable flight during the day when there is no real mission or training to accomplish.
DEATH PILLOWS	Ravioli
DEATH PUCKS	Hamburger Patty
DECK	Floor.

DECK APE	Non-designated enlisted person serving on the deck force, often as result of washing out of "A" school or being stripped of another rating.
DEEP SIX	Obsolete term for throwing something overboard.
DEPARTMENT	Highest organizational level in most naval commands. Common departments are admin, deck, engineering, operations, and maintenance. Broken up into divisions.
DEPLOYMENT	When your unit travels "over the horizon" and operates at the "pointy end of the spear" in support of national security.
DET	Short for detachment. When part of a unit leaves and operates at another ship or base. Also used in reference to some "workups" that involve the entire unit. Ex. NAS Fallon det.
DEVIL DOC	Term used by Marines to describe Corpsman that they like within Fleet Marine Force Units.
DFOB	(pronounced "dee fob") Dumbest Fuck On Board.
DICK SKINNERS	hands i.e. "get your dick skinners off my white hat"
DICKING THE DOG	putting "half-assed" effort into a task (refers to improperly securing the "dogs" on a watertight hatch when passing through)

DICKSMITH	Yet another derogatory term for hospital corpsmen.
DIG-IT	A device such as a Leatherman or Gerber multi-tool often carried by those who love the Navy.
DILBERT	Fictional and clueless cartoon character used in WWII era training material to demonstrate what NOT to do in naval aviation.
DILBERT DUNKER	Device used in water survival training ("swims") to teach aviators how to get out of the cockpit of a fixed-wing aircraft that has crashed or ditched at sea. Much easier than the dreaded "helo dunker."
DILDO	Nickname for a civilian teacher hired to train nuclear-field candidates in theoretical math, physics, chemistry, materials, and thermodynamics.
DING	Similar to "hit" (see below). Also, to cause minor damage to something (Ex. He dinged his aileron when he had a birdstrike on final to the boat.)
DINING-IN/DINING-OUT	Social functions, usually for officers and chiefs, where dinner dress is worn and certain "rules of the mess" are followed.
DINK	Acronym for married servicemembers with no children - Dual Income No Kids.
DINQ	Acronym for Delinquent In Qualifications. Ex: "That shitbird is dinq on ship's quals!" Also Delinquent In Nuclear Quals

DIPPER	An anti-submarine helo with a variable depth dipping SONAR. See "Dome."
DIRKA	Any term referring to the language, money, or products of the Middle East.
DIRT SAILOR	Nickname for Seabees who spend most of their time in a fox hole and never set foot on a ship.
DIRTBAG	A lazy and almost useless sailor. Produces substandard work-usually creating extra work for his shipmates. Accompanied by a bad attitude and desire to leave service ASAP.
DIRTY-DICKING	Wiping one's genital organ around the inside of a senior enlisted or officer's coffee cup. Laughter ensues when the junior crewmen watch the senior victim "enjoying" their beverage.
DIRTY-SHIRT WARDROOM	(Aircraft Carrier): Forward wardroom for pilots wearing (sweaty) flight gear. As opposed to formal ship's wardroom.
DISBO	Short for Disbursing Officer.
DISCO	Short for Disciplinary Officer. Usually works with Ship's JAG Officer
DIT DOT BOMB	A form of hazing by taking the round paper cutouts left from a hole punch and putting them in a box or other container rigged to open and rain down on another.
DITCH	To intentionally crash land an aircraft as "gently" as possible - usually into the water.

DITE	Acronym for "male appendage in the ocular". Usually reserved for undesirable tasks forced on one by superiors.
DITTY BAG	The term originates from seafarers and refers to a bag containing personal items such as a sewing kit, toiletry articles, and writing paper and pens.
DIVERS	Word passed every 15 minutes when divers are working over the side of a ship. It alerts personnel not to perform certain actions while divers are working.
DIVISION	Middle organizational level in most naval commands, below department and above branch.
DIXIE CUP	The canvas white hat Sailors wear with their dress uniforms.
DOCK JUMPERS	The unfortunates who would have to leap ashore to tie up when no "line handlers" are available.
DOG	A Soft Serve Ice Cream machine.
DOG VOMIT	A breakfast item made of tomato juice and hamburger, served on toast.
DOLPHINS	Submarine Qualification Device, called dolphins because of the dolphin fish used in the design.
DOME	A SONAR transmitter/receiver, either fixed or mobile.
DONKEY-DICK	Term used for various nozzle-shaped implements.

DOPEY	Green log book hidden in an engineering space where sailors vent frustration through prose, poetry, drawings, or cartoons.
DOUBLE NUTS	Name given to the CAG bird in each squadron in the airwing, with a side number ending with double zeros.
DOUBLE UGLY	Nickname for the F-4 Phantom aircraft.
DOUBLE-DIGIT MIDGET	Less than 100 days to EAOS (End of Active Obligated Service).
DOUCHE KIT	Container for toiletry articles such as shaving cream, deodorant, after-shave lotion, etc.
DOWN	Not working, out of commission, broken, or non-flyable.
DRB	Disciplinary Review Board, composed of Chief Petty Officers, where sailors who have committed infractions have their cases heard.
DRIFT COUNT	Monitoring the movement of the ship while at anchor.
DRIFTY	Sailor lacking the ability to stay focused while performing a given task.
DROP A CHIT	The act of filling out a chit.
DROP YOUR COCKS AND GRAB YOUR SOCKS	A saying yelled by the petty officer of the watch to wake everyone up.
DUCK DINNER	Slang for Dishonorable Discharge.
DYNAMITED CHICKEN	Slang for Chicken a la King or Chicken Cacciatore.

EAOS	End of Active Obligated Service, the normal end of enlistment.
EARTH SACK	Slang for a pile of feces.
EAWS	Enlisted Air Warfare Specialist.
ED'S MOTEL	Navy Filmmakers' acronym for Editorials, Motion Picture, and Television Department.
EMERGENCY BLOW	A rapid blowing of seawater out of a submarine's main ballast tanks to surface rapidly.
EMI	Extra Military Instruction, assigned as punishment for minor infractions.
END-OF-THE-WORLD PARTY	A party for a sailor about to leave on a cruise.
E-NOTHIN	Used to describe a junior Seaman, often someone right out of bootcamp or A school.
ENSIGN UPPER HALF	Alternative designation for those who fail to live up to the standards of O-2.
ENSWINE	Derogatory term for an ensign.
EOOW	Engineering Officer of the Watch.
ESFOAD	Acronym for "Eat Shit, Fuck Off, And Die."
ESWS	Enlisted Surface Warfare Specialist.
E-TICKET	When an officer has sex with an enlisted sailor.

EVEN NUMBERED CHIEF	Pejorative for an E-8 who is unable to advance to E-9 and refuses to let E-7's be promoted.
EVOLUTION	Navy preferred term for exercise.
EXPIRE BEFORE YOUR ID CARD	To die before being discharged.
F.A.W.C.U.	Focused After Watch Clean Up, post-watch cleaning period.
F.I.G.M.O.	"Fuck It, Got My Orders," refusal of a long or tough assignment.
F.U.B.A.	Navy female with an unusually broad ass.
F.U.B.A.R.	Situation that's severely messed up.
F.U.B.I.J.A.R.	Derogatory term for a reservist.
F.U.B.Y.O.Y.O.	Dismissive phrase indicating one's independence.
F.U.P.A.	Pejorative term for an overweight female sailor.
FAG	Fighter Attack Guy, also used derogatorily for Naval Academy graduates or submarine personnel.
FART SACK	Canvas mattress cover.
FART SUIT	Dry suit worn by aviators over cold water.
FATHER	Navigational aid on an Aircraft Carrier.
FATHER'S DAY	Confusing day in any Wardroom.
FEP	Fitness Enhancement Program, mandatory physical training regimen.

FIELD DAY	All hands clean-up.
FIELD SURVEY	To discard a worn-out item.
FIGHTING GEAR	Eating utensils.
FILIPINO MAFIA	Group of sailors of Filipino descent.
FILTHY FIFTEEN	Recruits assigned to maintain cleanliness.
FISH	Submarine qualification device or torpedo.
FIVE AND DIMES	Watch rotation with five hours on watch and ten hours off.
FLAG DECK	Command level on large ships for Admirals.
FLAIL	Major response to a minor problem.
FLAILEX	Pointless, flailing Exercise.
FLATHATTING	Flying in a dangerous manner.
FLATTOP	Aircraft carrier.
FLEET MEAT	Term for sexually active female sailors.
FLEET TAC	Fleet Tactical radio frequency.
FLEET UP	When a second in command takes over.
FLIGHT DECK BUZZARD	Chicken (food) on the Flight Deck.
FLIGHT LINE	Area where aircraft are readied for flight.
FLIP ME FOR IT	Pulling rank.
FLOAT CHECK	Throwing something overboard.
FLOAT COAT	Jacket with automatic flotation for flight deck personnel.

FLOAT SHE MAY, SHINE SHE MUST	Phrase expressing discontent with cleanliness tasks.
FLOAT TEST	Game of tossing non-floating items overboard.
FLOATING BELLHOP	Derisive term for a sailor.
FLYING BRAVO	Menstruating.
FNG	Fuckin' New Guy.
FOAD	Profane dismissal.
FOBBIT	Person unwilling to leave a Forward Operating Base.
FOBNOB	Abbreviation for "Friend of Only Black Nuke On Board," referring to a shipmate who is a friend of the only African American nuclear technician onboard a submarine.
FO'C'S'LE FOLLIES	Gathering of aviators on a carrier's forecastle.
FOD	Foreign Object Damage.
FOD WALK DOWN	Organized search for debris on a flight deck or runway.
FOOT SOLDIER	Navy female who trades favors for transportation.
FORM	Formation.
FORWARD	Direction toward the bow of the ship.
FOUR (4) BY EIGHT (8) WATCH	Watch section with challenging hours.
FOXTROT UNIFORM	Polite phonetic pronunciation of "Fuck You."

FRED	Profane term (Acronym) for an electronic device.
FRED (F*CKIN' RETARDED ENLISTED DUDE)	Profane term for an enlisted sailor.
FREEBOARD	Vertical distance between waterline and gunwale.
FREQ	Short for frequency.
FROCK	Procedure allowing a sailor to wear higher rank insignia temporarily.
FRS	Fleet Replacement Squadron.
FTN	Profane dismissal of the Navy.
FUFU JUICE	Perfume or cologne.
FUN BOSS	Morale, Welfare and Recreation Officer.
FUN METER	Imaginary gauge indicating one's level of enjoyment in a situation.
G.U.A.M.	Acronym referring to the remote island of Guam.
GEORGE	Junior officer requiring guidance.
GERBIL	Culinary dish resembling a small rodent.
GERBIL ALLEY	Nickname for Jebel Ali, UAE.
GERBIL GYM	Exercise area on a ship.
GET YOUR KHAKIS	Phrase indicating fraternization between enlisted personnel and officers.
GETTING SLANT-EYED	Euphemism for masturbating.
GHETTO	Open-bay barracks.

GHOST TURD	Sailor's term for a dust bunny.
GIG LINE	Visual alignment of uniform components.
GITMO	Guantanamo Bay Naval Station.
GLASSES	Binoculars.
GOAT HERDER	Person who pursues romantic interests onboard.
GOAT LOCKER	Lounge for Chiefs.
GOATROPE	Term for a chaotic situation.
GOES AWAY	Term used in combat aviation when an enemy aircraft is hit.
GOGGLES	Night Vision Goggles.
GOLDEN DRAGON	Sailor who has crossed the Prime Meridian or International Date Line.
GOLDEN RIVET	Mythical concept of a commemorative rivet.
GOLDEN SHELLBACK	Sailor who has crossed the equator at the 180th Meridian twice.
GOOD HUMOR MAN	Summer White uniform.
GOONED UP	To poorly execute a routine task.
GOUGE	Inside information or advice.
GRAPE	Easy or simple.
GREAT MISTAKES	Epithet for RTC/NTC Great Lakes, Illinois.
GREEN SCRUBBY	Mildly abrasive scouring pad.
GREEN TABLE TEA PARTY	Captain's Mast or Non-Judicial Punishment.

GRINDER	Area for corrective exercises in boot camp.
GRIPE	Maintenance Action Form.
GROG	Alcoholic brew served at social events.
GRONK	Term for overtightening a bolt or nut.
GROUND-POUNDER	Term for the Army or Marines, derogatory.
GUARD	Emergency radio frequencies.
GULFPORT SLAM HOUND	Derogatory term for local women in Gulfport, MS.
GUMBY SUIT	Brightly colored survival suit resembling the claymation character Gumby.
GUN BOSS	Head of the Weapons Department.
GUNDECK	To falsify records or reports.
GUNS	Sailor in the Gunner's Mate rating.
GUNWALE	Top edge of the hull on a ship's sides.
GUSSY	USS Augusta.
GYRENE	Derogatory term for a U.S. Marine.
HAC	Helicopter Aircraft Commander.
HACK	Unofficial punishment confining an officer.
HAJI	Anything Middle Eastern.
HALFWAY-NIGHT	Party night halfway through a submarine's patrol.
HAMSTER	Chicken cordon bleu shaped like a hamster.

HANGAR QUEEN	Aircraft chronically out of service.
HAOLE	Derogatory term for non-natives in Hawaii.
HAPPY SOCK	Soft sock brought for personal use.
HATCH	Vertical access between decks on a ship.
HAZE GRAY AND UNDERWAY	Surface ships engaged in arduous duty at sea.
HAZREP	Safety report after an unsafe incident.
HEAD	Bathroom on a ship.
HEAT SHIELD	Someone who is always in trouble, deflecting attention from others.
HEISMAN	Position assumed by young women when approached by sailors on liberty.
HELM	Steering wheel of a ship.
HELMET FIRE	When a pilot loses situational awareness due to task saturation.
HELO	Term applied to all naval helicopters.
HELO DUNKER	Training device simulating a helicopter crash at sea.
HERE TODAY, GUAM TOMORROW	Receiving orders to move from one island to another.
HINGE	Slang for an O-4, Lieutenant Commander.
HIT	Discrepancy or failing mark during an inspection.

HIT THE BEACH	Liberty.
HMFIC	Head Mother Fucker In Charge.
HOCKEY PUCKS	Swedish meatballs.
HOLLYWOOD SHOWER	Civilian-style shower aboard a ship.
HOLY CROTCH	Area in Dunoon, Scotland, which was a United States Navy base.
HOLY HELO	Helicopter used for transporting chaplains to other ships for services on Sundays.
HOLY STONE	Pumice stone used for cleaning a wooden deck.
HONCH HO	Term for female frequenters of the Honch.
HONCH RAT	Sailor who frequents the Honcho bar district.
HOOK	Short for "tailhook".
HOOKER	Sailor who lands aboard an Aircraft Carrier.
HOOLIGAN NAVY	WWII Navy pejorative for the Coast Guard.
HOOVER	Slang for the S-3B Viking aircraft.
HOP'N'POP	Physical exercise inflicted on officer candidates at OCS.
HORSE COCK	Large log of baloney or Polish Sausage served for meals.
HORSE SHOE	Area aft of maneuvering on submarines often used for telling sea stories.

HOT BUNKING	Sharing racks on submarines; climbing into a warm rack to sleep.
HOWEVER	Over-the-top method of expressing additional items.
HR PUFF AND STUFF	Nickname given to sailors appearing for duty in a disheveled manner.
HSC	Rate mostly comprised of junior sailors, often firemen.
HUMMER	Slang for the E-2C Hawkeye aircraft.
IA	Individual Augmentation/Augmentee: Program deploying sailors to the Middle East for 6-14 months.
IDIOT	Phonetic acronym for "Eye-Dee-Ten-Tango," used to mock inexperienced personnel.
IFBM	Instant Fucking Boatswains Mate: "A" school washout assigned to deck force.
IHTFP	Acronym for "I Hate This Fucking Place," commonly uttered by midshipmen at the Naval Academy.
IN-CHOP	To enter an area of responsibility.
INT WTF	Phonetic spelling for "Interrogative What The Fuck," used in text/teletype communication.
IRISH PENNANT	Loose thread on a uniform, originally a Royal Navy term.
ISLAND	Superstructure of an aircraft carrier.

IYAOYAS	Unofficial acronym found on the uniforms of Aviation Ordnance personnel.
IYARGOL	Term coined by nuclear personnel in response to Ordnance's navy pride.
JACK OFF CURTAIN	Small privacy curtain hanging on the outside of a rack.
JACK-O'-THE-DUST	Ship cook in charge of keeping track of the ship's food stores.
JAG	Judge Advocate General's Corps - Navy lawyers.
JARHEAD	Slang for a U.S. Marine.
JARTGO	Acronym for "Just Another Reason To Get Out."
JERKIN' THE GHERKIN	Slang for masturbating.
JG	Abbreviation for Lieutenant Junior Grade.
JO	Abbreviation for Junior Officer.
JO JUNGLE	Stateroom where lower-ranking JOs are billeted, known for lack of comfort and privacy.
JODY	Fictitious person who steals your spouse while you're deployed.
JOE NAVY	Term for a lifer with no life outside the Navy.
JOHN SORE PENNIS	Nickname for the aircraft carrier USS John C. Stennis.

JOHNNY CASH'S	Winter Working Blue uniform, named for Johnny Cash's preference for black attire.
JOPA	Acronym for group formed to provide guidance and support for young officers.
JORG	Junior Officer Requiring Guidance.
JORM	Junior Officer Retention Meeting, a forum for complaints about superiors.
JP5	Jet fuel used on all navy ships and air stations.
JROTC	Junior Reserve Officer Training Corps.
JSI	Junior Staff Instructor.
KHAKI SACKER	Slang for a person who brings their lunch in a brown bag.
KIDDIE CRUISE	A short cruise for reservists.
KING NEPTUNE	Senior "shellback" who presides over Crossing the Line ceremonies.
KISS THE CAMEL	To fall between ship and pier onto a floating log, which is often fatal.
KLOOSH	Anything unwanted or trash that makes a sound when dropped into the water.
KNEE-DEEP NAVY	Epithet for the Coast Guard, also referring to sailors of the Coast Guard.
KNEE-KNOCKERS	Passageway opening through a bulkhead at shin height.
KNIFE & FORK SCHOOL	Officer Initiation School in Newport, RI, for professionals entering the Navy.

KNIVES CLUB	Slang for the wives' club, known for infighting.
KNUCKLE BOX	Metal box used in the Navy for transporting supplies, often difficult to carry.
KNUCKLE BUSTER	Pneumatic tool used for removing paint from steel.
L.T.D.B	Often used sarcastically in reference to Naval lifestyle.
LADDERWELL	Stairs aboard a ship.
LAUNDRY QUEEN	Junior Non-Qualified submariner tasked with doing officers' laundry.
LAWN DART	Slang for F/A-18 Hornet aircraft due to its fuel consumption during takeoff.
LDO	Limited Duty Officer, typically a highly qualified enlisted person commissioned to continue working in their field.
LEAVE	Vacation time.
LETS CLEAN CONTINUOUSLY	Supposedly the actual meaning of the USS Mount Whitney's designator, LCC-20, known for non-stop cleaning.
LETTUCE BROWNER	Machine in the galley that gives lettuce leaves their brown color.
LEVITY SUPPRESSION TEAM	Imaginary group of sailors activated by the commanding officer to ensure low morale.
LIBERTY	Free time away from work or the ship, usually after working hours or in port.

LIBERTY BOAT	Boat assigned to transfer sailors to and from their ship when in a port that requires anchoring.
LIBERTY HOUND	A sailor who loves liberty more than anything else.
LIBERTY RISK	A sailor who loves liberty too much and puts themselves in danger.
LIEU-FUCKING-TENANT	Illustrates Navy practice of including a swear word inside another word.
LIFER	Derogatory term for those who plan to make a career in the Navy.
LIFER DOG	Derogatory term for someone who plans to make a career in the Navy.
LITTLE MANILA	Area on the mess decks where sailors of Filipino descent congregate.
LMD	Large desk, usually reserved for high-ranking officers ashore.
LOBSTER	Term for women in the Navy because all the meat is in the tail.
LOCAL TALENT	Derogatory term for females near a Naval Station who use sailors for money.
LOOP	Officer, usually a LT or LCDR, who is an admiral's aide.
LOST	Line Of Sight Tasking: when a senior officer tasks a junior officer with a time-consuming project.
LOVE BOAT	Term referring to a subtender comprised primarily of female sailors.

LSO	Landing Safety Officer or Landing Signals Officer, responsible for aircraft landing safety.
LST	Tank landing ship, or "Large Slow Target," a now-removed type of amphibious warfare ship.
LUCKY BAG	Collected unclaimed personal items or confiscated items auctioned to the crew.
LUCKY CHARMS	Nickname for Tripler Army Medical Center, used as a navigational aid.
MAIL BUOY	A fictitious buoy where mail for a ship is supposedly left.
MAKE A HOLE	Command to make way for a senior ranking person to pass through.
MANDO COMMANDO	Sailor assigned mandatory physical training for being overweight or failing the Physical Readiness Test.
MARINE	Acronym humorously describing the relationship between the Navy and the Marines.
MARINE CORPS TABLE CLOTH	Front flap on trousers part of the dress uniform for E-6 and below.
MARINE SHOWER	Changing clothes without bathing, usually just applying deodorant or cologne.
MASH	Physical exercises as punishment or correctional training.

MAST	Form of non-judicial punishment where a sailor stands in front of the commanding officer.
MAT MAN	Electronics Maintenance Man
M-BOMB(S)	Slang term for Motrin (Ibuprofen) distributed by corpsmen in Sickbay.
MCPOO	Title sarcastically given to someone stating the obvious.
MEAT GAZER	Individual tasked with ensuring urine samples in a drug test are legitimate.
MEAT IDENTIFIER	Side dish during chow that helps identify main dishes.
MEATBALL	Fresnel Lens Optical Landing System, a visual landing aid for naval aviators.
MEDEVAC	Evolution of transferring a sick person from a submarine to a helicopter.
MESS CRANK	Sailor working on the mess deck, not rated as a cook.
MESS DECK INTELLIGENCE	Rumors spreading throughout the ship.
MESS DECKS	Chow Hall or Eating Establishment onboard ship.
MID OR MIDDIE	Short for Midshipman, a college student studying to become a naval officer.
MIDNIGHT REQUISITION	To "borrow" a needed item, often condoned to get underway.
MID-RATS	Midnight rations, leftovers served at night.

MID-WATCH	Watch from midnight to 0400.
MILKMAN	Sailor wearing the working white uniform.
MISSILE SPONGE	Ship stationed on the outer ring of a battlegroup, likely to be hit.
MOBILE CHERNOBYL	Nickname for USS Enterprise (CVN-65).
MOM AND DAD	Commanding Officer and Executive Officer.
MOM AND POP NIGHT	Night before graduation from Boot Camp spent with family.
MONKEY	Nuclear Machinist's Mate.
MONKEY SHIT	Packing material used to seal openings between bulkheads.
MOTRIN	Magical pill dispensed by hospital corpsmen, believed to cure every ailment.
MOUSE HOUSE	Slang for areas occupied by Missile Technicians on Ballistic Missile Submarines.
MPA	Junior officer responsible for Machinery Division and main engines.
MR. VICE	Master of Ceremonies at a Dining-in/Dining-out event.
MTI	Military Training Instructor responsible for guiding future submarine sailors.
MUNG	Dark green/brown plant residue found in/on scuppers in submarine engineering spaces.

MUSTANG	Officer who rose from the Enlisted ranks.
MYSTERY MEAT	Term for unidentifiable meat eaten nonetheless.
NAFOD	Acronym critique given by the LSO to a student pilot who doesn't know his limits, especially while attempting to board the carrier.
NAMI WHAMMY	Slang for the comprehensive two-day flight physical given to prospective aviators.
NASTY CITY	Slang for National City, California, near Naval Station San Diego, known for its cheap dive bars frequented by "West-Pac Widows."
NAVAL AVIATORS' DISEASE	Term jokingly referring to the high percentage of female children fathered by naval aviators, attributed to various factors including electromagnetic exposure and lifestyle.
NAVAL INFANTRY	Derogatory term for the U.S. Marines.
NAVCMPAC	Designation for where form DD-214 transfers sailors, sometimes providing car fare for transportation.
NAVIGATORS BALLS	Two round pieces of metal (Iron) on either side of a ship's magnetic compass to correct for the magnetic field caused by the ship's metal surfaces, also known as Deviation.

NAVY	Acronym used humorously by disgruntled sailors for "Never Again Volunteer Yourself."
NAVY BALLS	Bravado displayed by sailors, especially when the threat of punishment from the commanding officer prevents action.
NAVY HO	Derogatory term used by male sailors/Marines to describe all women in the Navy, often used when slighted by a female.
NAVY SHOWER	A form of showering practiced underway to conserve fresh water, where water is turned on to wet down, then turned off to lather up, and finally turned on again to rinse off.
NEST	A number of small ships, usually small combatants, tied up outboard of each other at a pier.
NEW NAVY	Concept often depicted in posters for the Navy's alcohol de-glamourization campaign, symbolizing a shift towards a more restrained lifestyle.
NFO	Officer, who flies alongside the pilot as a weapons officer.
NIA	Acronym for "Navy-Issue Ass," referring to the wide posteriors Navy females tend to have or develop.
NIPPLES-TO-THE-RAFTER	Term for a dead piece of equipment that has no hope of being fixed.

NO GAS	Acronym for "No One Gives a Shit," used to dismiss junior personnel.
NO LOAD	A useless sailor who does not pull his share of the load.
NO-FUCK, VAGINA	Pejorative term for Norfolk, Virginia, often used to refer to the city itself.
NON-SKID	Rough epoxy coating used for grip on weather decks.
NOODLE-WINGER	Slang for a helicopter pilot.
NOONER	A short break during mealtime where sailors report to their rack or an undisclosed location for an hour of sleep.
NORS	Acronym for "Not Operationally Ready Supply."
NO-SHITTER	A sea story that is mostly fictional and unverifiable, often beginning with the phrase "Hey, this is no shit..."
NQP	Abbreviation for "Non-Qual-Puke," referring to a non-qualified crewman who is not yet able to stand watch.
NUB	Acronym with various meanings referring to newly reported sailors with no qualifications or experience.
NUC	Naval Sea Systems Command designation for Engineering Department crewmembers responsible for the safe and proper operation of a ship's nuclear reactor and its support systems.

NUCLEAR WASTE	Pejorative term for sailors who exit the Naval Nuclear Power training program before successful completion.
NUGGET	Term for the juniormost pilots or NFOs in a squadron who are fresh out of the Replacement Air Group (RAG).
NUKE	Slang term for a nuclear weapon or ordnance with large payloads, as well as for nuclear-trained members of a ship's Engineering Department.
NUKE IT	To overthink an easy task.
NUKE IT OUT	To reason out a problem by eliminating obvious wrong answers, encouraging someone to put forth more effort before giving up on a problem.
NUTS TO BUTTS	To stand close together in line, a practice from the old Navy where sailors would stand so close together that their bodies were touching.
NVG'S	Abbreviation for "Night Vision Goggles," used for seeing in low-light conditions.
OAFO	Acronym for "Over And Fucking Out," similar to "WTFO" (What The Fuck Over).
OBNOB	Acronym for referring to the only African American nuclear technician onboard a submarine.
OCCIFER	Derogatory term for officers in general, particularly junior officers.
O-CLUB	Officers Club.

OCS	Officer Candidate School, a 13-week program at NAS Pensacola that turns prior enlisted sailors and college graduates into Naval Officers.
O'DARK HUNDRED	Pronounced "oh dark". Referring to some point really early in the morning, like 0200
ODIE AND JODIE	Slang for Officer of the Deck and Junior Officer of the Deck underway.
OFFICER'S CANDY	Urinal disinfectant cakes.
O-GANG	Term coined by A-Gang for the Officers.
OLD MAN	The Commanding Officer or Admiral in command, regardless of gender, usually used when the CO has gained the respect of subordinates.
OLD SALT	Naval veteran.
OLY	USS Olympia (SSN-717).
ON REPORT	Initial discipline practice notifying an individual that he/she is being investigated for possible discipline.
ONE-EYED JACK	Slang for a slider topped with a fried egg, served at midrats.
OOD	Officer of the Deck.
OPERATION GOLDENFLOW	Command-wide urinalysis test.
O-RINGS	Pejorative term for junior officers, also referring to a sealant device.

ORM	Operational Risk Management, a principle emphasizing a common-sense sanity check before performing a task.
OS TRAINER	Derogatory term for a large Popsicle, implying Operations Specialists are expected to "brown-nose" officers more than other ratings.
OSCAR	The buoyant dummy used during man-overboard drills.
OUIJA BOARD	Flat board used on an aircraft carrier to indicate aircraft position and status.
OUT-CHOP	To leave an area of responsibility.
OUT-FUCKING-STANDING	An adjective emphasizing something as beyond outstanding, used seriously or sarcastically, often by RDCs in boot camp.
OVERHEAD	Ceiling.
P.A.P.E.R.C.L.I.P.	Acronym for "People Against People Ever Reenlisting Civilian Life Is Preferable," expressing dissatisfaction with enlistment or unity amongst sailors, often submariners.
P.B.	Short for Pacific Beach, California, a suburb of San Diego.
P.C.O	Acronym for Prospective Commanding Officer, referring to the incoming CO during a transition period.

P.C.O.D.	Slang for the last day of a long deployment when sailors could get laid and still obtain Venereal Disease cures before returning home.
P.D.O.O.M.A.	Pulled Directly Out Of My Ass, used by Chiefs when asked where they got a good idea.
PACKAGE CHECK	A common form of greeting in the Submarine Service where one man shakes another man's crotch, testing mettle and camaraderie.
PADDLES	Code word for the Landing Signals Officer (LSO).
PAPER ASSHOLES	Gummed Reinforcements (office supplies).
PAPER SUIT	Literally, a suit made of paper, preferred for cleaning up Otto II fuel spills.
PARE	A sailor of Filipino descent, used affectionately or pejoratively, depending on context.
PATROL SOCK	Term used for a spunk rag.
PAVY	A man who was a punk in real life but tries to act tough in the Navy.
P-DAYS	First 7 to 10 days of boot camp, the 'P' stands for Processing.
PECKER-CHECKER	Derisive term for a Hospital Corpsman.
PEOPLE TANK	On a submarine, the confines within the pressure hull, as opposed to other specific tanks.

PERMA-FIRST	A Petty Officer First Class (E-6) who, for various reasons, cannot get promoted to Chief Petty Officer (E-7) but remains hopeful.
PERMANENT HELP	Slang for a PH (Photographer's Mate) in a fighter squadron.
PERSO	Personnel Officer.
PFM	Acronym used to describe when things work but the reason is unknown.
PHANTOM SHITTER	Usually at least one per ship, a person who mysteriously defecates in inappropriate places onboard.
PHROG	CH-46 Sea Knight helicopter. Also referred to as the "Whistling Shitcan of Death."
PIECE	Rifle, as used in manual-of-arms (rifle drill).
PIER-QUEER	Air Force term for Sailor.
PIERWOLF	Nickname for the USS Seawolf (SSN-21).
PIG BOAT	Diesel submarine or the USS California (CGN-36).
PINEAPPLE FLEET	The Pacific Fleet, usually referring to the Seventh Fleet.
PING	To emit a pulse of sound energy from a SONAR transmitter.
PING JOCKEY	A derisive term for a SONAR Technician.
PINKY TIME	Half hour immediately following sunset or preceding sunrise officially counted as nighttime.

PIRATE	A sailor known for being good at their job but having poor military bearing.
PISS CUTTER	Slang for the garrison cap.
PISS TEST	"Whiz Quiz" or urinalysis.
PISSER	Urinal.
PIT	A sailor's rack or bunk, or the engine room on a ship.
POD	An official document issued by a command listing all activities for the day, including the Uniform of the Day.
POETS DAY	"Piss on electronics, tomorrow's Saturday," used to refer to any day before the start of the weekend by people in electronics ratings.
POG	A term used by Marine Infantry (Grunts) to refer to anyone who is not in their field.
POGEY BAIT	Candy, sweets, or ice cream used as bribes for non-infantry personnel.
POLISH A TURD	To make the best of a bad situation.
POLLYWOG	An individual who has not crossed the Equator and must undergo rituals to become a shellback.
POOKA	Any hidden space or cavity for stowing items.
POON	Petty Officer of the Navy - used regarding a junior Petty Officer who always offers opinions.

POOPIE PANTS	A pair of pants made by cutting off the top half of a coveralls uniform item.
POOPIE SUIT	Coveralls uniform item.
POOW	Petty Officer of the Watch - a term for a watch that is unremarkable.
POPPING YOUR PUP	Slang for masturbating.
PORT	Left side of a boat or ship.
PORT AND REPORT	A watch stood without relief, designated only for the port section.
PORT AND STARBOARD	A rotation of two duty sections, one designated port and the other starboard.
PORTABLE AIR SAMPLE	A snipe hunt gag in the Submarine Service where a newbie is sent to collect a non-existent air sample with a plastic garbage bag.
PORTHOLE	A window on a ship.
POTS LINE	Plain Old Telephone System, allowing users to make phone calls as if in their home port.
POWDER MONKEY	A sailor sent back and forth for an item, often tasked with retrieving something from below-decks.
PQS	Personal Qualifications Standards, a card carrying various qualifications for a warfare badge or similar.
PROP	Short for an aircraft's propeller.

PRT	Physical Readiness Test, assessing a sailor's physical fitness.
PT	Physical Training, a required exercise regimen.
PUCK CHOP	A Navy pork chop that is extremely overcooked.
PUCKER FACTOR	Tension caused by high stress during a difficult or dangerous situation.
PUDDLE PIRATE	Derisive terms for U.S. Coast Guard personnel.
PUNCH OUT	To eject from an aircraft.
PUS ROCKET	A form of food resembling sausage, containing ground fatty animal flesh and hot grease.
PUSHBUTTON	Term applied to a 6-year enlistee with advanced schooling who gains rank quickly through promotions.
PUSHIN' ROPE	Erectile dysfunction usually associated with a drunken visit to a brothel.
PUSSY PILLS	Sea-sickness pills.
PUSSY TO THE LEFT	A term used to remind sailors how to tie a dress uniform neckerchief.
P-WAY	Short for passageway or a hall.
QUARTER	Often preceded by port or starboard, the ? generally begins abaft the beam on both sides of the ship and extends in an arc aft to the stern.
QUARTERS	A gathering of all the people in the organization.

QUEER	Derogatory term used by sailors when referring to U.S. Air Force personnel.
R.O.A.D. PROGRAM	Retired On Active Duty, refers to someone who is approaching retirement so they don't care about getting any real work accomplished.
RACK	Bed.
RACK BURNS	Reddish marks seen on the face of a sailor who has just emerged from sleeping in his/her rack.
RACK MONSTER	A sailor that would rather stay in his/her rack other than participate in the everyday routine of the ship.
RACK OPS	A term describing a sailor that has been ordered SIQ (sleep in quarters) by medical.
RADCON MATH	Term used by Navy Nukes, generally ELT's, when numbers magically add up to equal the desired sum.
RADIOING THE LOGS	(Submarine Service, surface ships sometimes use the term "Blazing the logs," or simply gundecking)
RAG	Officially called the FRS (Fleet Replacement Squadron), although the former is still widely used.
RAILROAD TRACKS	Refers to the connected silver rank bars of a Lieutenant's khakis.
RAIN LOCKER	Shower
RAISIN	Recruit or junior sailor, predominantly heard at Naval Training Commands.

RAMP STRIKE	When an aircraft gets drastically low while attempting to land on a carrier and strikes the "round down," or stern of the ship, Often with devastating results.
'RATS	Short for "mid-rats"
READY ROOM	Large space aboard a carrier that is the focal point for each of the squadrons in the airwing.
REALITY CHECK	The act of taking a peek outside after many days or weeks below decks.
RED DEVIL BLOWER	A fan, painted red, used by damage control parties to de-smoke a space.
REDASS	Any task or evolution that is extremely painful or difficult to accomplish, often due to bureaucracy or red tape.
RED-ROPE	Slang for a Recruit Division Commander (RDC), in reference to the red rope worn around the left shoulder.
REEFER	Refrigeration ship carrying frozen foods.
REFRESHER TRAINING	The act of watching pornographic movies just before pulling into home port.
RELA	Nickname for a mythological group of malcontent nuclear electricians from the USS Nimitz.
RELATIVE BEARING GREASE	Another of the endless non-existing items new sailors are sent to find.

RENT-A-CROW	Term for a sailor advanced to E-4 because they graduated top of their "A" school class. The Navy 'rents' them for an extra year in return for being promoted.
RETENTION PREVENTION TEAM	Sailors who swear to never reenlist. Sometimes identified by wearing paperclips in the pockets of their dungaree shirts.
REWARD	Also known as dessert, meaning the meal was so poor that a reward was in order for just completing the meal. (submarine specific)
RHINO	Slang for the F-4 Phantom back in the day - presently slang for the F/A-18 E or F Super Hornet.
RICK OR RICKY	A "recruit" or Sailor-to-be still in boot camp.
RICKY BOXING	A boot camp term for sailors masturbating.
RICKY CRUD	One-night sickness in boot camp after receiving smallpox vaccination.
RICKY DIVE	Fast, effective method of cleaning in boot camp, consisting of wearing smurf suits inside-out and sliding, or being dragged, on the floor to pick up dust.
RICKY FISHING	A boot camp term for female sailors masturbating.
RICKY GIRLFRIEND	Your right hand. (AKA-Handeria)

RICKY HEAVEN	A number of restaurants and entertainment venues found in a single building at boot camp, so called because only graduates of boot camp may go there.
RICKY LAWNMOWER	Nailclippers, used to trim stray threads from uniforms. See "Irish Pennant".
RICKY MISTRESS	Your left hand. (AKA Palmala, Handeria's twin sister)
RICKY NINJA	A popular boot camp activity that involves several Rickies dressing up in all black, wearing the Navy issue ski mask, and stealing around in the middle of the night.
RICKY ROCKET	A boot camp "energy drink" made from an assorted mix of sodas, sports drinks, coffee, sugar and artificial sweeteners used to help keep the recruit awake.
RICKY SWEEP	Using a bare (or sock-covered) hand to gather dustbunnies and other dirt from a deck.
RICKY VACUUM	Using your hands to pick up dustbunnies and dirt from carpet. Similar to Ricky Sweep.
RING KNOCKER	A pejorative term for a graduate of the U.S. Naval Academy. So named from their large collegiate rings.
ROACH COACH	"Geedunk" on wheels. Mobile cafeteria van, often seen when on det to another base.

ROAST BEAST	Roast Beef, or any meat served aboard the ship that even the cooks who prepared it don't know what it is.
ROB	The act of "cannibalizing" a specific part off of an aircraft. (Ex. We didn't have a gyro in the parts bin so we robbed one off 614.)
ROCK	Used to define a sailor who has an intelligence quotient equal to or less than that of a basic igneous rock.
ROCKED BACK	Having to repeat a particular section of a school due to failing the exam at the end.
ROD	Retarded Officer Dude
ROGER THAT	A term of understanding and acceptance when given an order or other information.
ROLL-EM'S	Movie night, usually shown in the ready room or the wardroom
ROLLERS	Hot dogs
ROOF RAT	An Airedale that works on the flight deck of an aircraft carrier during flight operations.
ROTC	You get to go to real college on a full ride (shorter scholarships are also available) and only wear your uniform once a week.
ROTOR HEAD	Sailor who flies or maintains rotary-winged aircraft (helicopters).

ROUND DOWN	The approach end of the landing area on an aircraft carrier, which is directly over the stern of the ship.
ROYAL BABY	Usually the fattest "shellback" on the ship, this individual is part of the royal court and the initiation of pollywogs during Crossing the Line ceremonies.
RUBBER HOOEYS	Condoms
RUMOR CONTROL	The often wildly inaccurate rumors that concern fictitious changes to the ship's schedule.
S.H.E.	Stupid Human Error
S.N.O.B.	Shortest Nuke on Board, refers to the lucky nuke who gets out of the Navy next.
S.O.S.	Same as "Shit-on-a-shingle".
SA	Situational Awareness - the big picture. Losing SA, especially in flight, can lead to disastrous results.
SAIL RABBIT	Overcooked pork, or beef tenderloin.
SAILOR'S BALLS	See Navigator's Balls.
SALT AND PEPPERS	Short sleeve white dress shirt with black trousers and Combination Cap. Common in the 70's. Basically a less dressed up version of the Bus Driver Uniform.
SALTPETER	Chemical supposedly added to "bug juice" aboard ship to stifle libido, the stuff of urban legend.

SALTY	Old and experienced (or simply old and sea-worn, as in "my salty hat"). Can also refer to the traditionally profanity-laced language patterns of sailors.
SAND CRAB	A civilian in Civil Service positions working for the U.S. Navy. Very derogatory.
SANDBAG	A member of an aircrew who contributes little or nothing to the safe and successful execution of the mission - instead sits there like a sandbag and is just as useful.
SANDBOX, THE	The pier liberty facilities at Jebel Ali. Sandbox Liberty means travel outside the port of Jebel Ali is not authorized. All you get is a "beer on the pier". See "Gerbil Alley".
SAR	Search and Rescue
SCOPE DOPE	Radarman or Operations Specialist
SCRAMBLED EGGS	Gold embroidered oak leaves decoration on a Commander's/Captain's cover.
SCREAMING ALPHA	A sailor who is on fire and is running around screaming.
SCREW	A ship's or boat's propeller.
SCREW THE POOCH	To mess up in a big way. Usually followed by a visit with the old man.
SCULLERY	Washroom for eating implements such as knives, forks, trays, and cups.

SCUPPER	A funnel-like device used to collect rogue liquids usually from overflowing tanks in engineering spaces.
SCUPPER TROUT	A turd or other length of feces.
SCUTTLEBUTT	Drinking fountain or rumor (originated from the rumors that would be spread on board ship while gathered about the water barrel).
SEA AND ANCHOR DETAIL	Every sailor has an assigned duty station to be manned when the ship is either pulling into or out of port.
SEA DADDY	Senior, more experienced sailor who unofficially takes a new member of the crew under his wing and mentors him.
SEA GOING BELLHOPS	A derisive name for Marines. Refers to the fact that they pull guard duty aboard ship. A good phrase to use when picking a fight with a Marine.
SEA LAWYER	An argumentative, cantankerous, or know-it-all sailo using technicalities, half-truths, and administrative crap to get out of doing work.
SEA LEGS	Bodily adjustment to the motion of a ship indicated especially by the ability to walk steadily and by freedom from seasickness.
SEA OTTER	Seaopdetter; a member of a Sea Operational Detachment (SEAOPDET).
SEA PUSSY	A yeoman or personnelman - akin to a secretary - does clerical work.

SEA STORIES	Often exaggerated or embellished tales from previous deployments or commands told by seniors to juniors.
SEA SWAP	A recently initiated program where an American warship never returns to an American port.
SEABAG	The large green bag the army calls a "duffel bag".
SEAL	SEa Air Land operators nickname.
SEAMAN SCHMUCKATELLI	Generic name for a sailor, used in a similar manner as "John Doe".
SECURE	In general, to prepare something for stormy travel.
SENILE CHIEF	Slang for Senior Chief
SHAFT ALLEY	Field Day berthing aboard a Submarine. Also the compartment(s) containing a ship's propulsion shaft(s).
SHARK SHIT	A sailor who has fallen overboard and is lost forever.
SHELLBACK	An individual who has crossed the Equator.
SHERWOOD FOREST	(Submarine Service) missile area, on a boomer.
SHINBUSTER	Same as knee-knocker.
SHIP OVER	Re-enlisting.
SHIPMATE	Any fellow Sailor. Also used as a derogatory term against all junior enlisted personnel i.e. E-5 and below.

SHIPWRECK	Any fellow sailor. Used as a derogatory term.
SHIT CAN	Either the name for a trash can, or the act of throwing something into the trash.
SHIT CHASER	Name given to hull maintenance techs.
SHIT CITY	Norfolk, VA. See also "Asshole of the Navy".
SHIT IN A SEABAG	Stuffed green peppers.
SHIT RIVER	The creek that divided the base from the civilian side, in the Philippines, Between Olongapo City and Cubi Point Naval Base.
SHIT SCREEN	A shitbag who is so often the object of (negative) attention by his superiors that his shipmates' transgressions go relatively unnoticed.
SHITBAG	A derogatory term for a sailor who has been awarded punishment at mast, or any less-than-par sailor. Also known as "Shitbird".
SHITBOMB	Extremely unpopular topic brought up at the end of a (usually long and boring) meeting that requires a lot of work from everyone present.
SHIT-FACED	Drunk. The preferred state of consciousness for junior sailors, especially those visiting foreign ports.
SHIT-ON-A-SHINGLE	Creamed chipped beef on toast.

SHITTER	Toilet (or "Head," see above). Shipboard space where "shit" is both a verb AND a noun. Self-explanatory, really.
SHIT-THE-BED	Term used to identify that something is broken.
SHITTY KITTY	A slang word for the USS Kitty Hawk (CV-63), which is the worst ship in the United States Navy, and also the oldest.
SHOE	Derogatory term used by airedales in reference to "black shoes," or ship drivers.
SHOOTER	Catapult Officer aboard an aircraft carrier.
SHORT SEABAG	Reporting aboard without a full uniform; deficient in aptitude or intelligence.
SHORT TIMER	A sailor with less than 90 days until discharge or transfer and an attitude to match.
SHORT TIMER'S CHAIN	A chain that hangs from the belt of a "short timer" for all to see, with one link representing a day.
SHORT-ARM	Penis.
SHOWER TECH	Sonar Technician.
SHUTTERBUG	A Photographer's Mate.
SICK BAY	On larger ships like carriers and "gator freighters," this is a small hospital.

SICK BAY COMMANDO	A sailor who spends more time going to medical feigning ailments than doing work.
SICK IN QUARTERS	When a sailor is too ill or incapacitated to perform his duties and is required to report to his rack (quarters).
SIDE NUMBER	Unique 3-digit number assigned to every aircraft in the airwing.
SIERRA HOTEL	Phonetic letters for SH, which stands for "Shit Hot."
SIG	A signature on a qualification card. Also, Naval Air Station Sigonella, Sicily.
SIGNAL EJECTOR	A device on submarines that can shoot countermeasures, flares, and more.
SILVERWHALES	Refers to the rather large fat women near Bangor, Washington, that are from Silverdale.
SIMS	Simulators.
SINGLE DIGIT MIDGET	Sailor who has less than 10 days before getting out or transferring.
SKATE	Sailor who avoids work while not being detected.
SKATE GOLDEN	The ability to "skate" out of work while being assigned to a smaller working party undetected.
SKATER	Sailor who gets away with doing no work.
SKEDS-O	Schedules Officer.
SKEEVY STACKER	Storekeeper.

SKIMMER	Surface Sailor (used by submariners).
SKIPPER	Term used in reference to the Commanding officer of any Ship, Unit, Platoon, or Detachment regardless of rank.
SKITTLES	Sailors who work on the flight deck of a carrier.
SKIVVIES	Underwear.
SKIVVY SNIFFER	Ships Serviceman assigned to do the Ship's laundry.
SKIVVY WAVER	Signalman (because of signal flags).
SKOSH	Perilously close to minimum acceptable levels.
SKYLARKING	Not paying attention, due to "looking up in the sky" instead of on the assigned task.
SLEEP 'TIL YOU'RE HUNGRY, EAT 'TIL YOU'RE TIRED	The working day of an aviator as described by a surface sailor.
SLICK SLEEVE	A sailor in the E-1 paygrade who does not have a rating, and who has not yet graduated from Apprentice training.
SLIDERS	Hamburgers or cheeseburgers.
SLIME LIGHTS	NVG compatible exterior green lights found on aircraft that are almost invisible to the naked eye. Used in combat situations at night.
SLINGING GAME	Flirting with other people aboard the ship.

SLJO	Shitty Little Jobs Officer.
SLUF	Short Little Ugly Fucker, nickname given to the A-7 Corsair.
SLUFF	Short Little Ugly Fat Fucker, pejorative term for a sailor.
SLUGS	Term used to refer to Chief Petty Officer Selectees during their initiation and transition period.
SLURFF	Short Little Ugly Retarded Fat Fucker, someone that makes a SLUFF look good.
SLUSHING	Financial service provided by a shipmate where money is loaned out with high interest rates.
SMACKS	Anti-collision strobe lights on an aircraft.
SMAG	Simple Minded Ass Grabber or Small Minded Ass Grabber.
SMALL BOY	Term referring to smaller class ships, such as destroyers and frigates.
SMOKE PIT	Designated smoking area, almost always used when ashore.
SMOKING HOLE	What an aircraft becomes if it crashes over land.
SMOKING LAMP	Announcement specifying where smoking is permitted or prohibited during certain hours or operations.
SMOKING SPONSON	Designated smoking area aboard aircraft carriers.

SMOOTH CROTCH	Derogatory term for a nuclear Electronics Technician.
SMURF	A recruit who is in his first few days of boot camp who hasn't been issued uniforms yet.
SMURF SUIT	Set of blue sweatpants and sweatshirt issued on arrival at boot camp.
SNAFU	Situation Normal, All Fucked Up.
SNAKE EATERS	Special Forces personnel such as Navy SEALs, Green Berets, etc.
SNATCH IN THE HATCH	Term used to inform the crew that a female visitor is onboard.
SNIPES	Sailors assigned to Engineering rates.
SNIVEL	To request time off or to not be scheduled.
SNOB	Shortest Nuke On Board.
SNUGGLE UP	When two aircraft get very close while flying in formation.
SOCKED-IN	When the ceiling and visibility at an airfield or over an air-capable ship are below minimums for takeoff and landing.
SORRY I QUIT	Used to refer to a sailor who convinces a doctor to give them an SIQ chit.
SORTIE	A single flight of an aircraft.
SOUGEE	To scour; generic term for scouring powder.

SOUND OF ONE HAND CLAPPING	Masturbating.
SPACE	Refers to a room or compartment onboard ship.
SPANDAFLAGE	Overweight personnel squeezing into camo that is too small.
SPARKY	Radioman or Electrician's Mate.
SPLIB	Special Liberty, Comp-Time.
SPLIT TAILS	Female sailors, used more often in the early days of surface ship integration.
SPOOK	Usually a CT, IS or some kind of intelligence type.
SPU	Staff Pick-Up, refers to individuals that finish the training pipeline and stay behind to teach.
SPUNK	Cool Whip or anything like it.
SQUID	Submariner.
SQUISHY	State resulting from being at sea too long.
STAB	Any sort of unwanted, tedious work.
STARBOARD	Right side of the boat or ship (when facing the bow).
STAR-TIGHT	Same as "Gronk".
STATEROOM	Living quarters for officers aboard a ship.
STEEL BEACH PICNIC	Celebration on the weather decks of a ship.

STEW-BURNER	Sailor with the Culinary Specialist (CS) Rating
STICKS	The levers in the Maneuvering Room of a diesel submarine that are used to change the settings for the main propulsion motors.
STRIKER	Sailor receiving on-the-job training for a designated field (or rate)
STUFFED	A naval aircraft when its wings or rotors/tail pylon are folded and it is parked in close proximity to other aircraft.
SUBIC BAY	Philippines port also known as "Pubic Bay, the Asshole of the Orient."
SUCK METER	Similar to a fun meter, this fictitious gauge displays how shitty a given situation is.
SUCKBAG	Another name for a dirtbag or shitbag
SUCKING RUBBER	Extended periods wearing Emergency Air Breathing devices.
SUMMER CREASES	Military creases incorrectly or crookedly ironed into uniforms. "Some are here, some are there." (see Railroad Tracks).
SWAB	Mop.
SWAG	Scientific/simple Wild Ass Guess. Used commonly on Navy exams.
SWAP PAINT	Euphemism for a mid-air collision

SWEAT THE BULKHEADS	Indoor PT during boot camp which doesn't stop until the bulkheads are running with condensate.
SWIM CALL	Ship stops and off duty crew jumps in the ocean for a swim.
SWIMS	Aviation water survival training.
SWO	Surface Warfare Officer. SWOs are sometimes referred to as "SWO-dogs" or "SWO-Daddys".
T.A.R.F.U.	Things Are Really Fucked Up.
TACK ON	In an informal ceremony, when a sailor is frocked.
TAD	Temporary Assigned Duty
TAIL	Long cable containing a sonar array that is trailed out behind a ship or submarine.
TAILHOOK	Long metal hook that hangs below a fixed-wing aircraft as it attempts to land on an aircraft carrier.
TANGO LIMA	Phonetic of "TL," which is short for The Trophy Lounge, a club in National City, CA frequented by "WESTPAC widows" and sailors assigned to ships homeported at NAVSTA San Diego.
TAPE ZEBRA	Maddening condition aboard ship, especially aircraft carriers, where passageways are "taped off" so that they may be waxed, dried, and buffed in the middle of the night.

TARGET	Submariner term to describe the surface fleet or anything other than an identified friendly submarine.
TDU	Trash Disposal Unit. Sophisticated AN-DEEP-6 weapons system.
TEA BAGGING	Similar to rimjob but in this case the sailor dunks his nut sack in a beverage of an unliked individual.
TED	Typical Enlisted Dude.
TFOA	Things Falling Off Aircraft - when a piece of an aircraft falls off for no apparent reason during flight.
THE BEACH	"Terra firma." Any place that is not covered by water.
THE BLACK HOLE	Reference to the Navy's main base at Norfolk, Virginia, so called because "it's where sailors' careers go to die."
THE BOAT	(1) The Submarine; (2) Airdale term for the ship their airwing is attached to.
THE COW	The Commanding Officer's Wife.
THE GOO	Instrument Meteorological Conditions.
THE HOLE	Area on the deck of an aircraft carrier where helicopters are stored.
THE HONCH	Nickname for the Honcho bar district outside Yokosuka Naval Base.
THE LEANS	A mild case of vertigo experienced aboard a ship.
THE POINTY END OF THE SPEAR	Slang for being on deployment or cruise.

THE POND	Slang for the open sea.
THE TRADE SCHOOL	The U.S. Naval Academy.
THE ZOO	Nickname for USS Kalamazoo (AOR-6), a Wichita-class Replenishment Oiler that served the U.S. Atlantic Fleet from 1973 to 1996.
TIME MACHINE	A sailor's rack. Usually referred to by senior personnel without many daily responsibilities.
TIME ON THE POND	Refers to a sailor's sea time in terms of the number of cruises or patrols completed.
TIMMY	A name used for by RDC's when an anonymous recruit messes up and doesn't take credit for his behavior.
TIN CAN	Destroyer.
TIRE CHASER	Term used usually by Aviation Boatswains Mates to describe Blue Shirts or Chock Walkers on the flight deck and hangar bay of an aircraft carrier.
TITIVAION	Hour long field day held daily onboard USS Cape St. George (CG-71).
TITLESS WAVE	A yeoman or one who performs clerical duties.
TITS MACHINE	Old-school term for a kick-ass aircraft, usually a fighter, that consisted of little more than an airframe, minimal avionics, and a huge engine or two.

TITS-UP	Out of commission; hard-down.
TLD	Acronym for belt adornment, worn by nukes to see how much radiation is received in a period of time.
TOD	Typical Officer Dude. A weak attempt by TEDs to come up with a nickname for officers.
TOPSIDER	(Carrier) Anyone who is not a nuke.
TORPEDO SPONGE	Similar to "Missile Sponge", this refers to the smaller ships in a convoy, whose duty it is to protect the carrier, to the point of taking the torpedo hit for the carrier if needed.
TOUCH AND GO'S	Repeatedly falling asleep in a meeting or a class while trying desperately to stay awake.
TOWER FLOWER	Usually the SUPPO or another person with almost zero aviation experience who is tasked with manning the control tower on a small boy or supply ship.
TRAP	A fixed-wing arrested landing on an aircraft carrier. In the helo world, the Rapid Securing Device (RSD) on the deck of a "small boy."
TRICE UP	Make your rack. (rack = bed).
TRIPLE STICKS	Refers to the aircraft in the fighter squadron on a carrier with the side number "111".
TRIWALL	An extremely large cardboard box.
TROUT	See Scupper Trout.

TUBE STEAK	Hot dogs (also called "dangling sirloin").
TUNA BOAT	A submarine tender, or other non-combat ship that is comprised nearly completely by female sailors.
TURD	(Submarine Service) A surface ship.
TURD CHASER	An HT - Hull Technician. Renowned for their ability to find a clog in the ship's sewage treatment system.
TURKEY	Slang for the F-14 Tomcat.
TURN 'N BURN	Casual for "Get busy!" From formal daily announcement Turn to ship's work, often given as direct order Turn to!
TURN-TO	The command, normally given over the 1MC signaling the beginning of the work day.
TWEEKER	A very small screwdriver used by EM's and ET's to make meters indicate correctly.
TWEEKER	(Submarine Service) Electronics rating; any engineering rating not gronking a wrench.
TWEENER	(Submarine Service) Affectionate term for Missile Technicians on Ballistic Missile Submarines.
TWIDGET	Sailor in the Electronics or Electrical fields of job specialties.
TWO-BLOCK	To center or tighten; derived from tackle.

TWO-DIGIT MIDGET	Sailor with 99 or less days until his/her "End of Active Obligated Service", or EAOS.
UA	Unauthorized absence up to 30 days.
UN-ASS	To let go of, give up, or share something.
UNCLE SAM'S CONFUSED GROUP	Joke name for The United States Coast Guard.
UNCLE SAM'S MISGUIDED CHILDREN	Joke name for The United States Marine Corps.
UNDERWAY SOCK	A soft sock brought underway to comfort a frustrated submariner.
UN-FUCK	To correct something that is screwed up.
UNODIR	UNless Otherwise DIRected; enables TRUST-based management by exception (MBE).
UNREP	UNderway REPlenishment - Taking supplies from the supply ship by maneuvering alongside and passing lines between the two vessels. Differs from "VERTREP."
USS BACKYARD	Term for the sailor's home of record, to which he or she happily returns upon discharge.
USS LASTSHIP	Term for sailor's trying to tell a story, or give an example of how business was handled at their last command.

USS NEVERDOCK	Ship that seems to stay out at sea for unusually long periods of time. For sailors, this is usually their own ship.
USS NEVERSAIL	Mock-up ship found in boot camp, also called USS Recruit. Can also refer to real ships that seldom leave port, such as Sub-tenders.
USS NOTTAGAIN	Used by sailors separating from the Navy when asked which command they are going to.
USS USETAFISH	A submarine veteran's previous command.
VAMPIRE	Inbound missile to the ship.
VAMPIRE LIBERTY	Getting the day off for donating a pint of blood.
VERTREP	Taking supplies from the supply ship via helo pick up and drop off.
VERY WELL	Senior to subordinate acknowledgement.
VIRTUAL LIBERTY	The idea a sailor could walk off the ship and, instead of going into town, step on his crank, throw his wallet into the water and hit himself over the head with a blunt object.
VITAMIN M	Similar to Corpsman Candy above, but in this context relating to Motrin.
VOLUNTOLD	When a sailor is volunteered into a collateral duty by his superior.

VULCAN DEATH WATCH	A long evaluation or training drill onboard a submarine. It normally goes on for hours with no clear ending point.
VULTURES ROW	Place where people can watch flight operations without being in the way.
WARDROOM	Officer's mess, or dining room. Also used to collectively refer to all the officers at a command.
WARM AND FUZZY	A feeling that something has been done correctly and will produce the desired results. Most often used in the negative.
WARRANT	Short hand for a chief warrant officer. In the navy, these are generally older and more experienced than a commissioned line officer, much like an "LDO."
WATCH	A period of duty, usually of four-hours duration, with specific times for different watches throughout the day and night.
WATER WINGS	Surface Warfare Officer's badge (so named by aviators), a term pridefully used by non-carrier SWOs.
WAVE-OFF	In naval aviation, to voluntarily discontinue an approach to a landing or a hover due to unsafe or uncomfortable flight conditions.
WAXING THE DOLPHIN	Masturbating.

VULCAN DEATH WATCH	A long evaluation or training drill onboard a submarine. It normally goes on for hours with no clear ending point.
VULTURES ROW	Place where people can watch flight operations without being in the way.
WARDROOM	Officer's mess, or dining room. Also used to collectively refer to all the officers at a command.
WARM AND FUZZY	A feeling that something has been done correctly and will produce the desired results. Most often used in the negative.
WARRANT	Short hand for a chief warrant officer. In the navy, these are generally older and more experienced than a commissioned line officer, much like an "LDO."
WATCH	A period of duty, usually of four-hours duration, with specific times for different watches throughout the day and night.
WATER WINGS	Surface Warfare Officer's badge (so named by aviators), a term pridefully used by non-carrier SWOs.
WAVE-OFF	In naval aviation, to voluntarily discontinue an approach to a landing or a hover due to unsafe or uncomfortable flight conditions.
WAXING THE DOLPHIN	Masturbating.

WEAPONETTE	(Submarine Service) Pejorative term for the members of a submarine's Weapons Department.
WEATHER GUESSER	Term usually applied to personnel in the Aerographer's Mate (AG) Rating.
WEDGE	Nickname for someone so deserving. The simplest tool.
WEFT	Typically stands for "Wings, Exhaust (or Engine, for prop aircraft), Fuselage, Tail" and is a method by which ship's lookout stations can visually identify aircraft within the vicinity.
WESTPAC	While this usually refers to the western Pacific area of operations.
WESTPAC WIDOW	The wives of sailors who are on deployment, usually found in bars near their husbands' naval base.
WET SUIT CAMEL TOE	A disturbing sight caused by a (usually older and) fatter rescue swimmer attempting to squeeze into his wet suit for SAR duty.
WETTING DOWN	The promoted officer has to lay down a bar tab equal to the amount of his monthly raise for the enjoyment of his wardroom mates.
WHEEL BOOK	A small notebook, usually used by Division Officers or Chiefs to keep track of daily events and reminders.
WHEELS UP	Aviator's term for actual launch time (the wheels are up off the deck).

WHETHER LEAVE	Departing the command for an extended period whether or not official permission has been requested and/or granted.
WHIDBEY WHALE	Naval Air Station Whidbey Island (NASWI) variant of a dependent spouse who became significantly overweight.
WHISKEY-TANGO-FOXTROT	What the Fuck?
WHISTLING SHIT CAN OF DEATH	CH-46 Sea Knight helicopter, notorious for its mechanical issues and accidents during takeoff.
WHIZ QUIZ	Urinalysis for drug testing, commonly referred to as "Piss Test." Failing is known as "popping positive."
WIDOW/WIDOWER	Describes spouses of those deployed, effectively single until their partner returns. This can be specific to the type of deployment.
WINGS	Breast insignia for Naval Aviators, Naval Flight Officers, and Enlisted Aviation Warfare Specialists.
WIRE BITER	Electrician's Mate.
WOG	A naval term for someone who has not crossed the equator, part of a traditional ceremony involving both officers and enlisted personnel.
WOLF TICKET	Information that is dubious, exaggerated, or outright false.

WORKING PARTY	A group selected to handle the loading of supplies onto a ship.
WORKUPS	Training and preparation periods before deployment, involving various drills and exercises.
WRINKLE-NECK BASS	Another term for Scupper Trout.
WTFO	Expression for confusion or surprise, "What the Fuck, Over."
WUBA	Derogatory term meaning "Woman Used by All" or "Woman with an Unusually Big Ass."
WUBA CHARIOT	Elliptical exercise machines, often associated with female use.
WUBAFLAGE	Civilian clothes typically worn by those described as WUBA.
XOI	Form of non-judicial punishment where a sailor appears before the executive officer (XO) to review misconduct.
XO'S DOOR	A trophy humorously exchanged between engineering divisions on a submarine to pass time and alleviate boredom.
XO'S HAPPY HOUR	Daily hour-long mandatory cleaning evolution typically initiated by the executive officer via the 1MC communication system.

XOXING LOGS	In submarine service, the practice of entering engineering log data that is suspiciously similar to the previous hour's data, derived from "Xerox."
YOKO	Slang for Yokosuka, Japan.
YOUR BOY	A way to refer to someone when disclaiming ownership, responsibility, or relation.
ZARF	A simple cupholder on a submarine, often riveted to any available vertical sheet metal.
ZERO	Slang for an officer, referring to their pay grade starting with "O" (O-1, O-2, etc.).
ZOOM BAG	A flight suit.
ZOOMIE	Slang for aviators, particularly used for USAF pilots, originating from the term "blue zoo" at the USAF Academy.
ZOOMIES	Particle radiation emitted from naval nuclear power sources or nuclear weapons.
ZUT	A retired Morse radiotelegraphy procedure signal; former Radio Operators (RMs) might possess a ZUT certificate or tattoo.

Made in the USA
Middletown, DE
07 June 2024